Workplace Learning

Routledge Studies in Human Resource Development

EDITED BY MONICA LEE, LANCASTER UNIVERSITY, UK

HRD theory is changing rapidly. Recent advances in theory and practice, how we conceive of organisations and of the world of knowledge, have led to the need to reinterpret the field. This series aims to reflect and foster the development of HRD as an emergent discipline.

Encompassing a range of different international, organisational, methodological and theoretical perspectives, the series promotes theoretical controversy and reflective practice.

Workplace Learning

Concepts, Measurement, and Application

Edited by
Marianne Van Woerkom and Rob Poell

Routledge
Taylor & Francis Group
New York   London

First published 2010
by Routledge
270 Madison Avenue, New York, NY 10016

Simultaneously published in the UK
by Routledge
2 Park Square, Milton Park, Abingdon, Oxon OX14 4RN

Routledge is an imprint of the Taylor & Francis Group, an informa business

© 2010 Marianne Van Woerkom and Rob Poell

The right of Marianne Van Woerkom and Rob Poell to be identified as author of this work has been asserted by them in accordance with sections 77 and 78 of the Copyright, Designs and Patents Act 1988.

Typeset in Sabon by IBT Global.

Library of Congress Cataloging-in-Publication Data

Workplace learning : concepts, measurement and application / by Marianne Van Woerkom and Rob Poell.
p. cm. — (Routledge studies in human resource development ; 17)
Includes bibliographical references and index.
1. Employees—Training of—Congresses. 2. Organization—Congresses. 3. Organizational learning—Congresses. I. Woerkom, Marianne Van, 1971– II. Poell, Rob F. (Robert Frans), 1968–
HF5549.5.T7W6575 2010
658.3'124—dc22
2009050112

ISBN13: 978-0-415-48262-2 (hbk)
ISBN13: 978-0-203-85008-4 (ebk)

Contents

Figures

Tables

1 Introduction
Learning in the Workplace

Marianne Van Woerkom and Rob Poell

This book has arisen out of the need for an update on insights and perspectives on learning in the workplace, a topic that has received attention from both academics and practitioners since the 1990s. It contains 14 chapters based on recent research and practice aimed at an international readership of students, academics, researchers, HRD practitioners, managers, and policymakers interested in human resource development and workplace learning in specific. Most chapters in the book were part of the Workplace Learning stream of the Seventh International Conference on HRD Research and Practice across Europe, held at Tilburg University in the Netherlands, 22–24 May 2006, which was coordinated by the editors.

THE WORKPLACE AS A CONTEXT FOR LEARNING

Whereas 20 years ago learning in the workplace hardly received any attention from academics or practitioners, today workplace learning is a highly popular topic. Although workplace learning is a natural phenomenon that has always existed, the value attached to it has varied in history (see Van der Klink and Streumer 2002). In the Middle Ages workplace learning was the habitual way to develop in the trade. However, in the 20th century the focus changed to learning in schools. From the second half of the 1980s the learning potential of the workplace has been rediscovered, partly as a result of the growing costs and disappointing results of corporate training. In the 1990s many publications were devoted to the advantages and possibilities of workplace learning, in the context of both employee development and vocational education. The emergence of globalization and the knowledge economy, the aging of the workforce, fast technological developments, and different perspectives on the organization of work all strengthen the relevance of workplace learning. In the context of vocational education, dual trajectories (i.e., combining school and work) have become increasingly popular as they contribute to a better match on the labour market.

Studies into the learning potential of the workplace have shown that workplaces can be regarded as strong learning environments due to their opportunities for combining formal and informal learning as well as individual and teamwork, and for exchanges between novices and experts (Billett 1994; Darrah 1995; Velde and Cooper 2000). The workplace is still essential in transferring the 'mystery' of work and craft as well as work-related rules and habits to new workers (Engeström 2001). After more than 15 years of interest in workplace learning, however, it is time to draw up the balance sheet: What is the state of affairs regarding theory development on workplace learning, and what are promising new avenues for research? Have 15 years of research on workplace learning enabled us to make this concept more tangible and to identify variations in workplace learning activities and practices? How may the instruments developed be used in practice? To what extent are current work environments, such as team-based work and call centres, favourable for learning and what research-based recommendations can we make to boost the opportunities for learning in these contexts?

AIM AND SCOPE OF THE BOOK

In an attempt to evaluate the promises of workplace learning after more than 15 years of attention to workplace learning, this book addresses such issues by asking and answering the following related questions:

- What are current developments in the body of knowledge informing workplace learning research?
- How can learning in the workplace be operationalized?
- What is the impact of various workplace settings on workplace learning?

Very few books in the field of HRD to date are grounded in evidence-based research. Most HRD books are essentially textbooks and not research-based (although sometimes they are informed by research). HRD as an emerging field has a relatively theoretical knowledge base, which is reflected in the nature of its handbooks (Stewart and McGoldrick 1996; Hargreaves and Jarvis 1998; Wilson 1999, 2005; Walton 1999; Yorks 2004; Sadler-Smith 2006). The few research-driven books on HRD have been on very specific topics, for instance, HRD in the post-command economies of East and Central Europe after the fall of communism (Lee *et al.* 1996) or HRD in the health and social care sector (Sambrook and Stewart 2007). Stewart *et al.* (2001) focused on the research process and research design in HRD rather than on research findings, as did Swanson and Holton (1997). In general, therefore, the HRD literature lacks a strong empirical evidence base.

Much the same can be concluded about the topic of workplace learning. Although books in this area have been published as early as 1991 (Watkins) and even 1987 (Marsick), they predominantly focus on theory, how-to-do types of knowledge, and sometimes mere advocacy (Forrester *et al.* 1995; Garrick 1998; Boud and Garrick 1999; Rainbird *et al.* 2004). One recent exception was Streumer (2006), which brought together empirical research on the topic based on a set of 2001 conference papers predominantly written by Dutch authors.

The aim of the current volume is, therefore, to provide a comprehensive, up-to-date, and international overview of human resource development research in the broad area of workplace learning. It disseminates the results of a wide range of HRD research in order to contribute to evidence-based practice in the field of workplace learning. It provides a resource to inform teaching, learning, and professional practice. Specifically, its aims are as follows:

- To explore different perspectives on learning in the workplace and assess the various terms and meanings associated with it.
- To describe and evaluate various instruments that have been developed to measure workplace learning.
- To analyze the impact of various work settings on workplace learning, such as teams, action learning programmes, and contexts that are deemed problematic for learning, such as call centres.
- To provide a resource to academics and students researching HRD practice.
- To provide insights and glimpses of good practice for HRD practitioners.

The book is broken into three parts, preceded by this introductory chapter and concluded by one final implications chapter. The first part deals with perspectives on learning in the workplace (four chapters). The second part comprises three chapters about operationalizing learning in the workplace. The third part addresses learning in various workplace settings (five chapters).

OVERVIEW OF THE CHAPTERS

The first part of the book is concerned with theoretical developments in the body of knowledge underlying workplace learning and contains four chapters that present various perspectives on learning in the workplace. Chapter 2 is authored by Stephen Billett and deals with individuals' active and ongoing construction and remaking of the knowledge required for their work. He proposes a relational interdependence between individual learning and the remaking of the culturally derived work practices that individuals engage in. Neither the social nor the personal contributions alone are sufficient for the learning required to maintain competence throughout working life. The situated social experience is important for understanding the performance requirements of work practices and the processes of learning and remaking practice in work settings. However, personal and person-dependent factors, comprising their cognitive experience, also shape how individuals construe and construct what they encounter through work and throughout working life. It is these active and ongoing processes of knowledge construction through which learning and remaking of cultural practices occur.

The third chapter is written by Tara Fenwick and outlines practice-based conceptions of learning that might be fruitful sources for new directions in HRD's theories of learning. Fenwick argues that these theories still tend to be dominated by assumptions that learning is an individual process rooted in acquisition. However, in HRD practice learning is increasingly treated as a collective process rooted somehow in dynamic action. The chapter discusses three contemporary conceptions of learning: the participational perspective of situated cognition, the notion of expansion from cultural-historical activity theory, and the constructs of translation and mobilization presented by actor-network theory. While these are not particularly new to HRD, the contribution of Fenwick's discussion is to bring together these theories in a critical light to highlight selected dynamics that may be useful tools for HRD theory development.

Chapter 4 is authored by Peter Chin and colleagues. In their contribution, they explore several principles that they believe to be central to research on workplace learning. Research on workplace learning should have a broad focus and include the range from students in work-based education programs to adult workers, and the range from novice to proficient workers. The research is especially productive if it is aimed at inexperienced adult workers and learners in work-based education because they have not developed smoothly executable practices. The research needs to be attentive to all of the commonplaces of learning—learners, teachers, content, milieu—and should be inclusive with a focus on promoting learning for at-risk and exceptional learners. Research on workplace learning needs to document how the characteristics of the workplace fit the learner's individual needs, especially for vulnerable learners. Further, the authors argue that the complexities of workplace learning commend the development of populations of rich case studies as a research approach.

The fifth chapter is written by Paul Tosey with co-authors and deals with Gregory Bateson's framework of 'levels of learning', which has influenced thinking about workplace learning as well as thinking about learning in other contexts (e.g., higher education). However, in their opinion Bateson's framework is routinely misconstrued and misrepresented, meaning that its potential to synthesize a variety of ideas about 'learning to learn' and to provide an integrative view of individual and organizational learning is missed. The chapter aims to describe Bateson's framework and its origins and highlight ways in which literature misconstrues the framework, referring to the intersecting fields of education, management learning, organizational learning, and transformative learning. Furthermore, the chapter provides an alternative understanding of Bateson's model, highlighting the framework as a means of indicating multiple possibilities of learning from experience, and it identifies and discusses implications for workplace learning.

The second part in the book contains three chapters addressing recent developments in operationalizing learning activities in the workplace. This part starts with a contribution about antecedents of nurses' on-the-job learning behaviour by Marjolein Berings and colleagues (Chapter 6). This contribution discusses which elements of the famous Demand-Control-Support model developed by Karasek and Theorell (1990) influence the different types of actual on-the-job learning activities conducted by registered nurses. On the basis of a sample of 372 registered nurses working in different departments of 13 general hospitals in the Netherlands, the authors conclude that different types of learning are influenced differently by the psychological work conditions, with most effects for learning through talking with others. The role of the supervisor appeared to be extremely important, through providing sufficient job control and social support. Furthermore, Berings found that intrinsic work motivation plays an important direct role in on-the-job learning behaviour and also mediates key parts of the impact that the psychosocial work environment has on on-the-job learning.

Individual and organizational learning processes are highly contingent upon how individual workers gather information from their internal and external workplace contexts. Chapter 7 is written by Yu-Lin Wang and Andrea Ellinger and describes the development of an instrument to assess information acquisition activities. The chapter discusses the development of a new measure to assess internal and external information acquisition activities, drawing upon Dixon's (1992) conceptualization of information acquisition, which has been identified as a construct of organizational learning. The findings from the validation process demonstrate that the factors empirically derived from factor analysis mostly correspond to Dixon's framework. This newly developed instrument can be a useful tool in assessing how individuals obtain information as part of their informal workplace learning. It also represents the operationalization of one of the constructs that can advance our understanding of organizational learning, which has been hampered by a lack of available measurement tools.

Mistakes can provide important opportunities for workplace learning. Chapter 8 is authored by Johannes Bauer and Regina Mulder and discusses the development of an instrument that measures learning from errors at work. The authors argue that while there are strong traditions of research on human error and safety management—focusing primarily on organizational learning—there are only a few studies on how and under which circumstances individuals learn from errors encountered in a naturalistic work context. A special problem is how to investigate the engagement in learning activities after an error, because errors are unpredictable events. The authors introduce a conceptualization of learning from errors at work, which is based on theories of experiential learning at work and provides the basis for their instrument. Further, they present findings from a pilot study and from a larger study in nursing that aimed to test the feasibility of their approach. They conclude that learning from errors can be measured by asking workers about activities that they engage in after an error in order to analyze causes and to develop strategies for preventing similar errors in the future. Also, they argue that questions about the engagement in error-related learning activities should be based upon concrete error cases that represent a specific type of error, because different types of errors offer a different potential for learning.

The third part deals with learning in various workplace settings and contains five chapters. Besides workplace learning taking place in the context of organized programmes, it is also a process that simply emerges from the interaction between individual and the workplace setting. Therefore, we need to develop an insight into which workplace characteristics influence workplace learning. This part considers the implications that various workplace settings may have for employee learning. One specific type of setting is that of team-based structures, in which teams rather than individuals are responsible for getting the job done. This implies that by working together, employees can develop both individual and collective competencies in a process of exchanging information, advice, feedback, and different perspectives. Chapter 9 is written by Marloes Van Engen and Marianne Van Woerkom and deals with learning in the setting of work teams. They argue that in work teams the knowledge and skills of various team members will always differ to a certain extent as a result of their work experience and education. On the one hand this diversity in expertise in the team may have a positive effect on team learning and team performance, because when relevant expertise is brought together this may enhance the quality of decisions and actions. However, on the other hand differences among team members may also result in social categorization processes or in similarity attraction processes leading to professional rivalry, emotional conflict, and other dysfunctional affective processes in the team. On the basis of a survey among 624 respondents, working in 88 teams in seven different organizations, they conclude that the benefits of expertise diversity are greater than the costs. If team members report that they see differences in expertise in their team, they perceive their team as learning more, and consequently as performing better, and as being more innovative.

Workplace learning may also take place in project contexts. Chapter 10, by Rob Poell and co-authors, deals with two perspectives on project-based learning in work contexts, the first one being the critical-pragmatist perspective and the second the actor-network perspective. Despite their conceptual similarities, they are based on different classifications; the dominant actor is what differentiates learning projects in the actor-network perspective, whilst in the critical-pragmatist perspective the learning projects differ in their level of reflection. Eight case studies were conducted to find out whether there is a relationship between the dominant actor and the level of reflection in work-related learning projects. No clear-cut pattern emerged from the analysis, however, and the authors conclude there must be several other factors influencing the way project-based learning is organized, including individual agency and the learning climate in the organization.

Whereas in some sectors socio-technical design principles (e.g., self-managing teams) are prominent, other sectors develop in the opposite direction, bringing neo-tayloristic principles in practice. These kinds of organizations pose a major challenge for workplace learning. Chapter 11, by Eira Andersson and Anna Jansson, deals with workplace learning in the setting of call centres. They argue that the work situation in call centres is dominated by management principles that generate poor and problematic working conditions, such as monotonous work, high demands, low control, limited social support, and few opportunities for participation and learning. On the basis of qualitative interviews with local managers at nine call centres, the authors argue that learning in call centres can be described as focusing mainly on training and updating of daily tasks and can be discussed in terms of adjustmental learning, whereas organizational learning aiming for employee development does not seem to be implemented in these organizations. Based on these findings, they develop and test outlines for developmental learning in a call centre context by initiating such learning processes and introducing new tools for this purpose in collaboration with one call centre. The authors conclude that it is possible to implement developmental learning activities in a call centre environment and that these can counter the negative aspects of this environment by providing opportunities for variation and participation.

Another important context in which workplace learning is relevant is that of higher education, since many of these institutes are implementing workplace learning as an important part of their curriculum. This means that school learning is combined with paid work in a real company, which is assumed to be an effective learning environment for developing professional skills. Chapter 12, by Paul Smith and David Preece, examines current government strategies for higher education in the UK and the strengths and weaknesses of the work-based learning approach. The chapter explores the views of policy advisors and university staff with a detailed analysis of policy issues, comparing them to what is actually happening in practice through three case studies. The research data are drawn from interviews with policy advisors and academics at three post-1992 British universities. The main themes emerging are resistance to work-based learning programmes and a disjuncture between government policy and practice.

Chapter 13 is written by Marianne van Woerkom and deals with workplace learning in the context of teaching. Traditionally, teachers have a relatively autonomous but also isolated position within their classroom and their school organization, making it difficult to learn from each other by observing colleagues and exchanging feedback. However, teachers are being confronted with many pedagogical changes that require them to engage more in collaborative learning. The author argues that student teachers should therefore be prepared not only for their didactical and pedagogical role but also for the role they can play as a team member in the development of their school organization. Consequently, teacher educators should play a role in preparing student teachers for this new role. On the basis of a survey among 146 teacher educators in the Netherlands, Van Woerkom argues that if we want to prepare future teachers for their collective responsibility for processes of school innovation, they should be educated and coached by teacher educators who see school development and educational innovation as key parts of their job and who are actively involved in professional development themselves.

In the concluding chapter of this volume (Chapter 14), the editors pull together a number of threads from the preceding chapters, analyzing similarities and differences and potential reasons for these, and identifying common emerging themes and contradictions.

Part I

Perspectives on Learning in the Workplace

2 The Relational Interdependence between Personal and Social Agency in Learning and for Working Life

Stephen Billett

Currently, there is great interest in and expectations for learning through work and throughout working life. As a consequence, the concept of lifelong learning has been recast. Its principal purpose has become the maintenance of individuals' workplace competence (Organisation of Economic Co-operation and Development 1996). Governments' and employers' initiatives to mobilize workers' ongoing learning are attempts to realize national and enterprise competitiveness, in an increasingly globalized economy (Field 2000). The expectation is that by engaging workers in work-related learning throughout their working lives their workplace effectiveness will be sustained and their chances of redundancy will be reduced. This expectation includes developing the capacities to effectively respond to new workplace and occupational challenges as they arise and to adapt to new forms of work when occupational transitions are necessary. In part, government and enterprise interest is directed towards making lifelong learning occur through attendance in courses and programmes aimed to secure these outcomes. Yet, engaging in work learning, including that through and for work, occurs inevitably and continuously through workers' engagement in their daily tasks and interactions, and often in the absence of anyone directly guiding that learning (Billett 2001b). There is no difference between the processes of everyday thinking and acting and the process of learning (e.g., Lave 1993; Rogoff and Lave 1984): it occurs continuously as we think and act. The process of learning occurring continuously throughout our lives has been described as microgenetic development (Rogoff 1990). It comprises the moment-by-moment learning occurring incrementally, continuously, and, sometimes, transformatively when contributing to individuals' lifelong process of change: their ontogenetic development (Scribner 1985b).

The kinds of incremental and transformative learning that occur during individuals' engagement in everyday goal-directed work activities (Billett 2001b) are shaped by the degree of familiarity of these activities for workers. Familiar activities and interactions are likely to provide experiences that incrementally refine and hone (i.e., develop further) what individuals know and can do. Yet, activities and interactions that are novel to individuals can be generative of new knowledge structures, and are thereby personally transformative. This ongoing and pervasive process of learning that hones and extends what we know likely constitutes most of individuals' learning throughout their working life. Importantly, it arises through everyday work activities.

For those interested in promoting workers' lifelong learning, this form of learning, which occurs almost gratuitously through work life, is worthy of careful consideration. Therefore, acknowledging, improving, supporting, or directing that learning in particular ways may achieve the kinds of outcomes in which governments and employers as well as workers themselves are interested. As learning throughout working life becomes more important for all workers, it is worthwhile understanding further the ongoing and everyday process of learning. In particular, understanding the distinctive qualities, variations, and strengths and limitations of both the processes and outcomes of this learning is important. Such an understanding may provide pointers as to how best this learning can be organized and can contribute to governments', enterprises', and workers' goals for learning throughout working life.

In addressing this need, this chapter makes two contributions to understanding learning through work. Firstly, the process of lifelong learning is advanced as being an interdependent negotiated process between personal and social contributions (Billett 2006a). The contributions constitute a duality comprising the affordances of workplaces and the engagement of workers. Studies of learning through working life have identified how workplace affordances—those that invite workers to participate, through the provision of access, support, and reward—are generative of the kinds of robust learning required for effective and changing work (Billett 2001b). Such affordances comprise access to work activities and interactions that provide opportunities for new learning as well as those for refining and honing what is already known. They occur through processes of observation, access to and engagement in work activities that are authentic instances of the tasks to be learnt. Yet, beyond the contributions afforded by workplaces, individuals' personal agency, subjectivity, and intentionality exist. These personal factors mediate how individuals construe, construct, and engage with what is afforded by workplace settings. Therefore, rather than just focussing on how workplace settings afford support for workers, it is essential to consider how personal factors contribute to and shape (i.e., negotiate) relationally this learning.

Secondly, although there is an interdependence in the learning process, it occurs relationally between personal and situational factors. That is, learning will occur in different ways across and between kinds of workplace circumstances, and in distinct ways for workers. For instance, in work settings that lack close guidance by experts, the learning of new knowledge and transformations of work practices still proceeds, yet it may be premised much more on learners' agency and intentionality than access to experts (Billett *et al.* 2004). More generally, workers' cognitive experience shapes how they construe and construct what they experience and, therefore, learn, and in ways that are person-dependent. Hence, learners' capacities and interests become more central to their learning. So beyond the potency and diversity of learning experiences and outcomes arising from different kinds of workplace affordances is the central role of the learner. The chapter seeks to extend accounts of the kinds and outcomes of inter-psychological processes that comprise learning through work through a consideration of these two points.

THE THEORETICAL CONTEXT: THE PERSONAL AND SOCIAL CONTRIBUTIONS TO LIFELONG LEARNING

Learning is acknowledged as comprising a process through which individuals deploy and change their ways of knowing, or cognitive experience, through participating in activities and interactions (e.g., Rogoff and Lave 1984; Sfard 1998). Consistent with cognitive theory, workplace experiences that are novel for individuals are likely to be generative of new knowledge. This includes means of categorization and classifying what is known, and ongoing processes of refinement or embellishments in human performance when re-engaging with tasks previously undertaken (e.g., Anderson 1993). Hence, different kinds of ongoing learning arise ordinarily through individuals' participation in work. Nevertheless, the processes and outcomes of this learning will, by degree, be person-dependent. For instance, what will be for one worker a novel work task, from which she/he might learn new knowledge and categories of knowledge, might be quite familiar for another worker. Thus, engaging in the same activity for the second worker leads to the refining or reinforcement of what they already know or can do. So, there will be distinct kinds of processes and outcomes arising for each of these workers engaging in the 'same' task.

Yet, because these work activities are socially shaped, the change in individuals arising from these activities and interactions realizes social legacies (Billett 2003). It is helpful here to be reminded of Rogoff and Lave's (1984) earlier proposition: activity structures cognition. That is, there a legacy in the form of what is learnt (an intra-psychological attribute) that arises from the socially shaped activities in which we participate (inter-psychological processes). For the learning of occupational practices that have developed through history, and reflect cultural needs and situational (i.e., workplace) requirements, the opportunity to access this socially derived knowledge through work experience is particularly important. Workplaces also shape these participatory processes, through their invitational qualities, which shape the access and support that individuals are provided with to secure occupational knowledge through workplace activities and interactions. The process of learning through participation, however, also needs to include how individuals construe and construct what they experience in these settings. It is these person-dependent processes that shape and even determine how individuals engage in and learn through workplace activities (Billett 2003). Individuals, by degree, elect how they participate with what they are afforded by social practices. Just as school students elect to engage in different ways with what is afforded by their schools, so too workers elect how they respond to what is afforded them by their workplaces. How individuals interact with the social experience of their workplaces is premised in their cognitive experience (i.e., how they experience and construe the social and physical world they encounter in the settings), which comprises their subjectivities as well as their conceptual and procedural learnings.

As foreshadowed, this learning through everyday participation at work constitutes negotiated and relational interactions between social and personal contributions: those of the setting and of the learners. These negotiations are shaped in relational ways. On the one hand, workers need to engage in the socioculturally derived and supported practices to secure the knowledge required for their work. This necessity drives workers' learning and participation. Yet, this relatedness ranges from total involvement to being wholly disengaged (Valsiner 1994). For instance, individuals may not even be aware of the social press, subjugation, discourse or other social forms in ways that influence the responses of others. On the other hand, workplaces afford workers opportunities to learn the procedures and goals required for effective performance to different degrees: they have different invitational qualities.

The interactions between the personal and the world beyond the person are mediated by individuals' cognitive experience, which has been shaped by their earlier (i.e., pre-mediate) engagements with the social world (Valsiner and van de Veer 2000). Consequently, these negotiations should not be viewed as the individual versus the social, because individuals' knowing has personal-social geneses. Yet, it is these personal, socially derived cognitive experiences (i.e., how and what they know) that shape individuals' construal and construction of what they experience in work and throughout working life. This is not to deny the potency of the immediate social experience of workplaces, including their occupational practices and techniques, norms and discourses. These have arisen and been sustained through history and reflect cultural purposes and needs. Importantly though, individuals' construal and construction of workplace and their capacities shape how work practices are enacted within work practices, albeit bounded by workplace imperatives, constraints, and monitoring, (and often despite these).

Beyond changes to individuals (i.e., their learning) that occur through these negotiations, the same constructive and interactive processes also bring about change in work activities and practices. This is because the processes constitute the active remaking and transformation of the culturally derived practices that comprise paid work. This occurs, like learning, continuously as workers deploy their capacities and construals of the work tasks they enact and at particular moments in time. So, there are two key changes occurring through participation in work-related activities: individuals' incremental or transformative learning and the remaking and/or transformation of work activities.

Yet, these changes—individual (worker) and cultural (workplace) development (learning and change to work)—occur through relational processes. Individuals' personally unique interpretations and enactments of their work and workplace reveal the limits of social agency or suggestion. The capacity of the social world to project and secure its suggestion is neither comprehensive nor complete because it is limited by individual interpretation (Valsiner 2000). The cultural psychologist Valsiner (2000) refers to the personal experiencing of each event and the capacity to rebuff much of what we experience through the social world, which would otherwise overwhelm us (Valsiner and van der Veer 2000). Yet, conversely, individuals' freedom and capacity to secure their intentions are limited by the activities and interactions their work affords them. Moreover, the workplace's invitation and projection of its contribution is exercised in different ways and forms depending upon workplace circumstances and individuals taking up of those suggestions (Billett *et al.* 2005).

In all, the account of learning advanced here focuses on inter-psychological processes. These are negotiated between individuals' personal cognitive experience and the social world, including the norms, discourses and practices, including forms of close and indirect guidance that comprise the social suggestion. As noted, personal subjectivities, gaze and discourses to which individuals have access are constituted as part of individuals' cognitive experience that shapes how they mediate their engagement in and learning through work (Billett 2006b). Individuals' engagement, learning and remaking of practice is also shaped by their dispositions, including interest, and the brute facts of their energy, strength and their limits, as in exhaustion. Therefore, just as personal agency is constrained by strong social suggestion, surveillance and control, the press of the social world can be constrained. This can occur by individuals' capacities to suppress its suggestion (Berger and Luckman 1966), or even its rebuttal by individuals (Valsiner 2000). Moreover, given the limits and ambiguities in how the social world projects its suggestion (i.e., its contributions, norms and practices), individuals have to actively construe and construct the meaning being suggested by the social world (e.g., the requirements to practice effectively). The inter-psychological process of learning is, therefore, necessarily individually and relationally negotiated because personal histories or ontogenetic development (i.e., learning across life) is personally unique.

It follows that it is now important to understand something of the ways in which the personal and social contributions are enacted differently across instances of work. For instance, much of the research that has been used to promote the social constructivist case (i.e., that there are social contributions to individuals' knowledge construction) has been undertaken in relatively rich social settings (e.g., educational institutions and large workplaces). Such settings afford accessible direct and indirect social guidance. Yet, much of work life learning (and learning throughout life generally) occurs in situations where the social suggestion is weak, including the absence of direct guidance by more expert partners. This is but one variation, albeit an important one, in the kinds of inter-psychological processes that might occur in workplaces and repeatedly be experienced throughout working life. Consequently, there is a need to know how learning occurs in circumstances that afford limited close interpersonal guidance by more expert workers as well as those where more informed social partners are easily accessible.

In the following sections some instances of learning through work are discussed under two broad headings: (a) those that afford access to the close guidance of experts and other contributions that make them socially rich learning environments, and (b) those where close guidance is absent and social contributions are weaker. The purpose is to identify variations in inter-psychological processes within the former and to understand how these processes occur in the later.

RESEARCH AND FINDINGS: RELATIONAL INTERDEPENDENCE AT WORK

As noted, much enquiry into the social contributions to learning has occurred in social settings that provide both close and more distance forms of social guidance, and by expert partners. Drawing upon important and helpful contributions from anthropology, and anthropological methodologies, these kinds of social settings dominated enquiries into and theorizing about learning in the last decade. Much of the interest in situated cognition, for instance, was to improve teaching and learning in schools, that is, in settings which also provide access to close social guidance (Raizen 1991; Resnick 1987). However, as not all workplace learning occurs in such situations it is necessary to understand something of the different inter-psychological processes that occur in the absence of strong direct and indirect guidance by more experienced social partners. These processes need to be considered alongside the processes that occur in workplace situations where close social guidance of more expert others may be available. In the next two sections, these considerations are addressed.

Settings Providing Access to Proximal Guidance of Experts and Others

Hairdressing salons are socially constructed spaces that are ordered to fulfil the requirements of the culturally derived occupation of hairdressing. In many ways, they represent the kinds of rich social settings that have been the focus of inquiry in identifying social contributions to learning and development (e.g., Scribner, Rogoff etc.). These settings afford close guidance of more experienced and/or expert partners. They also provide rich bases for observation and imitation that furnish cues and assistance for learning, more indirectly. However, although hairdressing salons have a common culturally derived purpose (dressing people's hair), each workplace may have quite distinct goals and preferences for the enactment of hairdressing (Billett 2001a). This means that hairdressers participating and learning in these salons are afforded quite distinct kinds of experiences and interactions. In one salon, stylish and transformational haircuts were the core business. Here, there was an emphasis on 'cut and colour', and an emphasis on contemporary and fashionable hairstyling. The youngish and inner-city clientele frequented this salon because of its reputation for offering fashionable cuts and styling. Typically, in this salon the hairdressers had their own clients and the salon's work was organized around each hairdresser working with their own clients through the entire hairdressing activity. However, another salon had quite a different focus and mode of hairdressing work. Here, the key concern was to provide dependable (i.e., predictable) haircuts and treatments to local clients that were seen as being 'good value for money'. Such an emphasis was seen to be important in a country town, which at that time was suffering from a rural recession. At this salon, the hairdressing work was divided and distributed across the four or five hairdressers on the basis of each hairdresser's level of experience. The most available experienced hairdresser would undertake the most crucial hairdressing task, often taking over from a less experienced hairdresser, midway through a process. This meant that the less experienced hairdressers would typically perform less critical tasks than in the city salon, while more experienced hairdressers would complete the more complex and critical tasks. Yet, in this salon, neither experienced nor novice hairdressers had their own clientele. Nor were they allowed the same scope of discretion, for instance, in accessing supplies. So the goals for this salon were associated with providing good quality and value-for-money hairdressing that were provided through a process that the owner described as a 'production line' (Billett 2001b).

In these ways, these two salons, like the others investigated, had particular goals and practices that were shaped by situational factors, including owners' and/or managers' preferences. Thus, each salon afforded quite distinct activities and interactions through which the hairdressers participated (i.e., practiced and learnt). These affordances went beyond differences in the kinds of hairdressing that was enacted through the salons' particular 'culture of practice' (Brown, Collins and Duguid 1989). They included the kinds of discretion that were afforded and means by which hairdressers came to engage with their work. In all, there were distinct modes of participatory practices (Billett 2002) being exercised in each of the salons.

These work settings comprised socially rich learning spaces that afforded both close and indirect forms of guidance. Much of hairdressers' work is

conducted in the public space of these salons, making it easy for hairdressers to be observed, monitored and imitated. Indeed, hairdressers habitu-
ally observe clients entering the salon, the process of hairdressing, and the
finished haircut when they leave. In many ways, therefore, these workplace
settings might be thought of as restricting the workers discretion. Within
the constraints of the salons' culture of practice (i.e., 'what we do here')
there is evidence that hairdressers were able to exercise personal preferences in dressing their clients' hair. Yet, despite the close monitoring and
restrictive practices adopted in the second salon, each of the hairdressers
negotiated their own engagement and meaning within the setting. Indeed,
across these salons there was evidence of a cognitive legacy of the salon in
shaping how the hairdressers engaged in hairdressing tasks. Even in the
most strongly monitored salon, there was evidence of constructions of hairdressing tasks being shaped by hairdressers' preferences that lead to practice. This is what Evans (2002) refers to as bounded agency: the kinds and
degree of discretion available within the constraints of a bounded social
practice. Moreover, it was possible to identify the events in individuals'
ontogenies that shaped these preferences for practice. These differences
were evident in accounts of hairdressers' preferences about their work, how
they categorized clients and how they conceptualized clients' hairdressing
needs and provided particular treatments for them (Billett 2003).

The point here is that workers were engaged in close physical proximity,
where their work could be observed and monitored and in circumstances
that might promote shared understanding. Yet, by different degrees, each of
the hairdressers construed, constructed and engaged in their work in ways
that reflected different combinations of social and personal press. Some
hairdressers also had roles as owners and managers that gave them more
authority in decision making, yet required engagement with other kinds
of concerns and perspectives. Hence, their decision making about their
hairdressing salons included issues associated with its overall management,
profitability and performance. So, they had a wider and different set of factors (i.e., cognitive experience) to consider than those who were employed
as hairdressers. Others were novices, some of whom were concerned about
their standing with both other hairdressers and clients. Perhaps not sur-
prisingly then, given these differing positioning in the social practice,
their responses to 'the same' work-related activities were marked by both
similarities and differences. While there were similarities in approaches to
hairdressing activities, there were also distinct and personally based variations. Consequently, despite the close and monitorable circumstances of
their work, variations of practice were enacted. In all, there was verified
evidence of diverse forms of relational inter-psychological processes and
negotiations in the accounts of these hairdressers' work (Billett 2003).

Similar relational engagement and learning (i.e., interdependencies) were
identified in other workplaces where common work task and collaborative
ways of working occurred. This included teams of information technology

(IT) specialists and firefighters (Billett *et al.* 2005). In the information technology work space there was a standard operating system for all the workplace's computers. There was also a performance feedback and rating scheme that clients completed to rate the performance of the technicians. Given the immediacy of the knowledge required for work (e.g., viruses and software problems), there was an imperative for these technicians to collaborate and share knowledge about problems with or threats to the system. Responses and solutions to these threats and problems had to be enacted quickly, and be uniformly applied and then shared across the workspace, and with teams of workers conducting similar tasks. Moreover, because the technicians were co-located, there was a better prospect for sharing of this knowledge. Nevertheless, despite the similarity of the work and the uniformity of the operating environment, the technicians engaged in and completed their work activities in personally distinct ways.

Each IT worker participating in the study reported having quite distinct work life history and goals, and these were inconsistent with the goals of the work area, in two of the three instances. One was a very experienced electronics engineer who wanted to use his skills more widely than was possible within the constraints of a standardized operating system. He also had a preference for resolving clients' problems for the longer term, which meant he preferred having fewer and longer interactions with clients each working day. However, this was inconsistent with quantitative accounts of client satisfaction and responses to the immediate problem. Another member of this team was a new employee who had retrained only recently as an IT technician. Since his work ambitions were not being fulfilled through these work activities, he was planning and making contacts for a move to a different kind of IT work. Consequently, he minimized his engagement in the workplace's social activities, particularly those conducted outside of work hours. The third participant did much to keep the workplace interactions going and initiated some of the social events outside of work time. His work history and expertise was consistent with the work of the help desk centre, and management of standardized information processing systems. Hence, the three IT workers' subjectivities, interests and intentions were quite different. This shaped how they participated and learnt through their working lives. Within the bounds of what was possible, these workers exercised their agency in different ways.

Similar findings were identified in the firefighters' workplace activities. These workers also engaged closely with each other and over time as part of the firefighting team. When on shift, they worked, trained, slept and ate together in a common space in circumstances and ways likely to promote high levels of inter-subjectivity. Indeed, all three of the firefighters participating in the study shared a strong identity of being 'firefighters'. Indeed, maintaining and extending that identity was a key motivating factor in their participation and learning through work. Furthermore, the workplaces had strict norms and practices that needed to be adhered to for work organization and safety requirements, and were reinforced by a 'command and control culture'. This extended to conventions associated with the allocation of tasks and, even, seating arrangements in the fire engine and a battery of permissions and regulations that had to be honoured. These included mandatory induction training and examinations for promotions. One informant was an experienced firefighter from another country. Yet despite his experience, he had to complete the probationary processes and period, and be treated as a novice firefighter until he had satisfied probationary requirements. The second informant was a senior officer seeking to continue his career in the service, whilst maintaining his identity as an active and expert firefighter. The third participant had a set of specialist skills that already permitted him some autonomy and authority when fighting fires. He was also provided with significant workplace support by being given time off to address a family health issue and to prepare for examinations that would assist his promotion to a senior officer. Therefore, while there was a common form of work, and strong identification with that work, each of the three officers had distinct positions within the service and also premises for their engagement in and learning more about firefighting. Hence, despite working in a strictly regulated command and culture environment, there were quite distinct affordances and ways of engaging with that work. Once more, the issue of bounded agency was evident.

So, although workplace learning can be understood through the duality of affordances and engagements, it is unlikely to be uniform. Hence their diversities, that is, the different kinds of affordances that workplaces provide and the distinctive personally particular bases through which individuals will engage in these set of affordances, need to be understood. Importantly, even in the workplace which affords the richest of social guidance, this may be rebuffed by workers because these are not the premises through which individuals want to engage in work and learn. For instance, an occupational health and safety officer rejected rich forms of workplace support, because he believed himself to be more knowledgeable than an assigned mentor, and his processes of occupational practice to be superior to that practice in this workplace (Billett 2001b).

Settings Where Proximal Guidance and Regulation Are Weak

The preceding studies discussed participation in work settings that afforded rich and close social guidance. However, it is probable that most workers are employed in situations of relative social, physical or geographical isolation that do not afford this kind of support. For instance, in Australia as elsewhere, those employed in small businesses far outnumber those employed in large businesses. These workplaces are likely to offer more limited forms of access to close guidance by a range of more experienced co-workers. Yet, conceptions of individuals' learning new knowledge in social situations are often premised upon having access to direct guidance by others who have that knowledge and can enhance the scope of those who are learning. This is exemplified in the concept of the Zone of Proximal Development, where the more expert partner is held to enhance the scope of the novice's learning through joint problem solving and support. Therefore, it is important to understand what comprises inter-psychological process in workplaces where direct social guidance is limited or unavailable.

In particular, it is useful to consider how workers in relatively socially isolated circumstances learn concepts and procedures that are derived from the social world. The example discussed here is of small-business operators' learning about how to implement a goods-and-service tax (Billett *et al.* 2003). The small businesses that were the focus of this study had a diverse range of occupational focuses (e.g., beauty therapy, agricultural agent, bookseller, veterinarian, optician etc.), varied in their size (e.g., sole proprietor, micro-businesses, small businesses), spread of activities and geographical locations (i.e., city, provincial centre and small towns). Although faced with the identical task of learning to administer the goods-and-service tax, they had quite distinct goals for their learning because the tax had different impacts, meaning and implications across the businesses. The small-business operators used differing ways of engaging with social partners and sources of information in order to learn about the tax. Here, in particular, there was evidence of the exercise of operators' personal agency, pro-activity and critical engagement in determining what the tax meant to their business. This included consideration of what bases and for what purposes they engaged with others and independently in learning about the tax. As with the information technology workers, the role of subjectivity, interest and intentionality was evident in the workers' engagement and learning about the new taxation system. For some of the operators, the requirement was seen largely as a nuisance and not a primary consideration for their work. This was a case for those who were more interested in their occupational practice (i.e., an optician, a vet, an agricultural supplier) than in the details of running a business. Their interest was to gain an overall understanding and delegate its implementation to a bookkeeper. However, for those operators with businesses that were highly focussed on cash flow and profitability, such as those who were entrepreneurs or owners of businesses, there was a need to understand the entire process. Then, there were those small-business operators who, unlike the optician and veterinarian, could not afford accountants and bookkeepers. These operators had to exercise particular agency in learning more about and how best to administer the goods-and-service taxes in order to remove the financial burden of accountants and bookkeepers. Consequently, there were quite distinct and relational premises for these workers to engage with the task of learning about the initiative. For some, it was a nuisance, others a key imperative and for others again a potential impost upon their work activities, including its viability. Hence, there were quite distinct and relational bases for their engagement, focus for and scope of learning.

The key point here, as Valsiner (1994) suggests, is that there are qualitatively distinct and relational responses to the same social suggestion. These were shaped by the particular imperatives of the workplace (i.e., workplace goals and purposes) and the small-business operators' interests. Their responses were more than quantitatively different (i.e., by degree). They represented distinct goals for and, consequently, diverse construals and constructions, and, in turn, bases for learning about the initiative. Essentially, the inter-psychological processes (i.e., between the personal and the social) were quite distinct. The press of the social suggestion (i.e., the need to accommodate the goods-and-service tax) was able to be exercised in different ways. Conversely, the ways in which these workers construed, constructed and enacted that suggestion were relational, according to their workplace and personal needs.

There was also evidence of both agency and interdependence in the small-business operators' learning. They needed to engage with social partners and sources of knowledge about the initiative to be successful it addressing its requirements. This included what the taxation scheme meant to their particular business. This interdependence was often enacted selectively and in ways which were highly proactive, critical and engaged. For instance, while many of the small-business operators took the opportunity to engage with sources of advice about the goods-and-service tax from others (e.g., other small-business men, industry talks and presentations), their engagement was much more active than a passive acceptance of what was presented (i.e., afforded) them. Some operators referred to going to meetings and listening critically to and questioning what was being advanced by speakers. They also referred to making critical appraisals and judgements about the sources of advice, such as other small-business operators and informants. Yet, overall, rather than the quality and scope of the learning being shaped by more expert partners, it seems that it was the learners' agency, intentionality and effortfullness that was central to the process of the process of learning in relatively socially isolated circumstances. However, the exercise of this agency should not be seen as being necessarily appropriate. There were also negative outcomes for some of these small-business operators because of reliance upon their own agency. For instance, one small-business operator who owned a farm supply business was required to undertake a significant amount of learning to effectively administer the goods-and-service tax. Like some others small-business operators in the study, he had never used computers before to manage his business. However, his strategies were largely internal and the lack of active engagement with other sources of information that could assist him led to significant difficulties. Others proceeded too hastily, and without appropriate advice. However, while all this indicates the need for access to expertise, it also reinforces the imperative for these relatively socially isolated learners to be agentic and proactive in their engagement with experts.

Indeed, when effective, the learning of these small-business operators occurred without engagements with more expert others. Beyond external financial experts, there were examples of family members providing guidance on financial and technical issues. However, it was how the inter-psychological processes that underpin this learning were conducted that is most noteworthy. For most operators, it was less a case of reliance upon social partners and more a case of strong engagement and personal agency, including a gradual relinquishing of expert guidance. Indeed, for some of these small-business operators the key challenge was to manage without the kind of close guidance that was being offered (at a cost) by accountants and business consultants. Consequently, in the absence of close forms of social guidance in everyday practice, the balance in the inter-psychological processes was taken up by enhanced learner agency.

However, there is a caveat. Although the study indicated that learner agency was both important and successful for new learning under these circumstances, the actual learning circumstance may not be typical of what is required by socially isolated workers. This taxation initiative was supported by advice from government and industry associations as well as that provided by accountants and financial consultants. Moreover, many others were engaged in the same kinds of learning. Hence, there were numerous opportunities for peer support and learning. However, in earlier studies, other kinds of learning by geographically and socially isolated learners who were not engaged in the same task (Billett 2001b) revealed similar processes of active engagement by learners, but with some distinct nuances. In the absence of expert informants, these learners attempted to locate and discuss workplace problems with appropriate experts. Principally, there was agency in their efforts to gain access to experts elsewhere. That is, there was other evidence of selective and purposeful engagement with particular kinds of social partners.

In all, these cases suggest that inter-psychological processes connect individuals with the social world in ways that assist their learning. Yet, these processes are enacted in circumstances where direct social guidance is largely absent. This requires learners' personal agency to be far stronger in order to compensate for the lack of close expert guidance. In some circumstances, this agentic form of learning is likely to be richer than when arising through joint problem solving with an expert partner, and certainly from being taught didactically. This is because the learners' engagement, interest and intentionality are driving the learning process. Even the learning of new knowledge derived from social sources is not wholly dependent upon close guidance from a more expert counterpart. Instead, the prospects for and scope of new learning in workplaces and through inter-psychological processes are not wholly dependent upon the close guidance of more expert partners. Rather, the agency of the learner can compensate in some ways for the circumstances where social guidance is unavailable. This is perhaps most likely to be exercised when the worker engages with the learning task wholeheartedly. Put simply, unless the learner sees this new learning as a personal imperative, such agency is unlikely to be enacted. Of course, there are limits to individuals' constructive efforts, as experts can provide guided access to knowledge that individuals alone might develop over a life span. Yet, the point here is that learning new knowledge from the social world does not always have to be mediated by an expert partner. Instead, the learners' agency and interests can compensate in some ways.

CONCLUSIONS FOR RESEARCH AND PRACTICE: RELATIONAL INTERDEPENDENCE AT WORK

The notion that learning throughout working life comprises an ongoing inter-psychological process premised on a relational interdependence between the immediate social experience and individuals' construal and construction and mediation of that experience has been advanced in this chapter. Through a consideration of different kinds and degrees of workplace affordances and individual engagement that constitute inter-psychological processes, it has been argued that this conception offers a dualistic and relational base to understand individuals' learning and remaking of their work activities in a way that privileges neither the contributions of the learner nor the setting. Instead, it acknowledges the relationships between them and how this is enacted in circumstances where the agency of the social and the personal take different and unequal roles. To understand learning through work, then, it is necessary to account for the relational bases of this learning. However, a consideration of relational bases between the individual and the social is far from new. Baldwin (1894, 1898) gave particular attention to the selectivity, construal and engagement of the learner in his accounts of human development. Similarly, from a sociological perspective, Giddens (1991) has long opposed the polarization of agency and structure, viewing structures as enabling as well as constraining, yet acknowledging the key role of human agency in bringing about change in the social world. Valsiner (1994) and Bhaskar (1998), although acknowledging the ubiquity of social influence, also emphasize the relatedness between individuals' interests and goals, and those comprising the social suggestion. Indeed, at least one rendering of Vygotsky's work suggests that he also advocated learner agency as being central to expansive learning. In considering children's engagement in play, he allocated a greater contribution to the scope of their learning as being found in their energies, imagination and engagement than that provided by social partners. The conceptual contribution in this chapter is to extend and reinforce the relational duality that constitutes inter-psychological processes that are enacted in lifelong learning, albeit in the workplace.

The procedural implications advanced in this chapter are that governments, industry leaders and enterprise managers need to promote both affordances for learning and also the reasons for individuals to engage fully and agentically in that learning. This is particularly the case when the learning is new and requires effortful engagement. The potential for effective learning through work can be realized by increased levels of workplace support for learning by employers, and expanded means of learning support for those working in circumstances of social and geographic isolation. However, and importantly, the kinds of support provided and the targeted focus of support need to be aligned not only to workplace requirements but also to the learners' interests and goals. Educational goals and purposes directed towards interests other than those which engage learners are likely to have more limited impact on those which can effectively engage learners. Certainly, quite often, the goals for learning through work are consistent with those of workers. However, this is not always the case. It would be mistaken to assume that workers' direction, intention and focus for their lifelong learning will always be consistent with that which governments, employers and educators seek to secure. Importantly, what is proposed here suggests that providing support for learning for workers who are socially, geographically or otherwise isolated may be far more helpful than trying to provide appropriate and targeted teaching of what is to be learnt. Learning throughout working life has been shown to be a relational and negotiated process. Finding ways of engaging workers of all kinds in the effortful processes of learning new knowledge and honing and refining that knowledge further stands as an important premise for efforts to improve learning throughout working life.

KEY LEARNING POINTS

- Understanding learning through work is dependent, by degree, on the contributions of situation, culture and individuals. Situations afford particular opportunities for learning, culture provides particular privileging of work and learning, and individuals actively engage in the process of constructing meaning (i.e., learning) and remaking occupational practices.
- The process of learning through work can best be understood as being negotiated between the personal and social contributions (i.e., inter-psychologically) but in ways which are bounded by both personal and social agency.
- Whereas most studies and theorizing about inter-psychological processes have emphasized the influence of social settings on forms of social guidance, we also need to consider how workers learn in circumstances that have relatively limited access to direct guidance.

3   Beyond Individual Acquisition
Theorizing Practice-Based Collective Learning in HRD

Tara Fenwick

In the human resource development field, learning has long been recognized to be embedded in everyday work practice. Theorists such as Watkins and Marsick (1993) have helped push HRD to consider the entire organization, its objects, people and structures, in terms of continuous collective learning activity. Much subsequent HRD research has employed theories of systemic informal and incidental learning, action learning, and conceptions of the "learning organization" as a site of continuous collective knowledge production. However, this important work seems to have been overwritten somewhat by theories returning to focus on the individual. In a recent review of work-learning literature published 1999–2004 in 10 journals (organization/ management studies and adult education as well as HRD), the only area that continued to feature a strong emphasis on learning as individual acquisition and development was HRD (in *Human Resource Development International* and *Human Resource Development Quarterly*) (Fenwick in press).

In this chapter I argue for a return to conceptions of learning as inherently collective, practice-based, and mutually constituted with/in systems of activity, discourses, objects and history. Indeed, I suggest that understandings of work learning within HRD theory can be fruitfully enriched by incorporating more fully a range of practice-based theories that are enjoying increasing uptake in broader fields of organization studies, new sociology and technology studies, and critical management studies. Practice-based theories have emerged both through application to learning issues of theories derived from new social and natural sciences and through ethnographic studies of learning in various work organizations (Beckett 2001; Belfiore *et al.* 2004; Gherardi and Nicolini 2000; Sawchuk 2003). I have deliberately chosen to present three perspectives alongside one another rather than concentrating upon just one. This is because, in my view, a range of theoretical perspectives is critical to avoid totalization of the terms of debate, or reification of any particular approach or unit of analysis, by any one perspective. All theoretical perspectives are provisional and limited in ways that are only fully appreciated in comparison with other views. That said, I certainly do not argue for accepting all perspectives, for some have proven to lack analytic power and capacity to illuminate important dimensions of learning and cognition in organizations. Into this latter category I would place psychologistic views of learning as acquisitive, transferable and measurable (e.g., Bates and Holton III 2004; Enos *et al.* 2003; Wiethoff 2004) or as decontextualized individual development (e.g., Maurer 2002).

The chapter begins, therefore, with a discussion of individualist views of learning and their limitations. The next section overviews three very different practice-based perspectives that I suggest may be helpful for HRD researchers and practitioners. These perspectives have in common the assumption that individuals' learning is enmeshed with/in systems of continuous activity, and that learning emerges from *relations* and interactions of people with the social and material elements of particular contexts. *Context* is thus considered carefully in terms of its divisions of labour and power relations, environmental affordances, cultural disciplines, language, and so forth. One is the emergentist perspective of complexity science (Davis and Sumara 2006). Another perspective is the notion of expansion from cultural-historical activity theory (Engeström 2001). A third are the constructs of translation and mobilization presented by actor-network theory (Latour 2005). Some of these conceptions are not new to HRD professionals and learning theories, notably the complexity science perspective with its notions of emergence and self-organization.

The third section of the chapter discusses similarities across these perspectives, highlighting important dimensions such as identity and power relations. The final section returns to HRD theory to consider implications of the discussion for expanding conceptions of work learning as individuals with/in activity.

LEARNING AS INDIVIDUAL ACQUISITION AND DEVELOPMENT

In the acquisitive perspective, learning is characterized as an individual human process of consuming and storing new concepts and skills/behaviours, frequently in terms of translating learning to capabilities that add to organizational resources (Nafukho *et al.* 2004). Research has focused on how to "harness" or draw out and use the individual's acquired knowledge. Preoccupations include transferring acquired knowledge to practice, measuring competency (reliable valid measures and competence definitions are identified as problematic), and narrowing the gap between training investment and results (Bates and Holton III 2004; Enos *et al.* 2003; Wiethoff 2004). In the related human development perspective, learning is viewed as a more continuous process of developing personal knowledge, capability, beliefs and so on, but the focus is still clearly upon the individual (Jacobs and Washington 2003). Research preoccupations include how to promote the individual's self-directed learning capability and how to understand the relation of work to individual developmental processes (Clardy 2000; Straka 2000).

Some recent publications, particularly in the *Human Resource Development Review,* have moved beyond these wholly individualist perspectives to address collective work activity but, as I showed in Fenwick (2007), these discussions tended to stop short of actually acknowledging and theorizing the learning dynamics of the collective. Little analysis addresses important questions raised in the broader fields of organization studies about knowledge emergence in collective practice, the power relations circulating in all learning endeavours, and the complex constructions and choices—and their effects—of different individuals with/in collective material activity and social interaction.

But what is wrong with models of work learning as individual acquisition or development of knowledge? Why should learning theories expand and enrich their analyses of the dynamics of activity? First, acquisition implies that learning is additive, and that knowledge is a preexisting substance ingested by the learning individual. Yet critics have shown individuals' apparent inability to carry knowledge across space and time (Hager 2004). Folk wisdom simply admits, "use it or lose it": human experience suggests knowledge is embedded in everyday action, not in heads or even in bodies as dislocated skills. Acquisition does not often account for how people construct, individually and collectively, different meanings of their experiences. Nor does it dwell on how adults revisit and re-construct these meanings, resist or ignore certain meanings, or how they often experience transformation of identities and knowledge through collective action and reflection.

Individualist developmental perspectives, while useful for attending to personal sense-making and emotions in work learning, tend to overemphasize and undertheorize the role of individual reflection. Experience is often cast as a fixed thing, separated from knowledge-making processes. What become prominent are individual mental representations of events, static and distinct from the interdependent commotion of people together, in action with objects and language (Fenwick 2003). Further, the notion of "development" has been criticized as rooted in hierarchical and deficit-oriented assumptions: that the individual worker moves from less to more complete, as determined by the gaze of the educator or perhaps the HR planner, in a progressive and isolated trajectory (Fenwick 2007).

Generally, this focus on the individual fails to fully acknowledge the central role of sociocultural participation, the collective interplay of minds, bodies, tools and action in work learning. Studies of work communities show that knowledge tends to be distributed among participants, rather than being concentrated within individuals (Cook and Yanow 1993). In fact, there is general consensus now that instead of considering what and how work knowledge is acquired or even developed, research ought to focus on what and how environments and forms of participation produce particular practices of activity and knowledge (Billett 2004). Some posit that capabilities exist as chains of behaviour that are holistic and embedded in collective activity (Chaiklin and Lave 1993). Learning to use a hammer effectively, for example, is influenced by the carpenter's value ascribed to the hammering task in relation to the overall project and the specific task difficulty. Hammer use is also affected by the network of activity, both material and social, of which the hammering is part. Cultural norms of hammering and tools shape the learner's hammer use, as do specific situational distractions and pressures. In fact, recent spatial concepts of work learning have shown how particular spatiotemporal architectures function as pedagogies that invoke particular work knowledge and behaviours (and subjectivities) (Edwards and Nicoll 2004). Punch clocks and lockers at the workers' entrances to factories, presentation rooms dominated by screen and lectern (where a large group of learners may be squeezed into one-half the space while the instructor occupies the front half), mobile phones required by some firms to be worn by employees 24/7—these are just a few examples of how arrangements of objects and spaces control workers' activity in terms of movement, duration and tempo.

Critics also have shown how conventional apolitical approaches to workplace learning ignore the power relations that determine hierarchies in what learning is most valuable, what counts as skill, and what knowledge remains marginal or unnamed. Feminists have long called attention to gendered determinations of work knowledge that persist (Mojab and Gorman 2003; Probert 1999). Class hierarchies also obscure important work knowledge. Power relations in organizations configure arrangements of activity and social divisions that enable some kinds of learning for some people, and constrain many others (Jackson 1991; Sawchuk 2003).

The problem for HRD practice is that unless it is based on learning models that adequately theorize the actual individual/social dynamics articulated in everyday practices, it risks underestimating the complexity of these dynamics and thus either repressing or being subverted by them. That is, the progressive possibilities for both individual and social change remain vague unless these dynamics are more closely understood. For these reasons, contemporary theories of learning in work tend to have shifted from individualism to social learning perspectives (Sawchuk 2003), from acquisitional to practice-based conceptions (Hager 2004), and from atomistic to comprehensive systemic analyses that also account for micro-interactions within activity (Engeström 2001). In addition, power relations are increasingly analyzed so that learning theories address politics of knowledge, production and social difference that shape everyday activity and the learning generated within it.

CONTEMPORARY PERSPECTIVES ON LEARNING AND KNOWLEDGE IN WORK

Recent scholarship in work learning tends to accept that the learning process is simultaneously both individual and collective, and occurs in various contexts: everyday action, planning, conversation, projects, problem solving, instruction, reading, and online activity (Sawchuk *et al.* 2005; Wenger 1998). Three perspectives have been selected for discussion here: complexity science, cultural-historical activity theory, and actor-network theory. While very different in orientation and argument, these perspectives share concern for how learning emerges as individuals interact and negotiate three main elements of practice: contextual structures and culture; dynamics of activity at different levels of analysis (language, group activity, collective change); and movements of knowledge. All analyze learning as individuals with/in activity, and all have been employed explicitly to analyze learning in work contexts. Each is rooted in different, often contested, positions about the nature of knowledge, the nature of being, the relation of learner to object, and the nature of practice. Some try to totalize the debate. But their various contributions suggest fruitful openings for reconsidering processes through which learning in work adapts, expands and changes. Because these three perspectives are each complex and internally contested, an extended dialogue among them is not possible within the confines of the present discussion. This discussion is limited to an introductory presentation and comparison of the perspectives.

Learning as Emergence of Collective Cognition and Environment: Complexity Science

Complexity science is actually a heterogeneous body of theories originating in evolutionary biology, mathematical fractals and general systems theory, and including enactivism, cybernetics, chaos theory, autopoietic theories, and so on. The present discussion draws from educators and organizational development analysts who have theorized complexity science in terms of human learning (e.g., Davis and Sumara 2006; Karpiak 2000; Kauffman 1995; Osberg and Biesta 2007; Stacey 2005). Complexity science provides one approach to understanding learning processes in a system such as a work organization. The first premise is that the systems represented by person and context are inseparable, and the second that change occurs from emerging systems affected by the intentional tinkering of one with the other. The key theme is *emergence*, the understanding that in (complex adaptive) systems, phenomena, events and actors are mutually dependent, mutually constitutive, and actually emerge together in dynamic structures.

Davis *et al.* (2000), among others, have applied these concepts to human learning, showing how "environment" and "learners" emerge together in the process of emergent cognition. For example, like other phenomena such as flocking behaviour, tornados and stock markets, human conversation is an example of emergence. As each person contributes and responds within the activity, she changes the interactions and the emerging object of focus; other participants are changed, the relational space among them all changes, and the looping back changes the contributor's actions and subject position. This is "mutual specification" (Varela *et al.* 1991), the fundamental dynamic of systems constantly engaging in joint action and interaction. The resultant coupling changes or "co-specifies" each participant, creating a new transcendent unity of action and identities that could not have been achieved independently. These interactions are recursive, continuing to elaborate what is present and what is possible in the system. These interactions also form patterns all by themselves—they do not organize according to some sort of externally imposed blueprint—so complexity theorists describe such systems as *self-organizing*. That is, through the ongoing processes of recursively elaborative adaptation, the system can maintain its form without some externally imposed discipline or organizing device, such as hierarchical management.

In work organizations, people constantly influence and adjust to each other's emerging behaviours, ideas, and intentions—as well as with objects, furniture, technologies, etc.—through myriad complex interactions and fluctuations. A whole series of consequences emerge from these micro actions. Most of this complex joint action leaks out of individual attempts to control what they are doing. No clear lines of causation can be traced from these interactions to their outcomes, because at any given time among all these interconnections, possibilities are contained in the system that are not visible or realized. This means, among other things, that humans are fully nested within and interconnected with many elements of the systems comprising them and in which they participate. They are not considered to be autonomous, sovereign agents for whom knowledge can be acquired or extracted.

And yet, in our observation and recall of such occurrences, the tendency is to focus on the learning *figure* and dismiss all its complex interactions as "background". Complexity science urges a refocusing on the relations *between* things, not the things themselves, to observe complex wholes emerge from improvisations among micro-elements. Out of these continuous and nonlinear interactions emerge dynamic structures that exceed their parts. Osberg and Biesta (2007) call this "strong emergence": conditions where the knowledge and capability that emerges is more than the sum of its parts, and therefore not predictable from the "ground" it emerges from. Johnson (2001) shows that this emergence is enabled in systems characterized by diversity, decentralization, redundancy, open constraints and feedback.

Overall, in complexity science knowledge and action are understood as continuous invention and exploration, produced through relations among consciousness, identity, action and interaction, objects and structural dynamics. New possibilities for action are constantly emerging among these interactions of complex systems, and cognition occurs in the possibility for unpredictable shared action. Knowledge or skill cannot be contained in any one element or dimension of a system, for knowledge is constantly emerging and spilling into other systems. No actor has an essential self or knowledge outside these relationships: nothing is given in the order of things, but performs itself into existence. In HRD applications of complexity science, attention would be drawn to the relationships among learners and the environment. For example, an organizational change initiative would focus on enabling connections instead of training individuals to "acquire" understanding of the new policy—connections between this initiative and the many other initiatives likely to be lurking in the system, between parts of the system, between the initiative and the system's cultures, and between people, language and technologies involved in the change. It would encourage experimentation among people and objects involved in the change, and would focus on amplifying the advantageous possibilities that emerge among these connections as people tinker with objects and language involved. Learning is defined as expanded possibilities for action, or becoming "capable of more sophisticated, more flexible, more creative action" (Davis *et al.* 2000).

Learning as Expansion of Objects and Ideas: Cultural-Historical Activity Theory

Cultural-historical activity theory tries to account for these ongoing dynamic interactions with an "expansive" view of learning, defined as change in the joint action of a particular activity system. Derived from activity theory with Marxist roots, this view helps show the importance of sociocultural interactions of individual perspectives, system objects and practice histories in generating knowledge. First it is important to understand that actual and possible action in an activity system is shaped by its "object", the problem at which activity is directed. Learning occurs as a cycle of questioning something in this activity system, analyzing its causes, modelling a new explanation or solution, implementing this model in the system, reflecting on it and consolidating it (Engeström 1999, 2001). This is a nonlinear process, not a problem-solving cycle. The process simultaneously involves the system's goals, mediating artefacts or tools, and perspectives of participants. In fact, much back-and-forth activity revolves around finding consensus about what exactly is the problem, and what can be tolerated as a solution or innovation within the politics of the system.

Thus Engeström (1999) shows how innovation and change are both rooted and reconstructed or changed in the sociocultural and historical activity systems in which individuals participate. What is viewed as novel or useful depends on what problems are perceived as uppermost in a particular time and space, what knowledge is valued most there, and indeed what knowledge can even be perceived, named and understood by its participants. Therefore, the innovative learning process must be understood as an interplay of individuals' choice-making and design within social relations constituted by material interests, cultural histories, and conflicting discourses. From within his theory of expansive learning in cultural-historical-activity systems, Engeström (1999: 384) explains innovative learning as the "construction and resolution of successively evolving tensions or contradictions in a complex system that includes the object or objects, the mediating artefacts, and the perspectives of the participants". The object (system objective), in particular, is constructed by actors to make sense of, name and stabilize a focus for their activities. These objects have histories and trajectories. They can provoke desire and resistance, and can generate identity or new forms of sociality. The creative potential of activity is closely related to moment-to-moment interactions among actors: they try to grasp the object or problem, redefine it, and seek openings for new possibilities within myriad constraints.

Sawchuk's (2003) study of technology learning among workers used cultural-historical activity theory. He showed how people participate in a wide array of computer-learning practices that are "integrated with everyday life and mediated by artefacts including computer hardware and software, organizational settings, oral devices, class habitus, trade unions, and working-class culture" (2003: 21). Encounters among participants are analyzed to reveal how their "patchwork" of learning opportunities unfolds in informal networks across overlapping systems of activity—at home, with buddies, in computer labs, on the job. It is here where Sawchuk finds an "enormous surplus" of knowledge production capacity as well as emancipatory potential for working-class people.

Wright (2002) also applied cultural-historical activity theory in his study of everyday learning and innovation in hi-tech teams (software developers). He found that it was almost impossible to separate individual skills and knowledge from what emerged collectively in the group. People and ideas were always moving in and out of each other's offices, and this interaction tended to circulate around the development of a prototype, which served as the "object" of the activity system and the centre of all the interactions. Bits of talk were usually accompanied by quick crude sketches, using desktop objects to expand an idea, moving back to the internet to snatch bits of data and statistics to check viability, calling others in to expand the idea creatively or to check constraints and standards. Thus, participation in collective action to define a problem and achieve an objective—with tools, language and action, individual and group—is interminably connected with skill transformation. Furthermore, this action alternates rapidly between creative, expansive activity and validating, critical activity, between what is present and what is not yet.

Learning as "Translation" and Mobilization: Actor Network Theory

Actor network theory (ANT) is also part of the shift from individualized, psychological approaches towards understanding learning and knowing as part of activity systems. However, it is distinguished from activity theory in taking knowledge generation to be a joint exercise of relational strategies within networks that are spread across space and time and performed through inanimate—e.g., books, journals, pens, computers—as well as animate beings in precarious arrangements. Both animate and inanimate "actants" are treated as materially equal—society and nature are not different domains, but one. The symmetry between inanimate and animate objects in actor-network theory arises because "human powers increasingly derive from the complex *interconnections* of humans with material objects . . . This means that the human and physical worlds are elaborately intertwined and cannot be analyzed separate from each other" (Urry 2000: 14). Learning is itself assembled, distributed and performed through a range of material networks within which one is interconnected, which in HRD are usually linked to institutional structures, everyday practices, and policies in different domains. In particular, learning and knowing are traced in the processes of assembling and maintaining these networks, as well as in the negotiations that occur at various nodes comprising a network.

Gherardi and Nicolini (2000) studied how cement-laying workmen learn safety skills, using actor-network theory to examine how knowledge is "translated" at every point as it moves through a system. For example, one workman would show another how to adapt a new safety procedure to make a task easier, or two together would adapt a particular tool to solve a problem, depending on who was watching, of course. At other points in the system, the crew foreman negotiated the language of the safety assessment report with the industrial inspector. Deadlines and weather conditions caused different safety knowledge to be performed and different standards of evaluation. The equipment itself, and the crew's culture, embedded or "grounded" a history of use possibilities and constraints that influenced the safety skills performed by those who interacted with the equipment. No skill or knowledge had a recognizable existence outside its use within the community.

Like complexity science, ANT is a family of theories, not one unitary conception (Latour 2005), with roots in critical post-structuralism and flowerings in society and technology studies. It explains that any changes we might describe as learning—new ideas, innovations, changes in behaviour, transformation—emerge through networks of actors. Edwards and Nicoll (2004) are among those applying ANT to understand workplace learning and pedagogies. Actants are acting entities (both humans and nonhumans) that have become mobilized by a particular network into acting out some kind of work to maintain the network's integrity. Each entity becomes an "actant" by *translating* another actant, mobilizing it to perform knowledge in a particular way, such as a worker translating a foreman into a disciplinarian through a particular set of behaviours. Each entity also belongs to other networks in which it is called to act differently, taking on different shapes and capacities. A written contract, for example, is a technology that embeds knowledge, both from networks that produced it and networks that have established its use possibilities and constraints. In any short-term employment arrangement the contract can be ignored, manipulated in various ways, or ascribed different forms of power. Thus, no agent or knowledge has an essential existence outside a given network: nothing is given in the order of things, but performs itself into existence. Recent branches of ANT theory (Law and Hassard 1999) have developed diverse iterations of these processes.

Another empirical example is evident in Biddle's (2004) study of everyday learning at a firefighting school. He used ANT to examine micro-processes of translation as the group integrated new technologies and adapted to new regulations. Particular innovations were enabled through strategies people used to interest, enroll, and mobilize others to perform particular skills. Fire—its risk and unpredictable danger, and its ability to paralyze newcomers—was also central. Fire and the tools of firefighting (the mantra was "put the wet stuff on the red stuff") "grounded" the community's interactions, shaping how people interacted with one another and the forms of knowledge that were possible. The firefighting culture that had developed over many years also grounded the knowledge transactions being negotiated. This was an aggressively masculine culture of humour, toughness and brotherhood that continually mediated many operational tensions (expensive errors, conflicts over process, resistance to technology) arising in changing practices, while creating new (gendered) tensions as women began to challenge the dominance of masculinized practices and images.

DISCUSSION: SYSTEMIC VIEWS OF
LEARNING AS PRACTICE-BASED

All three perspectives—complexity science, cultural-historical activity theory and actor-network theory—while deriving from very different theoretical roots and premises, bear three things in common. First, all three take the *whole system as the unit of analysis*, tracing human action and learning as enmeshed in a systemic web. Second, they all focus on closely tracing the knowledge that is produced, reinforced or transformed by subjects with/in activity. That is, they all trace *interactions among nonhuman as well as human* parts of the system, emphasizing both the heterogeneity of system elements and the need to focus on relations, not separate things or separate individuals. Third, they all understand human knowledge and learning in the system to be embedded in *practices*, rather than focusing on internalized concepts, meanings and feelings of any one participant. In other words, they do not privilege human consciousness or intention in any way, but focus on tracing what activity, objects and subjectivities emerge in activity. The questions of interest are around how practices emerge and become reconfigured, how they become entrenched, how different members of the system participate in practices and why, and how shifts in practices are linked to general systemic change.

Debate continues about where agency is located and how it is mobilized in relations among people, objects and discourses, and just how individuals and the collective interact in these processes of mutual constitution and reconfiguration. Some have shown that even when embedded in social structures, individuals retain a "durable disposition" to act (Mutch 2003), and workers organize their own learning regardless of management boundaries and innovation expectations (Poell and Van der Krogt 2003). Clearly, dynamics of individual volition are important within systems, as are individual differences in perspective, disposition, position, social/cultural capital, and forms of participation. Individuals' and groups' sense of their own knowledge in work, and the knowledge valued by the collective to which they see themselves belonging, form a critical element of their sense of identity (Christenson and Cheney 2005). Further, their participation in work practices is entwined with the identities they come to inhabit within a particular community (Wenger 1998). Learning is very much part of identity work—such as where people in work environments labour to discern subject positions available to them, how and what identities to perform, and how others perceive their identity (Chappell *et al.* 2003).

Further, power asymmetries exist in all human systems, which must be assumed to play out in workplace learning in terms of knowledge politics, contested interests related to what knowledge is most valued and by whom, how knowledge is shared and with whom, and inequities in access to learning opportunities. The three perspectives under examination in this discussion all address power relations and individual differences at play in systems of learning, although in different ways. Complexity science emphasizes the need for diversity if emergence (of new possibilities, innovations, practices) is to occur. Diversity is not to be "managed" towards producing greater homogeneity, as some approaches to HRD might advocate, but to be interconnected. In elaborating this with respect to human systems of learning, Davis (2006) explains that difference in a system needs to be recognized, which it often is not, and connected through redundancy or overlap built into the activities and tools shared among individuals, decentralized organizational processes, environments and projects that encourage continuous interaction, clear sites of linkage among difference, and multiple feedback loops across these sites.

In cultural-historical activity theory, the view of power relations echoes what I have elsewhere identified as a radical *view* (Fenwick 2008): organizations are viewed as sites of central contradictions and ideological struggle between those who control the means of production and those whose labour and knowledge are exploited. These are the Marxist roots of this theory, although it moves beyond binary conceptions of organizations as sites of class struggle between dominant and oppressed groups, where "learning" is conceived as either reproducing given power relations or transforming them through collective politicization and resistance. In cultural-historical activity theory, an emphasis is placed on the contradictions that are always carried within organizations, such as the common tension between emphasis on competency and control and injunctions for innovation involving risk and experimentation. Individual perspectives and interests are constantly at play in negotiating these contradictions, according to this theory. When these contradictions become sufficiently exacerbated or questioned through these negotiations, "learning" occurs—where learning is viewed as collective "expansion" of the system's objective and practices.

In actor-network theory, the post-structuralist origins become apparent in its approach to power: power is viewed as circulating through regimes of knowledge and discursive practices. Power is not possessed by particular people or institutions, but is constantly created and readjusted through relations among people, practices, objects, notions of what is normal and what is valuable. People in any system become "enrolled" in networks of practice that mobilize particular behaviours and then become "black boxed": everyone accepts them as given and everyone alters their behaviours according to the network demands. Examples would include organizational procedures that have long become entrenched whether or not they serve the collective interests, technologies such as PowerPoint software that embed a whole network of innovation and assumptions about communication, and artefacts such as blueprints and maps that define objects and structure users' perceptions in very specific ways. In actor-network theory, questions about power relations can destabilize the black-boxed networks and transfigure, dissolve, or initiate networks of practice. How do people and objects become part of the network? What identities and behaviours are mobilized by the network? How does space and architecture mobilize particular activity and repress others? What knowledge circulates, and what does not? Such questions unpick what appears to be stable, point to ambivalences, and can open productive possibilities for the system—all of which comprise collective learning.

IMPLICATIONS FOR WORK LEARNING THEORY IN HRD

The foregoing discussion has argued that theories of work learning as individual knowledge acquisition and as individual human development continue to have prominence in HRD journal publications, despite the availability of more systemic, multifaceted and action-based learning theories introduced to HRD over 15 years ago. Individualistic and acquisitive learning theories are argued here to be highly limited, usually apolitical and acontextual, lacking historical and sociological analysis of knowledge generation, ignoring cultural psychology and geography, and unable to account for the dynamic and often contradictory interactions of individuals with and in the turbulence of everyday activity. Towards expanded conceptions of work learning, three contemporary bodies of practice-based learning theory were discussed: emergentist perspectives of complexity science, expansion perspectives of cultural-historical activity theory, and translation/mobilization perspectives of actor-network theories.

For HRD, these theories point to specific multiple dimensions, forms and levels of work learning that can be useful in analyzing practical problems and formulating solutions. For example, the construct of "skill" is rooted in a conception of knowledge acquired by individuals, then applied or transferred to work tasks and problems. When workers are observed not to perform these tasks satisfactorily, causal logic diagnoses skill deficit in the workers and prescribes training to improve or transform skills. However, in real work environments, this logic and its underlying conception have proven faulty. Safety training, for example, does not necessarily reduce accidents because safety behaviours are influenced by a host of factors unrelated to workers' performance ability. One example would be affordances and barriers for particular practices embedded in work environments (Billett 2004)—such as, for example, an accident-disclosure policy that leads to worker punishment rather than to inquiry and problem solving. Other factors affecting safety behaviour that cannot be attributed to an individuals' "competence" in safety skills include tacitly accepted shortcuts and subversions of safety rules; conflicting expectations emphasizing, for example, faster production that compromises safety (Belfiore *et al.* 2004); and shifting micro politics among workers, foremen and safety inspectors (Gherardi and Nicolini 2000).

In many organizations, leaders perceive knowledge gaps between what existing workers can do and the skill transformations demanded by factors such as technological reshaping of operations, implementation of internationalized standards, and accelerated innovation in product and process to compete globally. A conventional response to understanding such gaps from an individualist acquisitive view of learning is to focus on the worker: the problem becomes recruiting or up-skilling individuals to fill the gap. However, from the perspective of the theories presented here, the problem is more complex. What we might observe and ascribe to an individual worker's skill performance actually has to do with the tools available and the system processes: whether the new software or the new safety cover for the cement mixer actually works effectively; whether the existing processes have been redesigned to incorporate them; whether there are bottlenecks, duplications or lengthy delays due to poor activity flow, poor communication between units, or bad delegation; whether the organization's cultural norms value and reward this particular skill. Even if it were possible to continually retrain workers or dramatically accelerate training, these approaches overlook the fact that many with needed skills can't get hired to matching jobs, and many in existing jobs say they have little opportunity to exercise the knowledge they already have developed (Livingstone 1999).

In other words, to analyze the issue of human learning and change in rapidly changing work environments, we must examine the whole system of continuities cut across by discontinuities at play. These analyses help illuminate how "skills" and knowledge are constituted in organizational nets of social/economic relations, how and why skill demands are perceived to be shifting in these contexts, how knowledge is actually generated and recognized by individuals and groups in different positions, and how skills are mobilized or enabled in different activities.

Taken together, the three theoretical perspectives discussed in this article raise further questions for HRD practice and research to clarify specific dynamics in learning processes occurring in work contexts. First are questions about what balance is created in different work contexts between processes of creating new knowledge, adapting/refining existing knowledge, and institutionalizing or stabilizing new knowledge. How do practices and objects emerge in these difference contexts, and how do they become reconfigured? What actions and identities are mobilized in these contexts? Second are questions related to the actual nature of the interplay between the structural (labour processes), cultural, collective and individual dimensions in generating and enacting knowledge. To what extent is a given work context more closed or more open to experimentation and adaptation through learning? What factors most affect the relative closure or openness of activity and therefore learning? Third are questions about the extent to which rapid change such as workplace technology is actually opening new possibilities and changing knowledge demands as opposed to fragmenting individual craft knowledge and whole tasks. How do the contradictory movements of "up-skilling" and "de-skilling" through technology affect the activities and therefore the learning of individuals and communities in a particular work context? What kinds of learning are most valued and encouraged, what kinds are not acknowledged, and how are judgments made that affect distribution and support of learning opportunities? Such questions draw attention to continuing dilemmas while opening new sites for dialogue and inquiry.

KEY LEARNING POINTS

Overall, these three different theoretical formulations point to elements in work learning processes that provide useful analytic tools for HRD.

- First, *multiple dimensions* involved in learning need to be acknowledged. Identity issues are very much integrated in how people see themselves as knowers, and perform knowledge. Language is key to how people recognize and represent knowledge, how they name and exchange it, and how they construct meaning together of their experience. Practices, the everyday cultural routines in which people participate, embed symbols, values, and goals that determine what counts as learning, what is useful knowledge, what is correct and what is an error. Power relations structure hierarchies of knowledge within a community, determine who gets to judge learning, who has access to knowledge and who can participate in knowledge creation. Power also positions the community and its collective knowledge in regard to other communities.

- Second, these perspectives shed light on *different levels and forms of work learning.* Complexity science demonstrates the emergence of innovation, and shows how patterns of organization at different nested levels of the system emerge unpredictably from disturbances that become amplified through co-specification. Actor-network theory provides a micro-level view of how knowledge is actually negotiated or "translated" at each interaction, and the politics influencing who or what can be seen and mobilized at any moment. Cultural-historical activity theory tries to link micro-interactions in practice to a macro-level view of how learning transpires over time, examining the historical emergence of a system's knowledge and tools, its structures of labour division and roles, and its changing objectives.

- These perspectives each theorize, in very different and very precise ways, the interactions and interconnections between different movements: between micro and macro levels of learning, between system structures and individual actions, between planned and emergent processes, and between continuity and discontinuity. Taken together, they demonstrate the very rich and multi-dimensional relations among individual(s)' participation and collective dynamics in learning processes. They also demonstrate the impossibility of certainty in explaining these relations. No one model of individual-collective connections can account for the complexities afoot. And no explanation that does not address power relations, artefacts and objects, identities, histories and contradictions held within the system, and the ongoing emergence of practices and spaces can be taken seriously as a theory of learning in work.

- For HRD theorists and practicing professionals, these explorations focus on understanding work-learning processes as practice-based: rooted in activity in particular contexts, and marked by multiple dimensions, forms, levels, and power relations in learning. As I argued at the outset, these conceptions are not new to HRD by any means: learning has long been acknowledged to be enmeshed in practice, culture, and ongoing collective knowledge. However, the continuing amount of HRD publication centring on the "individual" and on "acquisition" indicates that somehow we continue to be drawn back to old assumptions about how learning occurs and where knowledge lies. Until we can move beyond our Western heritage of overly individual-centric psychologistic theories of learning, HRD practice may find itself addressing the wrong questions in ways that advance neither human learning nor organizational well-being.

ACKNOWLEDGEMENT

This chapter is substantially revised and updated from "Towards enriched conceptions of work learning: Participation, expansion, and translation among individuals with/in activity", published in the *Human Resource Development Review* 5 (3).

4   Principles for Research on Workplace Learning

At the Intersection of the Individual and the Context

Peter Chin, Nancy L. Hutchinson, Joan Versnel, and Hugh Munby

Contributors to this part were asked to develop their chapters on the assumption that workplace learning (WPL) is a process that emerges from the interaction between the individual and the setting. In addition, we were invited to describe and to illustrate those workplace characteristics that influence learning. Within our Co-operative Education and Workplace Learning team (CEWL), twelve years of research on WPL have convinced us of the complexity of action knowledge in the workplace and of describing how it is acquired. For example, here is a high-school co-operative (co-op) education student explaining how she learned to restrain an animal on the examining table at the veterinary clinic.

Ruth: 'Well, if you put too much pressure, it'll hurt them and they'll start wriggling around. If you don't put enough pressure on, they'll think "Okay, I can break free," and they'll keep struggling and struggling. But if you put just enough, they'll know, "I can't go anywhere. It's not hurting me but I can't go anywhere."'
Researcher: 'How did you learn what "just enough" was?'
Ruth: 'Experiments. If you press down and they start squirming, it may be too hard; lighten up a little bit, and if they start squirming again, okay, just right in between there, and you can get them to stop. . . . It's just feeling around, knowing when it's comfortable and they're not moving.' (Interview, 10 April 1997)

Clearly, the kind of knowledge Ruth describes is different from the familiar declarative knowledge of the school classroom (Chin *et al.* 2004a). Ruth's learning is acquired as she works in a meaningful role, and as she engages in a peripheral (but not technical) task in which learning can be acquired only by doing. Also, in making explicit what is tacit, Ruth shows how the interactions between her and the elements of the clinic environment influence her learning in complex ways that challenge traditional learning theories in educational psychology (Munby *et al.* 2007a). In this chapter, we develop the basic assumption that WPL is interactional by suggesting that the interaction between the individual and the setting that gives rise to WPL is a deliberate, wilful one. We argue that efforts to understand this interaction and to identify how it may be influenced are deliberate and wilful—research is a deliberate interaction between individuals and settings. Thus WPL parallels research: both involve interactions between participants and settings, both involve participants trying to learn, and both activities are principled. In the current chapter, we explore six principles that we believe to be central to research on WPL:

1. Broad Focus: Research on WPL should include the range from students in work-based education programs (WBE) to adult workers, and the range from novice to proficient workers.
2. Salience: Research may be especially productive if it is aimed at the inexperienced because learning is more evident in inexperienced adult workers and in learners in WBE because the inexperienced have not developed smoothly executable practices.
3. Commonplaces: WPL research needs to be attentive to all of the commonplaces of learning—learners, teachers, content, milieu.
4. Inclusion: Research on WPL should be inclusive; a focus on promoting learning for at-risk and exceptional learners enhances WPL for all workers.
5. Richness: The complexities of WPL commend the development of populations of rich case studies as a research approach.
6. Congruence: Research on WPL needs to document how the characteristics of the workplace fit the learner's individual needs, especially for vulnerable learners.

Throughout this chapter we explore each principle and use our program of research, Co-operative Education and Workplace Learning, as a source of examples for each principle in action.

PRINCIPLE 1: BROAD FOCUS

Our first principle concerns the breadth of the focus of research on WPL: it acknowledges that, in addition to adult workers, the research participants include students enrolled in work-based education (WBE) programs. Work-based learning experiences can take many forms such as job-shadowing, entrepreneurship, co-operative education, school-based enterprise, and leadership courses. Some of the learning takes place in school settings, while the workplace provides an authentic context for other curriculum outcomes. As well, there are distinctive differences among work-based learning experiences in terms of duration, supervision, and compensation (Stasz and Stern 1998).

In co-op education, students are enrolled in full-time study and earn high school credits for extended periods of unpaid experience in workplaces that form partnerships with their schools. Although there are varying degrees of engagement within WBE programs, we characterize secondary co-op students and those involved in school-based enterprises as novice learners in the workplace. Learning in the workplace was once assumed to be concrete, rote, general, and individualistic (Pillay *et al.* 1998). Yet recent research suggests that work-based learning is complex, cognitive, context dependent, and involves initiation into a community of practice (Billett 2001; Wenger 1998). Workplace learning is informal and embedded in the routines of the workplace, and much of the knowledge required for success is tacit (Hung 1999). Recent research in workplaces suggests that learning can be enhanced when novice workers are made aware of the routines implicit in the workplace (Munby *et al.* 2003), and are mentored or guided in their workplace learning (Billett 2003; Darwin 2000).

Billett (2001) recorded how five workplaces afforded opportunities for learning and how individuals elected to engage with the guidance provided by the workplace. He found that for adult workers, the readiness of the workplace to afford opportunities for individuals to engage in work activities and enjoy the benefits of direct and indirect support was a key determinant of the quality of learning.

These and other findings from research on WPL with adults are reflected in our research with high school students in the workplace. The opening extract from our study of Ruth in the veterinary clinic reminds us that learning in WBE differs markedly from learning in school. We have argued (Munby *et al.* 2003a) that school knowledge tends to be propositional (declarative) while workplace knowledge tends to be action knowledge (procedural), and that unlike the sequential nature of the school curriculum, the organization of workplace learning is centred on clusters of tasks that tend to be introduced early in the work placement. We observed that much of Ruth's learning in the veterinary clinic occurred at the beginning, and that her daily routines enacted and improved on her performance of these tasks (Chin *et al.* 2000). Further, the main purposes of school are focused on learning, but the primary purposes of the workplace are focused on the production of goods and the delivery of services. Thus all learning and tasks in the veterinary clinic were directly related to patient health and recovery, and Ruth's learning was aimed at contributing as a team member to this goal. Research on WPL needs to include a focus on groups that represent a broad range of age and experience in workers because we can benefit from the insights of both adults and youth learning.

PRINCIPLE 2: SALIENCE

The second research principle is salience. We take the position that WPL is more evident in high school students in WBE programs and in adult workers who are new to a workplace context (in contrast to those adults familiar with a workplace who are learning a new task). In a study by Chin *et al.*

(2004b), we provide two snapshots of Denise, a high school co-op student who is placed in a dental clinic for half of each day for the entire five-month semester. In the first snapshot, Denise is in her seventh day at the dental clinic and is observing a dental procedure over the shoulder of the preventative dental assistant. During that observation, Denise feels faint and quietly leaves the room. In the second snapshot, which occurs about six weeks later, the researchers observe Denise performing all of the dental assisting tasks for the dentist while the preventative dental assistant looks over her shoulder. The stark contrast between these two snapshots highlights the richness of researching WPL with workers who are entirely new to a setting. In contrast to looking at experienced workers learning a new task, focusing on people totally new to a workplace affords researchers the opportunity to use theoretical frameworks that can address physical, cognitive, and social elements of WPL.

Billett (2001) argued that workplace knowledge is, at root, tacit or opaque. To novices, workplace routines are not necessarily self-evident, and one almost needs to be looking for regularities in order to observe them and learn them. Certainly, the behaviours of workers do not readily reveal the underlying routine that these behaviours are enacting. Billett's (2001) work has shown that the use of guided strategies embedded in everyday work activities has enhanced the development of knowledge needed for successful workplace learning and performance.

The conceptual lens of legitimate peripheral participation (Lave and Wenger 1991) captures the learning that novice workers experience within the workplace. Novices can begin to learn a complex routine by participating in one small subroutine, because participation provides a vantage point for observing and understanding the events that initiate, sustain, and terminate the larger routine. The routines also provide the novice with a broader understanding of how a particular role fits within the larger organization. In a study exploring the utility of well-developed instructional strategies to enhance a worker's understanding of a workplace, Munby *et al.* (2007b) found that the strategies were useful to both novices and experienced workers alike. Torraco (1999) claimed that it is important to view working and learning as reciprocal processes: 'the opportunities and constraints afforded in actual work contexts are indispensable for improving . . . skilled performance, for it is the learner who ultimately must translate these experiences into expertise' (1999: 10).

WPL can be understood utilizing theoretical frameworks that emphasize the active and pro-active role of the novice within the workplace setting. Hung's (1999) framework of epistemological appropriation highlights how a novice becomes part of a community of practice through a sequential self-regulating process of submitting to the authority of the experienced practitioner, mirroring the practitioner, and constructing independently patterns of actions and beliefs within the community. This self-regulatory process is enhanced by the teacher/mentor's support in scaffolding, modelling, and coaching.

Test *et al.* (2005) developed a framework of self-advocacy that depicts how individuals articulate their own interests, needs, and rights, and how they can be agentic within their workplace contexts. Although initially developed for students with disabilities, the researchers argue that this can be used with other populations where the goal is self-advocacy. Test *et al.* (2005) conceptualized self-advocacy as having four components: (a) knowledge of self, (b) knowledge of rights, (c) communication of one's knowledge of self and rights, and (d) leadership (communicating for self and others). The concept of self-advocacy serves as a backdrop to our own research on instructional materials to enhance meta-cognition, on the factors that contribute to creating successful learning contexts, and on the congruence of a program with the learner's needs. Such explorations are not only helpful to the learning of novices in the workplace but have direct benefits for the learning of experienced workers as well.

PRINCIPLE 3: COMMONPLACES

The third principle we recommend to inform research on WPL concerns context. We have found it helpful to adapt Schwab's (1972) four commonplaces as windows on learning in the workplace. Not only do these commonplaces––learners, teachers, content, milieu––help us to identify salient research questions; they also prevent us from overlooking important features of the workplace.

For example, our questions about learners who are co-op education students focused on their purposes for participating in co-op education, their expectations for the co-op placement, and their success in learning at their co-op placement. Attention to such learners also reminded us of their diversity of ability, and of how such differences need to be reflected in our instructional work with them—both in school and in work settings. Our questions about teachers drew attention to the importance of the role of the supervisors in assisting the learner within the workplace context. The content of the worker's role within the workplace itself attuned us to the purposes of the worker within the broader organization, and to how learning occurs. Finally, attention to the milieu reminded us of the many important stakeholders involved in work-based learning, and also focused our attention on the impact that the knowledge economy has on today's workplaces. Attention to the milieu reinforces the central importance of context within WPL.

The focus on commonplaces also enables researchers to distinguish among differences between what is intended (as espoused in policy documents), what is enacted (as interpreted and taught by teachers/supervisors), what is experienced (by the learner), and what is desirable (so that learners of all abilities can be successful). Such versions of the commonplaces are evident within the day-to-day experiences of learners, novices and experts in the workplace (Chin *et al.* 2000). As illustrated in Table 4.1, merging the

Table 4.1   A Heuristic of the Commonplaces

	Learner	Teacher	Content	Milieu/Context Stakeholders
Intended				
Enacted				
Experienced				
Desirable				

different versions of the commonplaces provides us with a heuristic of the various dimensions that could potentially draw our research attention.

Our early research explicitly attended to the different versions of the commonplaces such that each year of one of our three-year grants focused on either the intended, enacted and experienced, or desirable commonplaces. It becomes clear that our added attention to the different stakeholders has resulted in a research program that addresses many of the dimensions in the heuristic. It is important to mention that few of our studies focus exclusively on one stakeholder, although often one stakeholder is of primary interest. For example, a case study of a co-op student in a workplace may focus on the student, but invariably involves the co-op supervisor, the co-op teacher, and the learning context.

We also recognize that, for various purposes, different research methods are appropriate. For example, some examinations of the intended commonplaces have involved document analyses of content or policy, some examinations of the experienced commonplaces have relied on in-depth case studies of workplace learners, and some studies of the desirable commonplaces have involved focus groups with employers while others have relied on large-scale surveys (e.g., Hutchinson *et al.* 2001; Zanibbi *et al.* 2006). Of course, the research methods for each study that we have conducted are determined by the research question(s) to be answered, with the implicit understanding that the overall goal is to develop knowledge to enhance workplace learning of co-op students.

The commonplaces of 'the learner' and 'the content' invite attention to theoretical frameworks which are grounded in contemporary theories of learning. Among these are the appropriation of workplace knowledge (Hung 1999; Lave and Wenger 1991), co-participation (Billett 2001), and meta-cognition (Davidson and Sternberg 1998). Since CEWL's work focuses on how novices learn within the workplace, we believe that these broad theoretical frameworks capture the relationship between experience and knowing, and capture the processes and features involved in workplace learning. By focusing on the commonplaces, our own work within WPL has been guided by a heuristic that enables us to systematically examine the complexities of learning in the workplace.

PRINCIPLE 4: INCLUSION

The fourth principle for research in WPL is inclusion. Promoting learning and creating contexts for success for at-risk youth and youth with disabilities can inform workplace learning for all individuals (Hutchinson *et al.* 2006). Youth with disabilities face a variety of barriers when making the transition from school to productive participation in employment and in the community (Human Resources Development Canada 1998; Turnbull *et al.* 2003). At-risk youth are often involved in a cycle of disengagement and failure and, like their peers with disabilities, face poor post-school outcomes (Cho *et al.* 2005). Access to workplace learning opportunities for at-risk youth and youth with disabilities is one of the strongest predictors of their participation in competitive employment, higher earning potential, and even successful high school completion (Levine and Wagner 2005).

Positive outcomes in workplace learning for at-risk youth and youth with disabilities do not occur spontaneously. Through an extensive multidisciplinary review of literature on workplace accommodations in the fields of education, psychology, rehabilitation therapy, sociology, social work, disability studies, policy studies, epidemiology, nursing, and psychiatry, we identified six factors that contribute to creating successful learning contexts (Hutchinson *et al.* 2005; Versnel *et al.* 2008).

These six factors influence the negotiation of accommodations for workers with disabilities and our research has demonstrated that using the six factors as a framework for creating workplace learning contexts contributes to success for at-risk learners as well (DeLuca *et al.* 2008; Versnel *et al.* 2008).

The six factors identified in our multidisciplinary literature review include: access and disclosure, structural affordances, social context, cognitive problem solving, motivation, and social policy (Hutchinson *et al.* 2005). These factors have been shown to apply to Canadian educational and employment contexts and are likely to apply in other jurisdictions. Access and disclosure draw attention to the rights of employees to reasonable accommodations in the workplace with a concomitant obligation to disclose the disability in order to evoke the right (e.g., Canadian Human Rights Commission 2003). Structural affordances include modifications to the physical environment in the workplace, as well as other accommodations like flexible scheduling and telecommuting options (Gates 2000). Social context refers to the involvement of supervisors and co-workers in the activation of natural and designed social supports for individuals with differences (Williams *et al.* 2004). Cognitive problem-solving includes shared decisions about routines in the workplace that can provide structure to the learning and enable the transfer of knowledge from expert to novice workers (Munby *et al.* 2003b; Shaw and Feuerstein 2004). Motivation relies heavily on goal-setting, self-regulation, and self-advocacy. This is key for individuals with disabilities and to their ability to sustain the effort necessary to implement, and monitor the efficacy of, the accommodations they receive (Chin *et al.* 2007; Madaus *et al.* 2003; Versnel *et al.* 2008). Finally, social policy that governs and influences the experiences of individuals with disabilities in the workplace must be considered (Smith *et al.* 2003).

Workplace learning differs from school learning and is frequently embedded in the routines of the workplace (Munby *et al.* 2003b). Much of the knowledge in the workplace is tacit and requires explicit articulation for the novice learner (Hung 1999). For at-risk youth and youth with disabilities to benefit from workplace learning opportunities, mentorship and coaching are essential. Using principles of teaching and learning through the support of educational personnel, workplace supervisors and mentors can learn to scaffold and set challenging yet realistic expectations that align with the goals of the worker and the employer. Novice employees, like at-risk youth and youth with disabilities, benefit from opportunities for communication and interaction with experienced workers (Hutchinson *et al.* 2007).

Our observational studies in a wide range of workplaces have suggested that efficient workers recognize the organizing influence of routines in the workplace. They acknowledge that routines help to meet the purpose of the workplace. These individuals can identify the cues that: (a) alert them to begin a routine, (b) indicate that a routine needs to be aborted or altered, and (c) confirm that a well-executed routine is coming to a close (Munby *et al.* 2003b; Versnel and Hutchinson 2001). The opportunity for a youth with a disability or an at-risk youth to work along with an experienced workplace mentor creates a context for direct guidance and indirect support in how the specific routines of a workplace can be learned. In one of our recent studies, an at-risk youth moved from being on the verge of dropping out of school to serving as a mentor for other at-risk youth under the direct guidance of an effective caring teacher/supervisor in a WPL program (DeLuca *et al.* 2008). This interaction of workplace mentors with at-risk youth and youth with disabilities must be deliberate and planned to ensure success and to implement accommodations that sustain the ability of the youth to contribute to the workplace specifically and to society in general (Versnel *et al.* 2008).

Accommodations for youth with disabilities in school settings are identified through a formal process which includes the development of an individual education plan for each youth. While the accommodations for youth in schools are realized through this formal process, these youth may require similar accommodations in a workplace learning setting (Hutchinson 2007). The negotiation of such accommodations must be deliberate and should involve the school, the workplace, and the at-risk youth or youth with disabilities. Workplace learning can and frequently does take place in contexts which may not be adequately prepared to recognize the need for accommodations. Using a framework that identifies the factors which can help youth and workplaces negotiate the accommodations needed for success can create a successful learning context for students as well as a positive working context for experienced employees who require accommodations. When a workplace has had positive experiences with a worker with a disability, the likelihood of the workplace hiring employees with disabilities is increased (Hutchinson *et al.* 2005). It is apparent that, for many reasons, inclusion serves as a guiding principle for research on WPL.

PRINCIPLE 5: RICHNESS

The fifth principle that informs research on WPL is richness. We emphasize both rich case studies using multiple perspectives (reflecting the commonplace principle) and the richness that derives from producing a population of case studies. Stake (2000) speaks of a 'population of cases', and in our work we have used a population of cases to explore comparisons and patterns to generate insights that we might not otherwise be able to claim. Three examples illustrate this feature of our work.

First, we were struck by the similarities of actions taking place within a veterinary clinic, a dental clinic, and a hospital ward. As our research team's interest in routines grew, we undertook a series of short (one- to three-hour) observations of different workplaces and conducted interviews with workplace supervisors to determine if the tasks there could be construed as routines and to discover further characteristics of routines (Versnel 2002). From this population of cases we advanced an argument about the meta-cognitive function that workplace routines serve in a student's learning (Munby *et al.* 2003b): We argued that work can be conceptualized as routines, that routines can be taught, and that such attention to routines serves a meta-cognitive function in the co-op student's learning.

Second, our explorations of several science-based workplaces began to reveal that the co-op students saw few links between their learning in the workplace and their science classroom learning. These empirical data were then used to craft an analytic argument that depicts the differences between school science and workplace science in terms of the different forms and functions of science in each context (Chin *et al.* 2004). A framework emerged that afforded the development of instructional strategies with the goals of enhancing the quality of students' WPL experiences, and of the students' understanding of the relationships between school science and workplace science.

Third, by treating our research studies as a population of cases, we conducted an analysis of the findings from our case studies even though the cases did not utilize identical methods, theoretical frameworks, or constructs. Specifically, we revisited our studies with a focus on the implications for instruction that were reported in each research paper and, in turn, looked for commonalities among the instructional implications suggested for students in co-op settings. This resulted in the development of robust themes about workplace learning, with each theme having a list of instructional implications for students in co-op education. The five themes are: (a) routines (i.e., the role played by repetitive patterns of tasks), (b) purpose (both the student's purpose/goal and the workplace's purpose), (c) next steps (where there is always something else to do), (d) hiddenness (of the reasons behind work activities and of required workplace accommodations), and (e) community (or belonging). These concepts were translated into instructional materials that were brief, easy to read, and accessible to co-op students, co-op teachers, and workplace supervisors. Each theme was developed through a big idea, what that idea looks like in the workplace, and how the idea could be used. Munby *et al.* (2007b) reported that co-op students and workplace supervisors found the instructional materials to be helpful, in contrast to co-op teachers, who found the materials to be less useful. Workplace supervisors reported they could see the potential of using the big ideas with experienced employees.

In each example, it is clear that the findings and the potential instructional materials that enhanced the WPL experience could only be generated through a research stance that treated our extant case studies as a population. The sixth principle, which follows, serves as the latest articulation of our understanding of WPL that has only been possible to develop because we have been able to analyze a rich set of cases.

PRINCIPLE 6: CONGRUENCE

The sixth principle that can inform research on WPL is congruence. It is vital for enhancing learning that the characteristics of the workplace are a good fit to the worker's individual learning needs, especially when promoting learning in the workplace for new workers and vulnerable learners. The world faces a growing youth employment crisis: worldwide, youth are three times as likely to be unemployed as adults (International Labour Office 2006). And as the world and its workplaces change, increasing numbers of experienced workers find themselves needing to retrain for a second (or third or fourth) career (Karmel and Maclean 2006). WBE in its many forms is one of the most frequently recommended solutions in Canada and around the world for both disengaged youth (e.g., Canadian Career Consortium 2007; Quintini *et al.* 2007) and displaced adult workers (e.g., Ontario Ministry of Training, Colleges and Universities 2008; Park and Dhameja 2006). The result has been a plethora of varied WBE programmes and diverse youth and adult workers who might benefit from such programmes with no apparent means of matching the needs of these youth and adults to the programmes most likely to effect change for them. We argue that without a concerted effort at both the conceptual and practical levels, focused on the 'fit' required for effective WPL, we will continue to see these disengaged youth and adult workers on a path to social exclusion, and developed and developing countries without the workers necessary to sustain their economies.

Focus group research conducted by CEWL has reported the characteristics of WBE programs that have been recognized by experts in the field as most effective for preparing at-risk youth, who have been disengaged from school, for employment. These characteristics include: providing responsive social supports to individuals; enabling youth to advocate for themselves when acquiring experience in the workplace; and emphasizing, in every aspect of the program, the connections between what is learned in WBE and what is needed for success in the workplace (e.g., Hutchinson *et al.* 2006). However, our case studies demonstrate that a program that is effective in promoting learning for one youth can fail another youth. Zanibbi *et al.* (2006) observed one youth, in a water treatment plant, who received a structured learning experience, which increased her responsibilities as she showed herself to be competent and willing. In contrast, another student who lacked initiative repeated the same routine, uninteresting tasks throughout his entire placement in a gym, and was never observed being encouraged to learn more or requesting increased challenges. Thus it is critical to describe the person-context fit while examining the features of workplace experience in a systematic manner. Our data suggest that effective WBE programs gradually increase the complexity and accountability demanded of novice workers learning in the workplace, while including them in a community of practice that provides authentic experience in combination with mentoring (e.g., Hutchinson *et al.* 2008; Munby *et al.* in press; Zanibbi *et al.* 2006).

Recently, we conducted two case studies with novice youth workers who had been disengaged from school before enrolling in separate WBE programs (DeLuca *et al.* 2008). The specific purpose of this study was to describe and compare the experiences of these two at-risk youth learning in the workplace, placed in workplaces likely to promote resilience because each WBE program had been recognized as exemplary for at-risk youth (Hutchinson *et al.* 2006). We reported a multiple-perspective case study for each focal youth, which included the perspectives of the youth, the workplace employer, and the WBE educator. In one case, a responsive educator used deliberate planning to structure and scaffold learning for a young man who had to be re-engaged when he arrived in a program that taught students how to upholster. The teacher provided feedback, encouragement, and adjusted instruction and expectations to meet learners' needs. While the student we observed, Tim, was highly successful in learning upholstery and at securing employment, the teacher was clear that not all his students thrived in the program. And while many students thrived in the highly regarded co-op education program in which the second student, Ashley, was enrolled, the match to Ashley's needs for a structured curriculum, close supervision, and high accountability was not ideal. In spite of onerous demands for independent writing and other academic tasks, the WBE program attracted Ashley to return to school and enabled her to earn high school credits so she could proceed to a vocational program in community college. Although she was not observed to be learning much about aesthetics in her placement, Ashley did earn credits, which allowed her to meet some of her own goals. In a follow-up 12 months after the end of the initial study, Tim was working successfully in the field of upholstery, and Ashley was working full-time in a service industry and applying to a business program at a community college for the upcoming year, hoping to focus her studies on marketing. Following their experiences in WPL, Ashley and Tim were more able to set realistic, proximal goals for themselves and to direct their own learning to reach these goals. These two cases highlight how supportive adults in a workplace and an at-risk youth engage in interactions that facilitate the emergence of resilience in the workplace.

Our emerging population of cases highlights the importance of structuring WBE so the program and workplace experience meet the individual needs of vulnerable learners in the areas of planning for learning, communication, and social support in order to promote WPL. When WBE accomplishes this, vulnerable workers can transform themselves from timid observers to confident participants, assuming increasing responsibilities in a dental clinic (Chin *et al.* 2004b), a veterinary clinic (Chin *et al.* 2004), a travel agency (Hutchinson *et al.* 2008), or a water treatment plant (Zanibbi *et al.* 2006). When the optimal 'fit' is not there, between the needs of the individual and the characteristics of the program and placement, vulnerable workplace learners can flounder in the workplace where they are novices and in WBE just as they have in formal schooling or in their previous workplace, which has declared them redundant (Versnel *et al.* 2008).

We are currently embarking on a program of conceptual and empirical work to develop and explore the viability of a robust person-context model that will answer the vexing questions about which program characteristics in the plethora of varied WBE programs are likely to benefit individuals with diverse characteristics who have grown disaffected and disengaged from school or from their previous workplace. Because similar trends are being seen worldwide, we will analyze documents from many countries describing macro and micro responses to the challenges in order to develop our model, and then work toward specifying the model for particular contexts and validating the model through focus groups, interviews, and case study research in varied contexts.

CONCLUSION AND KEY LEARNING POINTS

The purpose of this chapter was to contribute to our understanding of how the process of WPL emerges from the interaction between the individual and the setting and to contribute to our understanding of those workplace characteristics that influence learning. Our 12 years of research on WPL suggest that the interaction between the individual and the setting that gives rise to WPL is deliberate and wilful as well as principled. In this chapter, we articulate six principles to guide research on the interaction between individual and setting, and we use examples from the ongoing research program of the Co-operative Education and Workplace Learning team at Queen's University to illustrate how these principles can inform research on WPL.

- The first principle, broad focus, highlights the importance of including a range of workers, from novice to expert, and of WPL experiences, from brief and introductory to lengthy and intensive, to developing a comprehensive understanding of the learning that arises in the inter-action between individual and context.
- Salience, the second principle, points to the light shone on the interac-tion and the learning when procedures are not executed automatically, when contexts are not understood, and when learners are finding their way toward comfort and competence.
- The third principle, commonplaces of learning, reminds researchers of the many aspects of learning that require attention for full accounts of learning—who is learning, who is teaching, what is learned, and the milieu in which learning takes place—as well as the different versions of learning to which researchers might attend to ensure thorough and informative accounts of WPL. These include the intended, enacted, experienced, and desirable versions of learning or curriculum.
- Given the increasing diversity in most societies, the emphasis on equi-table treatment of all, and the growing demand for well-educated problem solvers in the knowledge economies of the 21st century, the fourth principle of inclusion is gaining steadily in importance. Accounts of learning must be able to clarify the WPL experiences and needs of persons with disabilities as well as persons at risk for social exclusion. This emphasis on inclusion is related to the last two principles—richness and congruence.
- The fifth principle, richness, recognizes that WPL researchers must develop a well-rounded, rich collection or population of deeply described cases that allows one to consider each case and its lessons in this informing context. A population of cases enriches interpretation, when each can be understood in the context of all the others, and high-lights constraints that can only be seen within a finely drawn pattern.
- The final principle is congruence. In order to fully understand what characteristics of the workplace influence WPL within the all-important interaction between individual and context, researchers must consider that the characteristics of the individual learning worker may be criti-cal. The more vulnerable the worker is as a learner, the more important it is to recognize what learning needs of the individual must be met by the context and the structures that support learning.

Demanding as such principle-driven research might be, we ignore these issues at a cost. The inclusion of those who are at risk for social exclusion and of workplace learners who are vulnerable for any reason is one of the greatest challenges of the 21st century as we strive for equitable societies that can sustain our economies. Understanding the characteristics of workplaces that enable WPL is essential because workplace learning is deliberate as well as interactive, research on WPL is complex, and principled studies are much more likely to produce robust findings to guide practice.

ACKNOWLEDGEMENT

The chapter is prepared as part of the research grant Individual and Contextual Factors in Work-based Education Programs: Diverting At-risk Youth from the Path to Social Exclusion (Nancy L. Hutchinson, Peter Chin, and Joan Versnel, investigators) funded by the Social Sciences and Humanities Research Council of Canada. More information about the work of the research team is available at http://orgs.educ.queensu.ca/cewl/.

5   Bateson's Levels of Learning
A Framework for Transformative Workplace Learning?

Paul Tosey, Dawn Langley, and Jane Mathison

It is widely acknowledged that 'learning' is a problematic concept in human resource development, for both theoreticians and practitioners. In this chapter we consider Gregory Bateson's theory of 'levels of learning' as a fruitful yet enigmatic framework that offers a radical conceptual perspective on issues of workplace learning. We explore the origins and substance of Bateson's theory, which differentiates between types of learning; consider three examples of its potential relevance to issues of workplace learning; then review variations in notions of 'learning to learn' in the light of Bateson's thinking. Finally, we appraise the theory in the light of subsequent commentaries.

Our research approach combines a scholarly reading of Bateson's work (Bateson 1979, 2000; Bateson and Bateson 1988) and related commentaries such as Brockman (1977), Charlton (2008), Keeney (1983), and Visser (2003), with application of Bateson's framework in a consultancy project, and within a doctoral study of arts organizations in crisis (Tosey *et al.* 2008).

THE ORIGINS OF BATESON'S THEORY

Gregory Bateson (1904–80) was an English academic, the son of geneticist William Bateson (Lipset 1980). In 1936 he married Margaret Mead, with whom he conducted anthropological fieldwork in New Guinea and Bali, and took up residency in the USA in 1940.

Bateson and Mead were prominent participants in the Macy conferences (Montagnini 2007), which began in the USA in 1946 and which laid the foundations for the interdisciplinary science of cybernetics, a way of thinking in which systems are organized according to feedback (see, e.g., Capra 1996: 51–71). Bateson's particular development of this work emphasized the ecological nature of human systems. He was passionately interested in issues of epistemology—that is, how we know what we know: 'The processes with which Gregory was concerned were essentially processes of knowing: perception, communication, coding and translation. . . .' (Mary Catherine Bateson, in Bateson 2000: 5). Among other things, he argues that 'mind' resides in connections and relations in systems, not in the brains of individual people:

> Consider a man felling a tree with an axe. Each stroke of the axe is modi-
> fied or corrected, according to the shape of the cut face of the tree left by
> the previous stroke. This self-corrective (i.e., mental) process is brought
> about by a total system, tree-eyes-brain-muscles-axe-stroke-tree; and it
> is this total system that has the characteristics of immanent mind.
>
> (Bateson 2000: 317)

In the 1950s, human communication became the main focus of Bateson's work. During this time he developed the famous 'double bind' theory of schizophrenia (Bateson *et al.* 1956). From 1964–72 he was director of the Oceanic Institute, Hawaii. There, he was inspired by his observations of the way dolphins were trained (Bateson 2000: 276–8) to develop his theory of levels of learning (see also Visser 2003).

In the standard training method, whenever the trainer noticed behaviour that she deemed desirable for the dolphin to repeat in front of an audience, it was marked by the reward of a fish. This type of learning could be thought of as classical conditioning, in that the dolphin was learning to associate specific behaviours with the reward of food. However, once a particular behaviour was established in the dolphin's repertoire, the reward would be withheld. Bateson observed that initially this appeared to cause the dolphin some discomfort and frustration. Then, perhaps to some extent as a result of its agitation, the dolphin would eventually produce a new behaviour, which the trainer would reward as before.

This pattern continued over a series of sessions, until:

> In the time out between the fourteenth and fifteenth sessions, the dol-
> phin appeared to be much excited; and when she came onstage for the
> fifteenth session, she put on an elaborate performance that included
> eight conspicuous pieces of behaviour of which four were new and never
> before observed in this species of animal. From the animal's point of
> view, there is a jump, a discontinuity, between the logical types.
>
> In all such cases, the step from one logical type to the next higher
> is a step from information about an event to information about a class
> of events. Notably, in the case of the dolphin, it was impossible for her
> to learn from a single experience, whether of success or failure, that
> the context was one for exhibiting a new behaviour. The lesson about
> context could only have been learned from comparative information
> about a sample of contexts differing among themselves, in which her
> behaviour and the outcome differed from instance to instance. Within
> such a varied class, a regularity became perceptible, and the apparent
> contradiction could be transcended.
>
> (Bateson 1979: 137)

Here, according to Bateson, the dolphin's learning was of a different type; it was learning about *context*. The dolphin effectively learnt to distinguish between the *class* of behaviours that would be rewarded and the *class* of behaviours that would no longer be rewarded. This notion of *context* is tricky and contestable (Edwards 2006). It refers to a constructed, experiential reality. It is not merely about the physical location or practical setting in which learning takes place: 'for Bateson a context is the particular whole which a given part helps compose, not something separate from or abstracted from that part' (Bredo 1989: 28–9).

WHAT DOES BATESON'S THEORY OF LEVELS OF LEARNING SAY?

Bateson describes his theory as an attempt to illuminate 'the barriers of misunderstanding which divide the various species of behavioural scientists ... by an application of Russell's Theory of Logical Types to the concept of "learning" ' (Bateson 2000: 279). The theory of logical types distinguishes between a class (e.g., fruit) and members of that class (e.g., apples, oranges) and, in order to avoid logical paradoxes, stipulates that a class cannot be a member of itself; thus 'fruit' cannot belong to the class 'fruit'.

Altogether Bateson posited five levels of learning, as shown in Table 5.1. Bateson scarcely discussed *Learning IV*, commenting that it 'probably does not occur in any adult living organism on this earth' (2000: 293), indicating that it is likely to involve evolutionary change in a species. We therefore confine our discussion to *Learning 0* through to *Learning III*.

Table 5.1 The Levels of Learning (Adapted from Bateson 2000: 293)

Learning IV	' ... would be *change in Learning III*, but probably does not occur in any adult living organism on this earth.'
Learning III	... is *change in the process of Learning II*, e.g., a corrective change in the system of sets of alternatives from which choice is made.
Learning II	' ... is *change in the process of Learning I*, e.g., a corrective change in the set of alternatives from which choice is made, or it is a change in how the sequence of experience is punctuated.'
Learning I	' ... is *change in specificity of response* by correction of errors of choice within a set of alternatives.'
Learning 0	' ... is characterised by *specificity of response*, which—right or wrong—is not subject to correction.'

The relationship between successive levels is analogous to that between 'apples' and 'fruit', such that the levels represent qualitatively different *types* of learning. Bateson argued, however, that experience, which is located in time, would not reflect the neatness of formal abstract logic (Charlton 2008: 50). He also observed that 'Some of the most interesting aspects of communication may depend upon the use of contradictory messages at different logical levels . . . ' (Bredo 1989: 30).

Bateson's notion of *Learning 0* entails responding to stimuli but making no changes in response to these. This is like the initial response of the two mice in the popular business parable 'Who Moved My Cheese?' (Johnson 1998), who continue to look for their cheese in the same place each day even after it had disappeared—until, that is, the mice register that the cheese really has gone, and that they need to do something different. Yet *Learning 0* is also involved in skilled performance. The point is that it involves no change in behaviour; designating it numerically with a zero does not make it inferior to 'higher' levels.

Learning I denotes the changes in knowledge, skills, and attitude that comprise 'those items which are most commonly called "learning" in the psychological laboratory' (Bateson 2000: 288). Bateson included in this category habituation, rote learning, and Pavlovian conditioning. At this level of learning, for example, the dolphin responds to the trainer's actions by producing new behaviours.

Learning II is essentially learning about the pattern of the context; there is change in *the way events are punctuated*. The dolphin's apparent insight in the preceding story was into context—there was a new understanding of the relational pattern between itself, the trainer, and the activity in which they were engaged. This notion of context, and how people and animals communicate about context, is significant in Bateson's work. His question, during a visit to a zoo, about how monkeys that are play-fighting *know* that they are playing, and not fighting, is regarded by Ivanovas (2007: 847) as 'one of the milestones of Western science'. By analogy, we might ask (for example) how people in the workplace know whether to respond literally to a senior manager's invitation to give honest feedback about their actions. Thus the concept of *Learning II* introduces a reflexive aspect to learning; 'Instrumental conditioning tasks, for example, teach not only how to discriminate between particular stimuli, but also about instrumentality itself' (Bredo 1989: 36). With Bateson's notion of context also comes the recognition that learning is relational, social and constructed, since ' . . . *a way of punctuating* is not true or false' (Bateson 2000: 301).

Learning II is more profound and pervasive than *Learning I* (Cunningham and Dawes 1997). Bateson (2000: 300) identifies the phenomenon of transference as *Learning II*—for example, about the patterning of relationship between a child and a parent. The individual imports this patterning into other contexts in life without being aware of doing so, where its overlay represents *Learning 0*. Thus, 'this behaviour is controlled by former

Learning II and therefore it will be of such a kind as to mould the total context to fit the expected punctuation . . . this self-validating characteristic . . . has the effect that such learning is almost ineradicable' (Bateson 1973: 272). New *Learning II* happens when the individual becomes able to enact a new pattern of relating that no longer replicates that past context.

With *Learning III*, we are challenged to consider what it may mean to say 'one not only learns, but simultaneously learns how to learn, *and* simultaneously learns how to learn how to learn'. Bateson added the section on *Learning III* to his essay in 1971, noting that at this level, 'the concept of "self" will no longer function as a nodal argument in the punctuation of experience . . .' (2000: 304). Furthermore, *Learning III* is rare; ' . . . something of the sort does, from time to time, occur in psychotherapy, religious conversion, and in other sequences in which there is profound reorganization of character' (Bateson 2000: 301). Bredo notes that 'The "problem" to which third-order learning is a "solution" consists of systematic contradictions in experience' (1989: 35).

As a possible illustration of *Learning III*, we cite a meditation teacher's description of his experience of discovering a different way of knowing:

> One day . . . I was eating. I had been sitting, struggling for a number of days . . . I lifted my bowl and suddenly I understood completely . . . Everything is alright as it is. The whole world is completely profoundly whole. I didn't need to do anything. I didn't need to try so hard . . . . It was enormous, an astonishing revelation which instantly undercut all my questions and released me from the hundreds of ways I had always tried to change or fix myself or the world. There was an amazing physical dimension to it as well. My whole body dropped away, the self or container of myself vanished, the bottom of the world dropped out, I had no shape separate from the world. My whole way of being released and changed over the months that followed, so much that people began asking me what had happened.
>
> (Kornfield 2000: 93)

Some further observations about Bateson's theory are relevant. Some sources portray Bateson's levels as successive orders of cognitive reflection (e.g., Brockbank and McGill 1998: 41). Such a view could imply that his *Learning III*, for example, is broadly equivalent to a form of critical reflection (e.g., Mezirow and Associates 2000; Moon 2005). We believe that, according to the evidence of his writing, Bateson's levels are clearly not about cognition alone—nor are they about behaviour alone. He refers repeatedly to embodied, enacted change, in tune with recent theoretical notions of 'embodied knowing' (Lakoff 1999; Varela *et al.* 1993).

Furthermore it is not a stage theory of learning, whereby one 'progresses' from *Learning 0* to *Learning III*. Bateson's writing also suggests that all these levels may (but do not necessarily) occur simultaneously in experience.

Bredo observes, ' . . . the different levels of learning go in parallel' (1989: 32). While they can be distinguished logically in theory, in experience they may be happening together in time and space.

Nor is it the case that the higher one goes the better; *Learning II* and *Learning III* involve a questioning of meaning that can be uncomfortable and (according to Bateson) risky. Contu *et al.* (2003) identify a value-laden rhetoric in the field of management, such that 'learning' and related conceptions of 'the learning organization' and 'organizational learning' are seen as a universally 'good thing'. Contrary to this trend, Bateson conceives of 'learning' as potentially leading to either desirable or undesirable consequences.

APPLICATIONS TO ISSUES OF WORKPLACE LEARNING

We now give three illustrations of how Bateson's theory may be applied to issues of workplace learning.

A Consultancy Example

We begin with an example from a consultant known to us, who described her experience of using Bateson's theory in her work with an organization that exists to support other organizations to put customer relationship management (CRM) at the heart of their practice. In the consultant's words,

> *They've realized that in order to support others, they need to be putting CRM at the heart of their own practice firstly to be credible, secondly so they know what it really means and also to be able to support others. The question is how?*
>
> *I thought that it might help them to take a few steps back to understand the process that they were about to embark on. As part of one of the management team meetings I showed them Bateson's model of levels of learning.*
>
> *They were interested in the model and said that it made sense to them. They identified that they needed to learn CRM strategies, and also learn about the process of learning. They all chose learning tasks and agreed that they would reflect on how they learned in a journal. They had a month to complete the task and reflect on the process.*
>
> *When we met again they reflected on what they'd learnt:*
>
> • *They had never considered 'learning to learn' before they had seen the model. Learning was something that just happened 'unconsciously' or out of awareness unless it was something very tangible such as how to use a computer programme.*

- *They were interested in how they chose their tasks. A couple of people chose multiple tasks, some people chose a single task, others chose to learn about something they were going to do anyway. One chose to learn a new language.*
- *They reported that the process had helped them to be conscious of different types of learning activities and more aware of other people's approaches to learning.*

Retrospectively, we could portray these comments as indicating *Learning I*, about the chosen tasks. There is also evidence that they reflected on these tasks and engaged in a form of 'learning to learn'.

> *I do think they became more aware of how they begin to learn, barriers to learning, their own approach (how they avoid and how they embrace), how over ambitious some people can be, and how learning is both intensely personal and is possible to be a team experience.*

This awareness of learning as a dimension of the team's activities is one possible example of *Learning II*, a theme on which we expand next. *Learning II* also appears to enter the picture in comments such as:

- *Some people disengaged from the learning tasks they had set themselves, but in the group environment felt peer pressure to have learnt.*
- *Four people used their journal and found it helpful. Two of the people that didn't said that they felt guilty about it, perhaps not contributing to the team's learning.*

Identifying peer pressure is an example of attending to *Learning II*, since it concerns the pattern of relationship between individuals and team; meanings, rules, norms and expectations of the relationships between people. This recognizes a social and micro-political dimension to learning; 'No task instruction can be done in a socially neutral way . . . It must always . . . exemplify some form of social relationship. . . . Bateson's theory helps show how they are different aspects of a common process rather than different things' (Bredo 1989: 37).

Learning II can occur simultaneously with *Learning I*. It is not, as it were, timetabled separately on the curriculum of workplace learning. Any workplace experience could be said to involve overlapping and interpenetrating domains of learning, involving (for example) learning about self, about the overt task, and about the context at the same time. In the foregoing example, each manager could be gaining insight into themselves for personal development; learning about customer relationship management; and learning about (and co-creating) a context.

Organizational Learning

In the second example, Bateson's levels of learning were used as an interpretative framework as part of a doctoral study (Langley) of organizational learning in arts organizations that have survived financial crisis. Constructa (a pseudonym), a contemporary art gallery, was set up in a deconsecrated church and describes itself as *'a place where artists come to make new work'*.

When first opened in 1996 it was regarded as avant-garde. Some 10 years later it has been grappling to understand its present and possible future. It has prided itself on supporting artists who are keen to experiment, be adventurous and push the boundaries of their work—perhaps by changing, scale, method or materials.

The gallery had exhibited a particularly challenging exhibition both in terms of its content and construction. It involved the creation of an additional galvanized steel room in the centre of the space, an act that stretched the organization and its resources to its limits. In this room the audience was then confronted with questions about the ethics of mass media and photojournalism.

> *Flash! The image burns the screen. It takes a while for startled eyes to adjust. Into focus emerges a small African child, emaciated and curled in the dust. Less than a meter away stands a statuesque vulture. This is the only image in a text based installation that tells of the short, troubled life of Kevin Carter. His beginnings, his life as a photojournalist and his ultimate suicide brought on by the scenes he witnessed, captured and distributed. This is a nerve jangling, skin rippling, emotion wrenching experience. It is in your body before your thoughts form.*

To the researcher, the story of the exhibition's construction seems to mirror the process of renewal the organization has been through: it is a story of winning through against the odds, delivering in spite of a lack of resources; of inspiration and learning to innovate, to overcome the challenges.

Reflecting from the perspective of each of Bateson's levels, in order to identify possible examples of learning from her data, the researcher thought *Learning 0* may have been represented by the way many past routines were utilized. The gallery regularly produces exhibitions, so Constructa drew on existing capabilities. Behavioural patterns, possibly features of the culture, were also manifested. Drawing on Scott-Morgan's (1994) 'unwritten rules', the researcher identified rules about quality, delivering on time, giving all your effort, respecting the artist—above all, 'the show must go on'.

Learning I involves change in behaviour to meet stable or familiar goals (i.e., mounting the exhibition). There was evidence of people developing some new operational skills. The timescales and late decisions on funding meant that some processes and procedures needed to change; the extensive project management handbook was abandoned and they used existing networks to find emergency help.

Learning II is a change of pattern, the emergence of a new punctuation of events. The exhibit involved creating a new relational reality, with an international artist with whom they had not worked with before; the relationship was often mediated by a third party. The staff described how they tried to explain their ethos to the artist, but it was only the chair and vice-chair who succeed in sharing some of the culture at the end of the week, by just 'chatting' at the exhibition's opening night—'we want people to have a learning experience, we want people to grow' (chair, female).

The difficulties involved in constructing the box, and the emotional impact of the exhibit, resonated with the plight of the organization. A director recounted the complexity of the experience and another possible, albeit "negative", example of *Learning II*, the emotional containment the team learnt. The difficulties were 'undiscussable'. One of the gallery directors talked about a lack of time for reflection. Staff seemed unwilling to discuss the event—unable, apparently, to move into refection about it. It was a visceral, emotional experience.

Finally, other than the fact that a number of people, the researcher included, were profoundly moved by the work, the researcher did not identify evidence of *Learning III*.

This case, albeit described briefly, illustrates the possibility of using Bateson's theory as an interpretive framework in relation to issues of organizational learning. This helped the researcher appreciate better the multifaceted nature of learning in the organizations she has been studying.

Transformation: Reaching for the Holy Grail

Our third and final example illustrates Bateson's theory as a framework for critically analyzing issues of workplace learning, in this case the notion of 'transformation'. Indeed, initially we developed an interest in Bateson's theory as a possible framework to enhance the conceptualization of 'transformative learning' (e.g., McWhinney and Markos 2003; Tosey *et al.* 2005).

There appears to be a strong attraction in the Western world towards notions of 'transformation'. Transformation is the espoused goal of many managers, consultants, organizations, and even governments. At first glance, Bateson's *Learning III* would seem to offer the possibility of transformational learning. Yet as noted, Bateson said that *Learning III* is 'likely to be difficult and rare even in human beings' (2000: 301). It transcends, and potentially subverts, the whole basis of our perception and understanding of the world. Trying to grasp *Learning III* is, perhaps, like a fish trying to apprehend a world in which the sea does not exist.

The difficulty of this within Bateson's theory is that typically people seem to want transformation on their own terms. Yet *Learning III* is not something that can be pursued in an instrumental fashion. Bateson emphasized that 'even the attempt at level III can be dangerous' (2000: 305), leading to psychosis instead of enlightenment. He believed that both 'religious' and 'psychotic' experiences were examples of this kind of learning. He cites

(Bateson 2000: 461) the case of C. J. Jung, whose psychotic breakdown (or epistemological crisis, depending on your viewpoint) led to his writing one of the most problematic of his works, 'The Seven Sermons of the Dead'.

This leads us to a paradox. While business leaders may yearn for transformation, and many consultants may promise to deliver it, it is both perilous to attempt and beyond the capacity of mankind to produce through planned, conscious intent. Few writers on organizational learning appear to identify this problem, with the exception, for example, of Bartunek and Moch (1994), who liken this type of learning to mystical transformation through the experience of 'the dark night of the soul'. It is probably the projection of a hierarchical, goal-orientated mind-set to see *Learning III* as some kind of 'holy grail' (French and Bazalgette 1996) of learning; it is not guaranteed to be either benign or transcendent. Therefore if *Learning III* were to happen, it would not be controllable by management. It might disturb the very notions underpinning business organizations and their purposes, values, and operations.

LEARNING TO LEARN

One of the contributions of Bateson's theory is that it can help to unpack the notion of 'learning to learn', which according to Poell (1999) is a prominent theme of the learning organization literature. In management development, it has been said that 'Learning to learn . . . Will help you ultimately with everything you need or want to learn in the future' (Pedler *et al.* 2001: 260).

Using Bateson's framework we can identify at least four different aspects to this term. First, 'learning to learn' often refers to the acquisition of skills or knowledge pertaining to the intentional activity of learning or study. This, we suggest, is an example of *Learning I* in Bateson's framework, in the sense that it concerns of new behaviours and skills that provide new choices for action.

Second, 'learning to learn' can refer to reflection on, or increased awareness of the processes involved in, learning. In HRD a typical example could be through profiling one's learning style (Coffield *et al.* 2004; Honey and Mumford 1992); in higher education research there is contemporary emphasis on 'meta-learning' (Jackson 2004) and meta-cognition.

The question of where this form of 'learning to learn' can be located in Bateson's framework highlights a difficulty about the place of reflection within his theory, about which writers have expressed varying views. For example, McWhinney (2005: 28) describes *Learning II* as 'reflective knowledge'. However, since Bateson's writing about *Learning II* emphasizes *enacted* changes, this raises the question of whether reflection represents instead a movement in a different direction, as it were, laterally not vertically. For example, he referred explicitly to 'a stance at the side of my ladder . . . to discuss the structure of this ladder' (Bateson 2000: 308), which suggests that cognitive reflection such as written discussion of the theory is to be distinguished from the type of learning that is 'on' the ladder (Bateson used this metaphor of a 'ladder' to refer to the framework of levels).

For the same reason, there seems to be a good case for differentiating between a third sense of 'learning to learn', Argyris and Schön's (1978) concept of 'double-loop learning', and Bateson's *Learning II*. Double-loop learning involves questioning the goals or values being pursued through action. Whereas single-loop learning is concerned to improve the methods by which one pursues a goal, double-loop learning reviews the goal itself, or the values associated with it. It is essentially a cognitive process. Indeed, Argyris and Schön themselves distinguished double-loop learning from 'deutero-learning', the term coined originally by Bateson (2000: 167) and later abandoned by him in favour of *Learning II* (2000: 248–9). While Bateson and Argyris both built on cybernetics, Visser (2007) suggests that their divergence may echo their different understandings of Ashby's work. According to Harries-Jones (1995: 114), Bateson was especially keen to challenge the emphasis on control by original Macy conference participants such as Ross Ashby (1965) and Norbert Wiener (1965), whose work led to that branch of cybernetics that is concerned with artificial intelligence and control systems.

If we pursue this distinction between Argyris and Bateson, *Learning II* could be seen to represent a fourth sense of 'learning to learn'. Bateson referred to *Learning II* as 'learning to expect some sort of context', commenting that 'I equate that with the development of becoming test wise in experiments. That if you subject a human being or animal to experiments of a general sort, that subject becomes more skilled at dealing with contexts as it were' (cited in Ray and Govener 2007: 1028). Visser (2007) reaches a similar conclusion in his review of the concept of deutero-learning, which:

> . . . refers to the behavioral adaptation to patterns of conditioning at the level of relationships in organizational contexts. This form of learning is continuous, behavioural-communicative, and largely unconscious. It tends to escape explicit steering and organizing.
>
> (Visser 2007: 665)

Similarly, Snyder's (1971) notion of the 'hidden curriculum', cited as an example of *Learning II* by both Bredo (1989: 33) and Engeström (2001: 138), refers to the tacit expectations and rules for success of formal educational contexts, of which the teachers themselves may be unaware but which they also reinforce. 'Savvy' students are quick to discern and orientate to the hidden curriculum. Mary Catherine Batson offers a related example:

> I grew up being told that if I burned myself I should put butter on the burn. Then at a certain point they told me, no, don't do that, put the

burn under running water or even better put ice on it. Not only had I learned one version of how to deal with a burn, but in the process of learning that, I had also been learning about who to believe, about the nature of validity and authority.

(Bateson 2005: 18–19)

Bateson's writing about *Learning II* also conveys its embodied and aesthetic nature. Bateson placed much emphasis on the epistemological importance of art and the aesthetic, both generally in his writing (Harries-Jones 1995: 14), and specifically with reference to apprehending relations between the levels of learning: ' . . . art is commonly concerned with . . . bridging the gap between the more or less unconscious premises acquired by Learning II and the more episodic content of consciousness and immediate action' (Bateson 2000: 308). Bateson saw aesthetics, which has received recent interest in the field of human resource development (Gibb 2004), as enabling people to extend beyond the limitations of explicit, conscious knowing. His interest in the aesthetic dimension of learning appears significant and worthy of further exploration, as discussed at length by Charlton (2008). This contrasts, for example, with the metaphor of 'man as action scientist' that is espoused by Argyris *et al.* (1985), which emphasizes intentional, cognitive inquiry into contexts and their 'governing variables'. Similarly, Mezirow's emphasis on critical reflection as the route to transformative learning (e.g., Mezirow 1991) neglects the embodied and aesthetic modes that are implicit in Bateson's theory, as well as explicit in his writing.

APPRAISING BATESON'S THEORY

Bateson's theory of levels of learning has influenced and been discussed by thinkers in fields including education (Bloom 2004; Brockbank and McGill 1998; McWhinney and Markos 2003; Peterson 1999); organizational learning and change (Argyris and Schön 1978; Bartunek and Moch 1994; Engeström 2001; French and Bazalgette 1996; Roach and Bednar 1997; Tosey and Mathison 2008; Visser 2003, 2007; Wijnhoven 2001); and psychotherapy and personal development (Bandler and Grinder 1975; Dilts and Epstein 1995; Keeney 1983; Watzlawick *et al.* 1974). Typically, these authors have found Bateson's emphasis on qualitatively different types of learning evocative (McWhinney 2005: 26) and stimulating.

It also remains enigmatic. He did not develop his theory as far as he might have done; according to Bredo (1989: 36), the levels of learning are 'properly viewed as a framework and not an elaborated theory'. There is relatively little critique that engages directly and in detail with Bateson's theory. McWhinney (2005: 25), drawing on neurophysiological findings, interestingly argues that there is 'a neurological explanation of the difference between LI and models of LII and LIII'; yet this work 'does not support a typological difference between LII and LIII' (*sic*). Instead, McWhinney portrays *Learning III* as a temporary letting-go of existing assumptions about reality and causality, after which a person typically resumes more stable but modified patterns of *Learning II*. This reformulation could reduce the risk that Bateson's levels are seen as a simple hierarchy.

The centennial of Bateson's birth, in 2004, prompted reviews of his intellectual contribution in general, manifesting, for example, in special issues of the two journals *Cybernetics and Human Knowing* (2005) and *Kybernetes* (2007). Thomas *et al.* (2007: 872) report that the majority of Bateson's citations in the SSCI (Social Science Citation Index) are in the field of business and organization management, and affirm that his radical contribution is revered by many. Yet Ivanovas (2007: 848) argues that Bateson's ideas 'have not really become paradigmatic', because his underlying ecological approach has been ignored or misunderstood while his concepts have been assimilated into linear ways of thinking.

A major intellectual development that is relevant to Bateson's thinking in general is the 'Santiago Theory of Cognition' by the Chilean academics Umberto Maturana and Francisco Varela (e.g., Maturana and Varela 1998). Capra (1996: 170) comments that:

> The central insight of the Santiago theory is the same as Bateson's—the identification of . . . the process of knowing with the process of life. This represents a radical expansion of the traditional concept of mind . . . the brain is not necessary for mind to exist.
>
> (Capra 1996: 170)

Bateson's view of Maturana and Varela's position is discussed in Harries-Jones (1995: 183–91). Where Maturana and Varela depart from Bateson is that they regard the idea of a hierarchy of logical types, on which Bateson theory of levels of learning is based, as a property of human consciousness. Capra suggests that Bateson regarded these types as existing objectively in the world, and concludes (1996: 300) that this hampered Bateson from developing further insight into the nature of mind. Maturana and Varela's ideas, and their implications for Bateson's theory of levels of learning, represent one direction for future research.

CONCLUSION

Gregory Bateson's theory of 'levels of learning' has influenced a variety of writers on education, management learning, and psychotherapy. Yet Bateson's writing is complex, due to the issues of epistemology that he was attempting to explore and elucidate. His *Mind and Nature* (1979) is the most accessible of his books. As Mary Catherine Bateson comments, 'Every effort to know about knowing involves the cat trying to swallow its own tail' (foreword to Bateson 2000: xii–xiv). This means that what appears at first glance to be a straightforward, logical explanation leads rapidly into a recursive world, like a hall of mirrors.

While this can be daunting, we have also typically found it rewarding, and we believe that Bateson's theory offers a worthwhile and radical perspective on issues of workplace learning. Engeström (2001) argues that theories of learning are too often focused on the individual and identifies Gregory Bateson's 'levels of learning' as one of the few theories that attempts to address this problem. According to Bredo, simultaneous theoretical consideration of content and context is uncommon: 'Learning theorists tend to focus on individual task learning independent of social context, while socialization theorists focus on the effects of social context independent of the task' (Bredo 1989: 27). Bateson's theory combines the two; or perhaps more accurately, does not separate them epistemologically.

Bateson's theory may also account for some of the subtleties and paradoxes of workplace learning, for example, such that attempts to promote *Learning I* can produce contrary *Learning II*. We have explored its possible application to issues of workplace learning, and have suggested that it can help to distinguish between variations in the sense of 'learning to learn'.

KEY LEARNING POINTS

- Bateson's theory offers a simultaneous theoretical consideration of content and context. Learning, like 'mind', is relational; learning is both individual and social.
- Contu *et al.* (2003) criticize the discourse that promotes 'learning' as unquestioningly a good thing, which Bateson's theory avoids. Bateson argues that learning can have desirable and undesirable effects. It may be wise to be wary of the apparent attractions of the idea of 'transformation', since *Learning III*, for example, entails significant risk.
- The extent to which managers or human resource developers can choose or determine the type of learning that arises in workplaces is limited, as is the capacity to bring about *Learning II* and *Learning III* instrumentally.
- Bateson's theory emphasizes that learning involves embodied experience and aesthetics as well as cognition.

ACKNOWLEDGEMENT

We wish to thank Deborah Durrant, who kindly gave permission to use the consultancy example in this chapter.

Part II

Operationalizing Learning in the Workplace

6   Antecedents of Nurses' Actual Learning Activities

The Role of Psychological Work Conditions and Intrinsic Work Motivation

Marjolein Berings, Marc Van Veldhoven, and Rob Poell

One of the leading models in literature about the relationship between learning behaviour and psychological work conditions is the demand-control-support model (Karasek and Theorell 1990). The 'active-learning hypothesis' derived from this model assumes that employees with a high level of task demands, a high level of task control, and a high level of social support have opportunities to control these high task demands and can thus develop new behaviour patterns (learning). The demand-control-support model has been confirmed by many authors (e.g., Dollard and Winefield 1998; Karasek and Theorell 1990; Parker and Sprigg 1999; Taris and Feij 2005). The question can be raised, however, whether these studies measured 'active learning' properly. They mostly used rather passive indicators that do not reflect actual learning behaviour (e.g., self-confidence and job satisfaction). In this chapter we will investigate the influence of the psychological work conditions from the demand-control-support model on more active (behaviour-based) indicators of learning among nurses. Nurses are an excellent target group for such a study because they are very much involved in continuous learning. We will also investigate the mediating role of intrinsic work motivation on the relationship between these work conditions and learning, as a possible explanation for some inconclusive findings from previous studies.

THEORETICAL FRAMEWORK

Psychological Work Conditions

According to the active-learning hypothesis, the main factors determining workers' learning behaviour are job demands, job control, and job support. The concept of *job demands* refers to the difficulty of work, with respect to pace and mental load (de Jonge *et al.* 1995). *Job control* was originally a multidimensional concept, including job decision latitude and skill discretion (Karasek 1985). Since skill discretion (the degree to which workers make use of their skills) is operationally overlapping with some of the outcomes of active learning, such as skill acquisition and development, it is suggested by several authors to omit this concept from the measurement of job control (e.g., Schreurs and Taris 1998; Taris and Kompier 2004). Therefore, in this chapter we choose to measure job control using only one aspect of decision latitude: autonomy. This job characteristic indicates the opportunity or freedom that employees have to determine several elements in their direct work situation, such as the methods they apply and the order in which they conduct their job activities (de Jonge 1995; Taris and Kompier 2004). *Social support* refers to overall levels of social transactions offered by supervisors or colleagues, such as encouragement and the provision of such interaction possibilities (de Jonge 1995; Karasek and Theorell 1990). Whereas empirical studies testing the demand-control-support model show contradictory results regarding the first two variables (cf. Taris and Kompier 2004), recent studies agree that social support stimulates on-the-job learning (Ellinger *et al.* 1999; Eraut *et al.* 2002).

Active Indicators of Learning

Ironically, the active-learning hypothesis has mostly been investigated using rather passive indicators that do not reflect actual learning behaviour (e.g., self-confidence and job satisfaction). This has been criticized by many authors who claimed that more pro-active and learning-oriented indicators are needed in this line of research. Nevertheless, so far measures of learning attitudes and learning outcomes have been used rather than measures of actual learning behaviour. Examples of these attitudes and outcomes are perceived mastery and role breadth self-efficacy (e.g., Holman and Wall 2002; Morrison *et al.* 1998; Parker and Sprigg 1999; Taris *et al.* 2003). Authors using this type of measure for active learning claim that active learning cannot be observed directly, but must be inferred from its outcomes (cf. Taris and Kompier 2004).

Karasek and Theorell (1990) themselves were ambiguous on the exact concepts to use for measuring what they referred to as 'learning'. This has resulted in many different measurements by different authors testing the model. Taris *et al.* (2003) distinguished among four clusters of outcomes used in previous research: (1) job satisfaction, (2) job involvement and job commitment, (3) self-efficacy and mastery, and (4) job challenge. Indicators like self-efficacy and mastery are usually perceived as the most 'active' indicators; however, even these do not indicate actual learning behaviour. For these indicators significant results were not always found and some studies even reported negative effects (e.g., Holman and Wall 2002; Parker and Sprigg 1999; Taris *et al.* 2003). Even when the expected results were found, it is not clear what 'learning' entails in this context. Taris and Kompier (2004) explained: "*Workers may display blind trial-and-error behaviour as well as carefully planned experiments with alternative ways of dealing with new problems (and, of course, every-thing in between)"* (p. 157). Holman and Wall (2002) therefore suggested that future studies measure learning with clear process measures, indicating the actual learning behaviour.

Actual Learning Behaviour

Many activities that people perform on the job can be indicated as learning activities, such as dealing with the challenges of work itself and interactions with other people in the workplace (Eraut *et al.* 1998). Sometimes these learning activities are primarily working activities, with learning as a by-product, and sometimes these activities are primarily meant for learning (Doornbos *et al.* 2004). Karasek and Theorell (1990) distinguished between open-loop learning (developing new solutions for anticipated future problems) and closed-loop learning (routinization of already developed action plans).

In this study we focus on actual learning activities rather than the outcomes of learning. We assume that participating in these activities results in certain learning outcomes (cf. Kwakman 2003). In order to justify our measurement of the various types of learning activities that exist in working situations, we distinguish among six different types of learning activities (cf. Berings *et al.* 2007):

Learning . . .
1. . . . by doing one's regular job, such as taking care of patients or conversations with patients and family;
2. . . . by applying something new in the job, such as broadening tasks or job rotation;
3. . . . from theory, such as reading books or searching the Internet;
4. . . . from supervision, such as visiting information meetings, training, or coaching;
5. . . . from reflection by oneself, such as planning or looking back by oneself;
6. . . . by talking with others, such as asking informative questions or feedback, or looking back with others.

Relationship between Psychological Work Conditions and Active Learning

Based on the demand-control-support model, we expect a positive relationship between, on the one hand, perceived workload, perceived autonomy, and perceived social support from colleagues and supervisor and, on the other hand, learning activities. The question to be answered in this chapter is: *"Which psychological work conditions facilitate or hinder which types of actual learning behaviour?"*

People in active jobs with high demands will take steps to manage those demands (de Lange *et al.* 2005; Parker and Sprigg 1999), provided they have the necessary job control. In jobs with high demands, people consider it challenging to perform at the highest possible level, and thus they are willing to learn. This corresponds fully with goal-setting theory; for instance, Locke and Latham (1990) showed that relatively difficult goals lead to high performance, amongst others because they can be energizing and provoke persistence. People with high job control have opportunities to adjust to demands according to needs and circumstances (Karasek and Theorell 1990). They can choose adequate strategies to deal with new challenges, develop new action programs (Frese and Zapf 1994), explore different ways of solving problems (Bandura 1997), and learn new skills (de Lange *et al.* 2005). Social support on the job is needed to be able to grasp available learning opportunities (Ellinger *et al.* 1999; Eraut *et al.* 2002) and will enhance the effects of job control (Mikkelsen *et al.* 2005). Many studies suggest that on-the-job coaching by supervisors, often regarded as a management style, is essential to maximize employee learning activities and performance (e.g., Whitmore 2002).

Taris and Kompier (2004) conducted an inventory of 30 studies testing the active-learning hypothesis. Almost two-thirds of the studies supported the hypothesis, in that positive additive effects of both job demands and job control on learning outcomes were observed. Most other studies found only the relationship between job control and learning, and no relation between job demands and learning. The evidence for the influence of job control, therefore, seems stronger than that of job demands. The smaller impact of job demands may be explained by reasoning that both workers with low and those with high job demands can explore various ways of dealing with these demands, some of which may be conducive to learning (Bandura 1997). For example, workers with low job demands could use the available time for self-study. Looking more closely at the results of the analysis by Taris and Kompier (2004), it is striking that most positive effects were found in studies using relatively active learning variables, such as feedback-seeking behaviour, active problem solving, and participation in social and political activities.

Different studies found different effects of job demands, job control, and social support. The demand-control-support model also predicts synergistic effects between the three different work conditions, but in many studies these were not found. Many authors found additive effects rather than interaction effects (Taris and Kompier 2004). Karasek (1989) considered the exact form of the synergistic effect (additive or interactive) as relatively unimportant. Many authors regard both interaction and additive effects of the different work conditions as confirmations of the active-learning hypothesis (cf. de Lange *et al.* 2003; Taris and Kompier 2004). In this study we will only assess the main effects, for two reasons. The first reason is parsimony: we will already be considering a large number of relationships, to which exploring interaction terms would only add further. The second reason is the rather limited findings of previous studies.

The current literature about on-the-job learning and the active-learning hypothesis does not enable us to formulate specific hypotheses on the influence of psychological work conditions, as the learning variables used previously were not behaviour based. Other literatures have neither delivered any empirically validated theories on different ways of on-the-job learning (Van Woerkom 2003). Therefore, the current study explores how several specific psychological work conditions influence different types of actual learning behaviour.

Work Motivation as a Mediator

As the outcomes of the different studies have been so diverse, we suspect that an intrapersonal psychological mechanism that links several combinations of job demands and job control to learning behaviour must play a role (cf. Parker and Sprigg 1999; Taris and Kompier 2004).

Intrinsic work motivation could have an important mediating effect, as it determines how active a person is, under given circumstances, in work-related learning activities. Intrinsic work motivation is *"the degree to which a person wants to work well in his or her job in order to achieve intrinsic satisfaction"* (Warr *et al.* 1979: 135). Several theories in the field of organizational psychology consider intrinsic motivation an important mediator of the relationship between task characteristics and learning: the job characteristics model of Hackman and Oldham, the goal setting theory of Locke and Latham, and the self-determination theory of Deci and Ryan (Wielenga-Meijer *et al.* 2006). Also, empirical studies show that motivational orientation is the main factor for nurses to participate in continuing professional education (Waddell 1993) and that highly motivated nurses are more self-directed in their learning (Furze and Pearcey 1999). It is therefore imaginable that workers with a high intrinsic work motivation are also highly motivated to be involved in continuing learning activities. Studies that investigated relationships between motivation and learning outcome variables, however, showed different results (Taris and Kompier 2004). This may imply that the role of motivation is different in different work conditions and/or regarding different learning activities, which we will investigate in this study.

Karasek and Theorell (1990) regarded motivation to learn as a dependent variable. They described motivation to learn as *"an environmentally facilitated, active approach toward learning new behaviour patterns or solving new problems"* (p. 170). This motivation would then lead to active learning behaviour and related outcomes, such as feelings of mastery and self-efficacy. Karasek and Theorell (1990) showed that job demand, job control, and social support influence motivation to learn new work behaviour, new skills, and general work motivation.

The research questions of this study are as follows: *"Which types of nurses' actual on-the-job learning are influenced by job demands, job control, and job support? And what is the role of intrinsic work motivation in this relationship?"* The full model that is investigated in this study is presented in Figure 6.1.

RESEARCH METHOD

Participants

The nursing population forms an excellent target group to study work-related learning. Its professional working environment keeps on changing (cf. Allen 2001; Clark 2001; den Boer and Hövels 2001) and therefore continuous learning is needed during nurses' careers (Lawton and Wimpenny 2003) through courses, training, and learning on the job (Powell 1989). Continuing development is important for nurses to remain employable (Lawton and Wimpenny 2003) and their job is more attractive to nurses if they are given greater learning opportunities (Maurer *et al.* 2003).

We distributed questionnaires to nurses via contacts with nursing supervisors and HR professionals working in hospitals in the Netherlands who had visited a symposium about on-the-job learning in the health care sector that we had organized a year earlier. We asked them to distribute the questionnaires to the nurses working in their departments. Using snowball sampling, more supervisors were approached. In this way, the questionnaire was distributed to 912 registered nurses working in different departments of 13 general hospitals in the Netherlands. Of these questionnaires, 436 were returned, yielding an initial response rate of 48 per cent. The dataset contained a relatively large number of missing

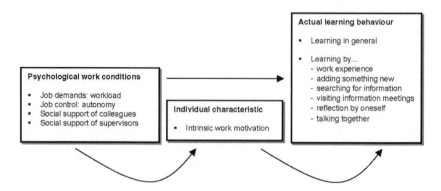

Figure 6.1 Adapted Demand-Control-Support model: Psychological work conditions influencing actual learning behaviour (variables used in present study).

data, which was probably due to the questionnaire's length. We therefore imputed the missing data for all cases where less than 10 per cent of the learning activities scores were missing. Other cases were left out of the analyses. Data imputation improves the efficiency of estimates and the 'power' of statistical tests (de Leeuw 2001). We used 'two-way imputation for separate scales', because in simulation research this method has proved to produce almost no bias in Cronbach's alpha (van Ginkel 2007). This left us with a final sample of 372 cases and a final response rate of 41 per cent, which is modest but useful.

Table 6.1 presents an overview of descriptive statistics for the sample, which was not completely representative of the population of all nurses working in general hospitals in the Netherlands. A nonparametric chi-square test revealed that males were overrepresented ($\aleph^2 = 7.30$, $p = 0.01$). One sample t-test showed that the nurses in the sample were a bit younger ($t = -4.41$, $p = 0.00$) and had a longer workweek ($t = 17.21$, $p = 0.00$) than nurses in the population.

Instruments

On-the-Job Learning Activities

Nurses' on-the-job learning activities were measured by 42 items of the OLSQN, a Dutch questionnaire measuring seven on-the-job learning activities conducted by nurses for six different learning contents in a nested situation-response design (Berings *et al.* 2007). This scale measures learning activities by asking respondents to indicate the extent to which a particular learning content has been mastered by engaging in

Table 6.1   Descriptive Statistics for the Control Variables (N = 372)

	N	%
Type of hospital	369	
- academic hospital	219	59.35
- other hospitals	150	40.65
Type of unit	365	
- ward	316	86.58
- outpatient department	49	13.42
Gender	368	
- male	61	16.58
- female	307	83.42
Level of nursing education	363	
- vocational education (Dutch mbo)	209	57.58
- higher education (Dutch hbo and post-hbo)	154	42.42

particular learning behaviour. An item example is '*In the last two years I have improved my technical nursing skills by asking my colleagues informative questions about this.*' The learning contents selected as well as the distinction in different types of learning behaviours were based on interview studies with nurses, their supervisors, and HR professionals in health care (Berings *et al.* 2008). The six-point response scale ranged from 1 = 'never' to 6 = 'always'. Based on the results of the factor analysis, two learning activities (learning by asking informative questions and learning by reflecting with others) were combined into one single learning activity: learning through talking with others. The other scales of the questionnaire represent learning by work experience, learning by adding something new, learning by searching for information, learning by visiting information meetings, and learning through reflection by oneself. We excluded 11 items in order to decrease ambiguity in the factor solution and to increase the reliability of the scales. Additionally, a general measure for learning was calculated, based on all 42 items. Nurses in the sample seemed to learn most often through reflection by themselves and through work experience, and least often through visiting information meetings ($p < .001$).

Psychological Work Conditions

We chose not to measure job demands using the original questionnaire by Karasek (1985), mainly because this instrument has been criticized for being too narrow. It measures job demands only in terms of pace and amount of work, neglecting qualitative job demands. We therefore operationalized job demands by perceived workload and used a scale taking qualitative demands into account. The scale consists of eight items from the Maastricht Autonomy Questionnaire, developed by de Jonge *et al.* (1995), which were measured on a six-point scale, from 1 = 'never' to 6 = 'always'. An example is '*At my ward, work is mentally strenuous*'. We deleted one item to improve the reliability of the scale.

Job control, operationalized by perceived autonomy, was measured with 10 items from the same questionnaire, on a five-point scale, from 1 = 'very little' to 6 = 'very much'. An example is '*To what extent does your work offer you the possibility to determine the order of your work activities yourself?*' We deleted one item to improve the reliability of the scale.

To measure perceived social support at work, a 10-item scale was derived from the VOS-D, a Dutch questionnaire on organizational stress (Bergers *et al.* 1986). An example is '*If there are any problems at work, can you talk about this with your supervisor/colleagues?*' Five items measured social support from colleagues and five similar items measured social support from supervisor on a six-point scale, from 1 = 'very bad' / 'very little' / 'never' to 6 = 'very good' / 'very much' / 'always'.

Intrinsic Work Motivation

Intrinsic work motivation was measured by means of six items from a scale originally developed by Warr *et al.* (1979) and translated and adapted by Tummers *et al.* (2002). The five-point response scale ranges from 1 = 'totally disagree' to 5 = 'totally agree'. An example is *'I perceive a feeling of fulfilment when doing my work well.'* We deleted two items to improve reliability of the scale.

The reliability of the scales and the means and standard deviations of the nurses' scores on the scales are shown in Table 6.2. Tables 6.3 and 6.4 show Pearson correlations among the different variables.

Table 6.2 Mean Scores, Standard Deviations, and Reliability Coefficients for Measures of Nurses' On-the-Job Learning Activities, Intrinsic Work Motivation, and Psychological Work Conditions (N = 372)

	Mean	SD	Items	Cronbach's alpha
On-the-job learning activities				
Learning (in general)	3.71	.73	42	.96
Learning by . . .				
Work experience	4.17	1.04	3	.79
Adding something new	3.60	1.11	3	.79
Searching for information	3.37	1.03	3	.80
Visiting info meetings	3.00	1.02	5	.87
Reflection by oneself	4.22	.86	5	.81
Talking together	3.83	.78	12	.89
Individual characteristic				
Intrinisic work motivation	5.21	.50	4	.73
Psychological work motivation				
Workload	3.23	.67	7	.88
Autonomy	2.70	.60	9	.83
Social support of colleagues	5.11	.58	5	.78
Social support of supervisor	4.81	.92	5	.89

Table 6.3   Pearson Correlations among the Predictor Variables (N = 372)

	Workload	Autonomy	Social support of colleagues
Work load			
Autonomy	-.23		
Social support of colleagues	-.05	.23**	
Social support of supervisor	-.09	.21**	.40**

* p ≤ .05 (two tailed)   ** p ≤ .01 (two-tailed)

Statistical Analysis

Figure 6.1 illustrates the model that we are investigating in this study. We conducted a regression analysis in order to describe the relationships between the predictor, mediator, and outcome variables after proving no multi-collinearity between the different variables exists. Four control variables were integrated in the analysis: hospital type, ward type, gender, and level of nursing education, to eliminate the effect of these background variables. For interpreting the evidence favouring mediation in the statistical results we used the protocol suggested by MacKinnon *et al.* (2007). In accordance with this protocol, we present two analytical steps. In the first step, the effects of the psychological work conditions on intrinsic motivation were calculated. In the second step, the effects of all psychological work conditions *and* the mediator intrinsic motivation on the diverse learning activities were calculated (see Table 6.5).

RESULTS

Looking at the control variables, nurses' learning activities were mainly influenced by the level of nursing education. The higher the educational level, the more the nurses learned on the job through work experience, adding something new to their existing tasks, and reflecting by themselves. Hospital and ward types had no significant influence and gender had an effect on learning through working experience only. Female nurses learned more through working experiences than male nurses. The control variables had no influence on intrinsic work motivation.

Figure 6.2 presents the significant results from Tables 6.4 and 6.5 together in a two-step model. All significant direct and indirect effects from the psychological work conditions on learning are shown. Workload and both types of social support had a significant impact on intrinsic work motivation. Social support by the supervisor also had a direct effect on five

Table 6.4 Pearson Correlations among the Predictor, Mediator, and Outcome Variables (N = 372)

	Intrinsic work motivation	Learning	Learning by . . .					
			Work experience	Adding some-thing new	Searching for information	Visiting info meetings	Reflection by oneself	Talking together
Work load	.10	.01	-0.3	-.04	.07	.00	.04	.01
Autonomy	.05	.16**	.08	.16**	.07	.14**	.08	.15**
Social support of colleagues	.29**	.24**	.10*	.26**	.13*	.23**	.19**	.22**
Social support of supervisor	.24**	.16**	.13*	.12*	.06	.11*	.11*	.21**
Intrinsic work motivation	-	.30**	.20**	.22**	.21**	.21**	.30**	.27**

* p ≤ .05 (two tailed) ** p ≤ .01 (two-tailed)

Table 6.5 Linear Multiple Regressions of Psychological Work Conditions Characteristics on Nurses' On-the-Job Learning Activities (N = 372)

| | | Learning by . . . | | | | | | | | | | | | | |
| Perceived | Intrinsic work motivation | Learning | | Work experience | | Adding something new | | Searching for information | | Visiting information meetings | | Reflection by oneself | | Talking together | |
	Beta[1]	Beta[1]	Beta[2]	Beta[1]	Beta[2]	Beta[1]	Beta[2]	Beta[1]	Beta[2]	Beta[1]	Beta[2]	Beta[1]	Beta[2]	Beta[1]	Beta[2]
0. Hospital type (0=academic; 1=others)	-.05	-.01	0	.05	.06	.03	.04	-.07	-.06	-.03	-.03	-.01	0	-.01	0
Ward type (0=ward; 1=outpatient department)	.04	.01	0	-.08	-.09	.01	.01	.07	.07	.06	.06	0.02	0.03	-.01	-.02
Gender (0=male; 1=female)	-.01	.06	.06	11*	11*	.01	.01	-.03	-.03	.01	.02	.08	.08	.09	.09
Level of nursing education (0=vocational ed; 1=higher ed.)	.01	.13*	.13*	19***	.19***	.17***	.17***	.01	.01	.01	.01	.17**	.17**	.10	.09

1. Workload	.13	.06	.03	0	-.03	.02	0	.07	.05	.05	.03	.08	.05	.05	.02
Autonomy	-.01	.12*	.12*	.05	.06	.12*	.12*	.07	.07	.11*	.11*	.06	.07	.11*	.11*
Social support from supervisor	.25***	.21***	.15**	.08	.03	.22***	.18**	.12*	.08	.19**	.15*	.18**	.12*	.17**	.12*
Social support from colleagues	.13*	.04	.01	.09	.07	0	-.02	-.01	-.03	.01	-.01	.02	-.02	.11	.08
2. Intrinsic work motivation	-	-	.25***	-	.19***	-	.16**	-	.18**	-	.16**	-	.28***	-	.21***
Adjusted R²	.10	.08	.13	.06	.09	.09	.11	.02	.04	.04	.06	.06	.13	.09	.11
R² Change	.11***	.08***	.05***	.03*	.03***	.07***	.02**	.02	.03**	.06***	.02**	.05*	.07***	.08***	.04***

$* \ p \leq .05$ $** \ p \leq .01$ $*** \ p \leq .001$

[1]Model including psychological work conditions tested against model only including control variables
[2]Model including intrinsic work motivation tested against previous model

out of seven learning behaviour indicators. Job autonomy showed a direct effect only, on four out of seven learning behaviour indicators only. Intrinsic work motivation had a consistent effect on all seven learning behaviour indicators.

Mediation effects of psychological work conditions on learning behaviour through intrinsic work motivation were confirmed for workload and social support by colleagues. For social support by the supervisor, direct and mediated effects were established. Job autonomy showed direct, unmediated effects only. Mediation by intrinsic work motivation was present for all learning behaviours. The direct links between social support by supervisor and autonomy are different for the diverse learning behaviours.

CONCLUSIONS AND DISCUSSION

Study Outcomes

Using a sample of nurses, with actual learning behaviour as an outcome variable, we have partly confirmed the active-learning hypothesis. We found direct effects on four out of seven measures of learning behaviour for job control (autonomy) and on five out of seven measures for social support by the supervisor. It is difficult to grasp why some learning behaviours were influenced by our independent variables and others were not, with this type of research still in an exploratory stage. However, like earlier studies (e.g., Taris and Kompier 2004), we did not find any direct effects from job demands (workload) on learning behaviour. The results of this study rather suggest that the job demands–learning behaviour relationship is mediated

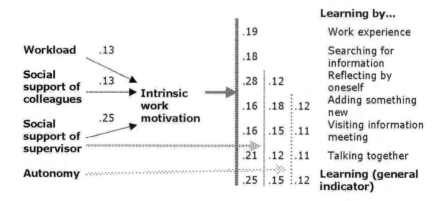

Figure 6.2 Significant Beta values for the model of psychological work conditions influencing nurses' learning, with intrinsic work motivation as a mediator.

by intrinsic work motivation. Three out of the four psychological work conditions in the Karasek model were found to influence actual learning behaviour through the mediator intrinsic work motivation, namely, job demands and both types of social support. The learning types reflecting by oneself and talking together were influenced most strongly by the psychological work conditions of the Karasek model. This may be due to the fact that these types of learning depend more on personal choices. Other types of learning that are more automatically integrated in daily work processes may be more task driven and thus less dependent on the nurses' perceptions of their working environment.

Overall, the independent variables social support by the supervisor and autonomy had most influence on nurses' learning behaviour. Like workload, social support by colleagues did not have any direct effects on learning behaviour. This may be explained by the relatively high average score on collegial support among nurses, together with low variance, which made relationships with other variables hard to establish in this sample. Also, social support by the supervisor and autonomy are, much more than workload and social support by colleagues, dependent on the management style of the supervisor and the organizational work system. It is interesting, therefore, to observe that management styles seem to have a major influence on individual learning behaviour. Managers providing sufficient autonomy and support stimulate nurses' on-the-job learning behaviour. This is in line with claims by other authors about the influence of transformational leadership on organizational learning (e.g., Arágon-Correa *et al.* 2007; Vera and Crossan 2004). Transformational leaders are inspirational, motivational, and provide responsibility and opportunities to change existing systems; they provide autonomy and support. It seems worthwhile to investigate this in further research.

Learning through searching for information is a type of learning that showed different results from the other types of learning. This type of learning was only influenced through an interaction effect of autonomy and social support by the supervisor, and not through main effects of psychological work conditions. For this type of learning, only the model that included the mediator intrinsic work motivation was significant. Here, the management style of the supervisor may be especially important, in that only when autonomy and social support by the supervisor are provided simultaneously, nurses are inclined to learn a lot through searching for information.

Study Limitations

The model showed many significant relationships; however, most Beta and R^2 change values were not very high. Amongst others, this may be due to the homogeneous sample that was used in this study. Looking at the discrepancy in terms of age and weekly working hours between our sample and the actual Dutch nursing population, it is possible that nurses who are more interested in continuous learning were more inclined to fill out the questionnaire. Therefore, our sample may represent a more homogeneous group of nurses interested 'more than average' in learning on the job and career development. Also, even though the nurses worked at different types of wards, they were all in the same profession, with many similar tasks and work structures.

Secondly, since both the independent and dependent measures were assessed by self-report methods, it is also possible that common method variance may have occurred, which reduces correlations between variables.

Thirdly, we looked at job demands as a one-dimensional concept. Mikkelsen *et al.* (2005) showed that different types of job demands (e.g., quantitative demands, cognitive demands, and social demands) have different—enhancing and reducing—effects on job mastery.

Finally, we analyzed the effects for actual learning behaviour. Actual behaviour is usually more difficult to predict than the attitude measures that were used in previous studies analyzing the Karasek model. A final reason is that nurses' learning behaviour does not only depend on the environment but also on their personal style (cf. Berings *et al.* 2007). Since this study was cross-sectional rather than longitudinal, we were not able to prove causal relationships, even though existing theory makes these very plausible (Karasek and Theorell 1990). It is recommended to conduct more longitudinal studies in future to investigate the role of intrinsic work motivation further.

Study Implications

This study has tested the Karasek model for the first time using actual behaviour measures for learning as an outcome variable. We have concluded that different types of learning are influenced differently by the psychological work conditions, with most effects for learning through talking with others. The role of the supervisor appeared to be extremely important through providing sufficient job control and social support. Intrinsic work motivation plays an important direct role in on-the-job learning behaviour and it also mediates key parts of the impact that the psychosocial work environment has on on-the-job learning.

In terms of practical implications, this study has shown that job control and social support by supervisors are main contributors to on-the-job learning; we therefore recommend that managers use a transformational/coaching leadership style, in order to enhance employee learning and performance. Also, the finding that intrinsic work motivation is a crucial indicator of on-the-job learning behaviour, mainly by stimulating individual reflection, underscores the importance of creating a supportive and challenging working environment.

KEY LEARNING POINTS

- Among nurses, different types of learning are influenced differently by various psychological work conditions, with most effects for learning through talking with others.
- The role of the supervisor in nurses' on-the-job learning is crucial, mainly through providing sufficient job control and social support.
- Intrinsic work motivation plays an important role in on-the-job learning behaviour by nurses and it also mediates key parts of the impact exerted by the psychosocial work environment.

7 The Development of a Measure to Assess Information Acquisition Activities

Implications for Workplace and Organizational Learning

Yu-Lin Wang and Andrea D. Ellinger

The importance of learning as a source of sustainable competitive advantage for organizations has been consistently articulated in the scholarly literature in the past decade (Kang *et al.* 2007; Voronov 2008). Learning may occur formally through sponsored training and education programs, more informally as learners experience challenges and integrate their learning with their daily work, may occur within teams and groups, and may manifest itself at the organizational level. Ultimately, learning at all levels is essential for organizations to adapt to internal and external environmental challenges (Casey 2005). Given the competitive global landscape, considerable attention has been given to learning in and with relation to work and organizations, and a base of literature has been growing on two scholarly traditions: workplace learning and organizational learning (Carrillo and Gaimon 2004; Elkjaer and Wahlgren 2006).

Workplace learning, which has its roots in adult education, is primarily focused on individual learning that occurs in the environment of work or the workplace (Elkjaer and Wahlgren 2006). It is often personal and highly contextual. Organizational learning, which has its roots in organization and management studies, is intended to foster learning, development, and change of the organization as a whole, "often by way of individuals" (2006: 16). Organizational learning is defined as the process of acquiring, distributing, integrating, and creating information and knowledge among organizational members (Dixon 1992; Huber 1991). The processes of organizational learning involve key components that support knowledge productivity processes, which include searching for information, assimilating, developing, and creating new knowledge on products, processes, and services (Verdonschot 2005). Organizational members not only need to have the capability to obtain information efficiently but also to create new knowledge which is an asset that can be managed to contribute to the firm's innovation and business performance (Bapuji and Crossan 2004; Lopez *et al.* 2005; Pham and Swierczek 2006).

Human resource development (HRD) is a field of study and practice that is concerned with optimizing workplace and organizational learning, development and performance improvement at the individual, group, team, and organization levels. The concept of organizational learning is most closely associated with HRD's learning paradigm, which stresses that organizations are systems that support multiple levels of learning. Developing and promoting an organization's learning capability is one approach that enables an organization to keep pace with the changing environment (Swanson and Holton III 2001). In the past, the HRD function has tended to be preoccupied with individual performance and training-dominated activities. More recently, strategic HRD practices focus on learning and knowledge creation to enhance individuals' competencies and collaboration within organizations (Harrison and Kessels 2003). Consequently, HRD professionals are increasingly serving as facilitators in cultivating learning infrastructures and cultures that encourage and promote learning at every level within organizations. Therefore, understanding organizational learning processes may enable HRD practitioners to more strategically facilitate approaches within their organizations that can impact workplace and organizational learning.

Among the organizational learning processes, information acquisition is an important mechanism for initiating organizational learning. Information acquisition refers to collecting information from a variety of sources, and often involves scanning the environment (Birdthistle and Fleming 2005; Casey 2005). Huber (1991) has acknowledged that information refers to meaningful data, whereas knowledge refers to interpretations of information that result in learning, but scholars have used these two terms interchangeably in articulating this organizational learning process in conceptual models and frameworks. Early organizational learning scholars viewed an organization as an interpretation system of its environment and indicated that individuals' attention to scanning the external environmental and searching for information have been very important for organizations to learn to prepare for external environmental jolts (Daft and Huber 1987; Daft and Weick 1984; Meyer 1982; Elkjaer and Wahlgren 2006). An organization can therefore improve its performance and adjust itself to the dynamic environment through the process of acquiring information from the environment (Gnyawali and Stewart 2003). This early information processing perspective has been influential in the development of organizational learning models that have been proposed in the 1990s and 2000s.

Organizational learning models have been underpinned by individual learning theories such as cognitive psychology or behavioural theory. Although many models and frameworks have adopted this perspective, researchers have acknowledged that the sum of individual learning is not equal to organizational learning. Organizational learning is not simply a collection of individuals who have learned, but rather reflects an entity that is capable of learning on a collective basis (Dyck *et al.* 2005). Learning may begin with an individual's cognitive process but organizational learning facilitating factors and mechanisms enhance individual members' learning and sharing in an organization (Dyck *et al.* 2005). More recent developments have come from a "holistic, integrationist perspective which suggests that organizational learning begins with the cognitive processes of *individuals* and is enhanced and preserved by organizational *processes*" (Dyck *et al.* 2005: 388). A social perspective on organizational learning argues "learning is an integral part of the practice in everyday organizational life and work. Learning is not restricted to taking place inside individuals' minds but rather comprises processes of participation in the organizational practices" (Elkjaer and Walhgren 2006: 21).

More recently, researchers have concluded that literatures on organizational learning fall into two categories: cognitive and social perspectives (Chiva and Alegre 2005). Consequently, some scholars' focus on organizational learning has shifted from a cognitive and behavioral emphasis to cognitive and social perspective. Both cognitive and social perspectives are being integrated into more current organizational learning models. For example, Gynawali and Stewart (2003) have suggested that organizational learning can be divided into two modes: informational and interactive. The informational mode is defined as the processes in which an organization collects, analyzes, and distributes information which reflect processes that have been embedded in Huber (1991) and Dixon's (1992) frameworks. The interactive mode of learning refers to learning that emerges from social interactions and actions among organizational members. Some of these processes have also been embedded in prior models and frameworks. Given recent organizational learning model developments, information acquisition is still an important organizational learning process (Dixon 1992; Gnyawali and Stewart 2003; Huber 1991).

Several scholars have acknowledged that organizations need to engage in broad information collection to create knowledge (Leonard-Barton 1995; Nonaka and Takeuchi 1995). Most organizations need to learn from external information sources, and, through their organizational members, firms often acquire information from diverse information sources, such as customers, distributors, suppliers, alliance partners, universities; and scholars have stressed the importance of keeping long term and stable relationships with these "learning partners", which can provide alternative perspectives and information sharing (Slater and Narver 1995). Moreover, Liyanage and Barnard (2002) have acknowledged that the information acquisition activity not only creates but also accumulates knowledge as a function of strategic learning activities in the workplace. Hence, organizations have opportunities to acquire and learn from these "learning partners" and transfer such learning outcomes within the organization for strategy development (Akgün *et al.* 2003).

PROBLEM STATEMENT

The concept of organizational learning has been examined since the 1950s and the base of literature has expanded conceptually, theoretically, and somewhat empirically during the past several decades (Dodgson 1993; Easterby-Smith 1997; Lipshitz *et al.* 2002). Most researchers have focused on the theoretical side of explaining organizational learning (Saru 2005). While there has been much theorizing about organizational learning processes, "there is actually very little empirical evidence to support the concepts and models that have been proposed" (Dyck *et al.* 2005: 388). Empirical studies on organizational learning have been limited (Easterby-Smith and Araujo 1999; Huber 1991; Tsang 1997; Dyck *et al.* 2005). It has been suggested that several reasons point to this scarcity of research. Organizational learning is a complex and multidimensional construct with various definitions, which cover broad ideas in describing the phenomenon (Crossan *et al.* 1995; Tsang 1997; Easterby-Smith 1997). In addition, suitable research sites have been difficult to access (Dyck *et al.* 2005), and there is limited instrumentation available that measures organizational learning processes (Santos-Vijande *et al.* 2005). Given the complex nature of organizational learning, challenges accessing relevant sites, and the limited available instrumentation, scholars have expressed concern about the insufficient empirical research base that exists. Therefore, the purpose of this study was to develop a valid and reliable measure of information acquisition, one of the most critical organizational learning processes previously identified in early and more recent organizational learning frameworks.

ORGANIZATIONAL LEARNING AND INFORMATION ACQUISITION LITERATURE REVIEW

Despite the various definitions of organizational learning in the literature that have focused on behaviour, cognition, and more recently social dynamics, scholars have tended to view organizational learning from a process perspective (Akgün *et al.* 2003). Huber's (1991) seminal model has been influential in conceptualizing organizational learning. Huber (1991) has articulated processes of organizational learning as being comprised of four main constructs: *knowledge acquisition, knowledge distribution, information interpretation,* and *organizational memory,* which view organizational learning as an effective process of acquiring, distributing, and interpreting information from the internal and external environment. Although Huber's (1991) organizational learning model has been viewed from a technical process perspective (Easterby-Smith and Araujo 1999), concepts of social interactions and processes have been somewhat presented in the processes and sub-processes of his organizational learning constructs.

His first "learning-related construct" is knowledge acquisition, which "is the construct by which knowledge is obtained" (1991: 90). Huber (1991) has indicated that organizations acquire information or knowledge through five processes: *congenital learning, experiential learning, vicarious learning, grafting,* and *searching.* In 1992, Dixon has further extended

Huber's (1991) framework and reconceptualized organizational learning into five elements: *information acquisition, information distribution and interpretation, making meaning, organizational memory,* and *information retrieval.* Dixon's (1992) information acquisition element is similar to Huber's (1991) knowledge acquisition construct except that Dixon (1992) has divided the information acquisition element into two processes: *internal information acquisition* and *external information acquisition.* In her discussion of information acquisition, she has acknowledged that "organizations obtain information both from external sources and by generating information internally" (1992: 33). This research study adopted Dixon's (1992) reconceptualization of information acquisition. Table 7.1 presents Huber's (1991) knowledge acquisition construct and Dixon's (1992) information acquisition processes and sub-processes. The following paragraphs delineate the comparison between these two concepts.

External Information Acquisition

Dixon's (1992) external information acquisition concept includes four processes: *borrowing, searching, grafting,* and *collaborating.* The terms "borrowing" and "*collaborating*" are what Huber (1991) defined as vicarious learning. Huber's (1991) vicarious learning refers to a learning approach that acquires secondhand experiences, strategies, or technologies from other organizations. *Borrowing* refers to organizations obtaining information from other organizations, such as attending conferences, employing consultants, and reviewing printed materials, such as literature reviews, industry related journals, and magazines. *Collaborating* refers to collaboration with other organizations in the forms of alliances and joint ventures. Several empirical studies have demonstrated that a collaboration strategy is beneficial to an organization's overall business and financial performance. For example, Antoncic and Hisrich's (2004) empirical study has demonstrated that an organization's number of strategic alliances is an important organization factor in fostering entrepreneurial learning and consequentially organization growth, profitability, and wealth. *Searching* refers to monitoring the external environment, including competitors, customers, and economic or technological or social environment reports. Huber's (1991) fifth process, *searching and noticing,* is comprised of three forms of searching: scanning, a focus search, and performance monitoring, of the external environment and evaluating how they are doing in comparison with their goals. Finally, Dixon (1992) has defined *grafting* as acquiring information through two sub-processes, mergers or acquisition, or by grafting new members into the organization. Grafting, according to Huber (1991), is an approach through which an organization gains knowledge by acquiring new members with new knowledge that does not currently exist in the organization, which he contends is much faster than imitating competitors or experiential learning.

Table 7.1   Processes and Sub-processes Associated with Huber's (1991) Knowledge Acquisition Construct and Dixon's (1992) Information Acquisition Element

Huber's (1991) Knowledge Acquisition Construct (p. 30)	Dixon's (1992) Information Acquisition Element (p.33)	
	External Information Acquisition	Internal Information Acquisition
1. Congenital learning 2. Experiential learning 2.1 Organizational experiment 2.2 Organizational self-appraisal 2.3 Experimenting organizations 2.4 Unintentional or unsystematic learning 2.5 Experience-based learning curves 3. Vicarious learning 4. Grafting 5. Searching and noticing 5.1 Scanning 5.2 Focused search 5.3 Performance monitoring	1. Borrowing 1.1 Conferences 1.2 Consultants 1.3 Printed materials 2. Searching 2.1 Reports, economics, technological, social 2.2 Consumers 2.3 Competitors 3. Grafting 3.1 New members 3.2 Acquisitions, mergers 4. Collaborating 4.1 Joint Ventures 4.2 Consortiums	1. Congenital 1.1 Founders 1.2 Prevailing technology 2. Experiential 2.1 Success and mistakes 3. Experimenting 3.1. R & D 3.2 Skunkworks 3.3 Pilot projects 4. Continuous process improvement 4.1 Process improvement teams 5. Critical reflection 5.1 Dialogue 5.2 Action science 5.3 Questioning assumptions

Internal Information Acquisition

Dixon's (1992) internal information acquisition concept includes: *congenital, experiential, experimenting,* and *continuous process improvement,* and *critical reflection.* Dixon's (1992) first internal information acquisition process, *congenital,* is the same as Huber's (1991) congenital learning definition, which is reflective of how an organization gains information or knowledge inherited at its conception that is influenced by the nature of its founders and prevailing technology. Next, *experiential* refers to learning from experiences, such as successes and mistakes (Dixon 1992). It is important to distinguish Dixon's (1992) *experiential* concept from Huber's (1991) experiential learning, which are not equivalent. *Experimenting* in Dixon's (1992) framework is classified under the term "experiential learning" in Huber's (1991) conceptualization. *Experimenting* relates to developing original innovations, inventing a new process to be adaptable, pilot testing, and deliberately creating (Dixon 1992). For Huber (1991), experiential learning is a result of acquiring knowledge through direct experience, intentional, or systematic efforts, including: organizational experiments, organizational self-appraisal, experimenting organizations, unintentional or unsystematic learning, and experience-based learning curves. According to Huber (1991), organizations or individuals are more adaptable in being "experimenting" agents in acquiring information. Dixon's (1992) fourth internal information acquisition element is *continuous process improvement,* which refers to process improvement teams that implement new processes to accomplish tasks, and introduce incremental change based on feedback from external environmental (Adams and Lamont 2003; Bedeian 1986). Finally, *critical reflection* relates to information that is generated by deliberately questioning assumptions and norms through dialogue, action science, and questioning assumptions (Dixon 1992). Despite some of the minor differences between Huber's (1991) knowledge acquisition construct and Dixon's (1992) information acquisition element that she divides into internal and external information acquisition, the overarching commonality is that information and knowledge can be obtained from diverse approaches that depend on both individual-level and organizational-level efforts.

RESEARCH METHODS

Design and Sample

The contribution of small and medium-sized enterprises (SMEs) to national economies has been recognized in European and Asian countries, such as the UK and Taiwan, in the past decade (Jones and Macpherson 2005). Yet, scholars have suggested that there is a compelling need to better understand individual and organizational learning in these smaller firms (Sadler-Smith *et al.* 2000). Past research, however, has tended to focus on Western and large organizations' perspectives in articulating organizational learning. In addition, SMEs studies have tended to focus on European countries as targets. Therefore, the study reported in this chapter shifted the focus to an Asian country, Taiwan, and more specifically on small and medium enterprises (SMEs) as the sample. SMEs account for 80 per cent of Taiwan's business, and they are increasingly transforming from labour-intensive industries to knowledge-intensive learning and innovative industries, especially the high-technology sector. George *et al.* (2001) have stressed that high-technology industries often face dynamic and fierce competition, and thus require diverse external information acquisition about external innovations. Consequently, 11 different high-technology firms in one specific science park in Taiwan were purposefully selected to serve as the sample population for this study. This science park is the place where most high technology industries in Taiwan are located.

The researchers contacted 11 employees at these firms to seek their assistance with identifying key respondents for the survey distribution. The 11 key contacts forwarded a letter from the researchers to 15–20 potential participants that he or she identified based upon the primary researcher's selection criteria. The primary researcher's selection criteria specified that respondents include: product developers, designers, engineers, and marketing personnel who have worked in the company for at least one year. A total of 192 letters were forwarded to the target participants requesting their participation in the study. These potential participants were able to contact the primary researcher directly to clarify additional questions or to visit the Web site that contained the online instrument by logging in using a specific password to complete the survey. Of the 192 participants, 123 participants completed the online instrument. The response rate for this study was 64 per cent.

Measurement

Based upon Dixon's (1992) theoretical contentions, her information acquisition element was divided into two dimensions: external acquisition and internal acquisition. Items representing Dixon's information acquisition element were derived from her operational definitions of both external and internal information acquisition. External information acquisition refers to the extent to which external sources are used to obtain information. External information acquisition was comprised of 14 items and contained four dimensions: *borrowing, searching, grafting,* and *collaborating.* Internal information acquisition refers to the extent to which the organization or individual generates information internally. Internal information acquisition was comprised of 15 items and included five dimensions: *congenital, experiential, experimenting, continuous process improvement,* and *critical reflection.* The information acquisition measure asks respondents to assess their perceptions about the extent to which individual and organization information acquisition strategies are used because individual-level efforts often contribute to organizational-level information acquisition (Dixon 1992; Huber 1991). Therefore, respondents were asked to use a 5-point rating scale to assess the 29 items using their perceptions of their own professional experiences and their perceptions of their organization's internal/external information acquisition activities. According to Dixon (1992), the sum of 14 external acquisition items was added together with the sum of the 15 internal acquisition items to derive the measure of information acquisition. Table 7.2 presents the 29-item pool of the information acquisition measure. Table 7.3 provides more details on the items as they relate to internal and external information acquisition.

Translation and Face Validity

An English version of the information acquisition measure was developed and reviewed by several faculty members at one research university in the US. After expert examination and several revisions, a sequential forward-back-translation approach was used for this cross-cultural measure. The content of the entire questionnaire was translated into Chinese and then back translated into English by the primary researcher. The co-author compared the back-translated version with the original English version and suggested only minor changes. Following this procedure and minor language adaptations, the researchers also had an independent reviewer, bilingual in English and Chinese, perform the same translation procedures to ensure that the measure was appropriate for the Taiwanese context and had face validity.

Psychometric Properties of the Information Acquisition Measure

Exploratory factor analysis and item-to-item total correlations were used in the first stage of analyzing the psychometric properties of the measure. After purifying the initial scale through exploratory factor analysis and item-to-total correlations, confirmatory factor analysis was employed to test the construct validity of the information acquisition measure.

Stage I Analysis: Exploratory Factor Analysis

Principal components factor analysis with varimax rotation was conducted for the exploratory factor analysis. This analysis resulted in eight factors that accounted for 69.32 per cent. The factors were: *searching* (5 items), *experimenting and improvement* (6 items), *experiential* (3 items), *grafting* (5 items), *borrowing* (3 items), *leadership on congenital learning* (3 items), *critical reflection* (3 items), and *archival documentation* (1 item). Since the *archival documentation* factor only contained one item (item 4),

Table 7.2   The 29 Item Pool for the Information Acquisition Measure

1. Attend industry-related meetings and join associations.

2. Attend instructional seminars, workshops, conferences or training programs.

3. Review technical publications in the high technology industry.

4. Review archival data of my organization.

5. Monitor economic, social, and technological trends in industry.

6. Systematically collect data on customers.

7. Systematically collect data on competitors.

8. Learn "know-how" from competitors' products.

9. Analyze competitors' products in detail while they appear in the marketplace.

10. Deliberately question organizational assumptions and norms.

11. I engage in dialogues with my colleagues at work to help me reflect.

12. I interact with my colleagues at work to help me gather information.

13. I acquire information or knowledge through my personal experiences.

14. I acquire information from successful working experiences.

15. I acquire information from mistakes happening during work.

16. Introduces incremental changes in existing practice based on feedback from external environment.

17. Implements continuous process improvement.

18. Builds process improvement teams.

19. Does pilot tests and experiments.

20. Develops original innovations.

21. Invents new processes to accomplish organizational tasks.

22. Acquires other organizations.

23. Hires highly specialized or knowledgeable personnel.

24. Builds alliances with other organizations.

(continued)

Table 7.2   (continued)

25. Forms joint ventures with other organizations.
26. Collaborates with other organizations.
27. The vision of the founder(s) is still highly influences business operations and management.
28. Current stock of information base is inherited from the period when the firm was established.
29. R&D is highly stressed.

the primary researcher deleted this item and conducted the exploratory factor analysis again. The results yielded seven factors with a 71.07 per cent extracted variance. Table 7.4 reports a seven-factor solution for the information acquisition measure. The factors covered include: *searching* (5 items), *experimenting and improvement* (6 items), *experiential* (3 items), *grafting* (5 items), *borrowing* (2 items), *leadership on congenital learning* (3 items), and *critical reflection* (3 items). Each factor accounted for 13.64, 12.19, 11.21, 10.03, 9.09, 8.72, and 6.19 per cent of the variance, respectively. Table 7.5 reports the item-to-total correlations that ranged from .309

Table 7.3   Information Acquisition Measure Development Summary

Variable	Measurement		Items	Total
Information acquisition	External information acquisition	Borrowing	Q1–Q4	14
		Searching	Q5–Q9	
		Grafting	Q22–Q23	
		Collaborating	Q24–Q26	
	Internal information acquisition	Congenital	Q27–Q28	15
		Experiential	Q13–Q15	
		Experimenting	Q19–Q21, Q29	
		Continuous process improvement	Q16–Q18	
		Critical reflection	Q10–Q12	
Total				29

Table 7.4   Seven-Factor Solution for Principle Component Pattern Matrix with Varimax Rotation for the Information Acquisition Measure

Items	Components						
	1	2	3	4	5	6	7
7	.876	.033	.022	-.053	.086	.066	.124
9	.856	.069	.047	-.019	-.018	-.032	.070
8	.843	.053	.066	-.034	-.021	.100	.153
6	.648	.106	.087	-.070	.265	.006	.153
5	.591	.013	.282	.088	.158	.211	-.171
20	.175	.744	-.072	.224	.163	.029	.029
21	.031	.742	.245	.122	.204	.042	-.002
17	-.164	.732	.194	.003	-.082	.178	.205
19	.223	.661	.212	.218	.008	.074	-.167
18	-.054	.657	-.071	.127	-.043	.094	.386
16	.113	.647	.244	.171	-.172	.078	.103
14	-.017	.130	.854	.016	.021	.053	.075
13	.125	.193	.810	.013	-.009	.016	.141
15	.146	.108	.775	.178	-.060	-.075	.123
24	.023	.133	.039	.878	-.066	-.048	-.030
25	-.015	.123	-.021	.774	.047	.130	.170
26	-.176	.115	.083	.730	.263	-.001	.128
23	.068	.362	.194	.628	.085	-.002	-.064
22	-.145	.166	.146	.632	.169	-.107	-.070
2	.072	.086	-.029	.076	.832	.126	.094
1	.084	-.072	-.031	.098	.808	.133	.020
3	.297	.076	.039	.08	.756	-.048	.067

(continued)

Table 7.4   (continued)

27	.025	.116	.110	-.087	.122	**.734**	-.067
28	-.040	.134	-.030	.093	-.015	**.685**	.073
29	.263	.028	-.104	.043	.121	**.665**	-.012
10	.286	.066	.146	.117	.162	.037	**.790**
12	.097	.106	.053	.069	.116	-.108	**.779**
11	.138	.201	.054	.047	-.052	-.001	**.667**

Note: Components 1–7 explain 71.07 per cent of variance of the total scale.

to .589, which were all significant at the .05 level. In addition, internal consistency reliability measures were assessed by using Cronbach's alpha. Cronbach's alpha for the multi-item measure was .853. Based on Bryman and Cramer (1997), Cronbach's alpha greater than .80 is classified as high reliability.

Stage II Analysis: Confirmatory Factor Analysis

Amos 5 with maximum likelihood estimation was used to perform a confirmatory factor analysis on the 28 aforementioned items (7 factors). Results from the confirmatory factor analysis indicated an adequate model fit (χ^2 = 459.081 with 327 df, $p < .001$, RMSEA = .048, CFI = .91, IFI = .91). In addition, each of the hypothesized factor loadings was statistically significant at the .01 level, and the standardized factor loadings were quite high (Table 7.6). Next, to confirm dimensionality of the information acquisition measure, a second-order confirmatory factor model was conducted. The second-order model was estimated to test whether external informational acquisition and internal information acquisition are affected by the higher-order construct, information acquisition. The results for the estimated model can be found in Table 7.6. The results indicated that the factor loadings of the second order model are significant at $p < .001$. The goodness-of-fit was good though slightly worse in the second order model (χ^2 = 469.341 with 330 df, $p < .001$, RMSEA = .051, CFI = .89, IFI = .89). In comparing these two models on their goodness-of-fit indicators, the researchers find that the best model would be the first-order model, which has a better CFI (exceed the recommended norm of .90) and RMSEA (recommended norms is smaller than .50). However, the differences between the first- and second-order models are minimal. Therefore, although the goodness-of-fit indicators in the second-order model are slightly worse, the results as a whole confirm the dimensionality of the information acquisition measure.

Table 7.5 Factor Analysis of Information Acquisition Measure

Factors	Factor Loading	Item-Total Correlation
Factor 1: Searching		
7. Systematically collect data on competitors.	.876	.456
9. Analyze competitors' products in detail while they appear in the marketplace.	.856	.486
8. Learn "know-how" from competitors' products.	.843	.512
6. Systematically collect data on customers.	.684	.487
5. Monitor economic, social, and technological trends in industry.	.591	.434
Factor 2: Experimenting and improvement		
20. Develops original innovations.	.744	.524
21. Invents new processes to accomplish organizational tasks.	.742	.589
17. Implements continuous process improvement.	.732	.423
19. Does pilot tests and experiments.	.661	.531
18. Builds process improvement teams.	.657	.497
16. Introduces incremental changes in existing practice based on feedback from external environment.	.647	.565
Factor 3: Experiential		
14. I acquire information from successful working experiences.	.854	.445
13. I acquire information or knowledge through my personal experiences.	.810	.512
15. I acquire information from mistakes happening during work.	.775	.498
Factor 4: Grafting		
24. Builds alliances with other organizations.	.878	.412

(continued)

Table 7.5   (continued)

Factors	Factor Loading	Item-Total Correlation
25. Forms joint ventures with other organizations.	.774	.465
26. Collaborates with other organizations.	.730	.409
23. Hires highly specialized or knowledgeable personnel.	.628	.538
22. Acquires other organizations.	.632	.524
Factor 5: Borrowing		
2. Attend instructional seminars, workshops, conferences or training programs.	.832	.406
1. Attend industry-related meetings and join associations.	.808	.334
3. Review technical publications in the biotechnology industry.	.756	.493
Factor 6: Leadership on congenital learning		
27. The vision of the founder(s) is still highly influences business operations and management.	.734	.334
28. Current stock of information base is inherited from the period when the firm was established.	.685	.309
29. R&D is highly stressed	.665	.312
Factor 7: Critical reflection		
10. Deliberately question organizational assumptions and norms.	.790	.543
12. I interact with my colleagues at work to help me gather information.	.779	.567
11. I engage in dialogues with my colleagues at work to help me reflect.	.667	.572

FINDINGS AND DISCUSSION

Exploratory factor analysis and confirmatory factor analysis were employed to empirically examine the items that represent Dixon's (1992) reconceptualization of Huber's (1991) knowledge acquisition construct from his

Table 7.6   Results of Confirmatory Factor Analysis

Items	Factor Loading
First order measurement model	
V9 ← Searching	.899
V8 ← Searching	.890
V7 ← Searching	.767
V6 ← Searching	.577
V5 ← Searching	.537
V21 ← Experimenting and improvement	.796
V20 ← Experimenting and improvement	.753
V19 ← Experimenting and improvement	.724
V16 ← Experimenting and improvement	.603
V18 ← Experimenting and improvement	.598
V17 ← Experimenting and improvement	.582
V13 ← Experiential	.827
V14 ← Experiential	.776
V15 ← Experiential	.776
V24 ← Grafting	.775
V25 ← Grafting	.716
V26 ← Grafting	.693
V23 ← Grafting	.673
V22 ← Grafting	.630
V2 ← Borrowing	.780
V3 ← Borrowing	.749
V1 ← Borrowing	.692

(continued)

Table 7.6   (continued)

Items	Factor Loading
First order measurement model	
V27 ← Leadership on congenital learning	.715
V28 ← Leadership on congenital learning	.622
V29 ← Leadership on congenital learning	.519
V12 ← Critical reflection	.888
V11 ← Critical reflection	.654
V10 ← Critical reflection	·605
Second order factor model	
Searching ← External information acquisition	.592
Borrowing ← External information acquisition	.662
Grafting ← External information acquisition	.583
Experimenting and improvement ← Internal information acquisition	.514
Experiential ← Internal information acquisition	.826
Leadership on congenital learning ← Internal information acquisition	.509
Critical reflection ← Internal information acquisition	.843

Note: χ^2 = 459.081 with 327 *df* (p < .001); RMSEA (root mean square error of approximation)= .048, CFI (Comparative Fit Index) = .91, IFI (Incremental Fit Index) = .91

Second order model: χ^2 = 469.341 with 330 *df* (p < .001); RMSEA (root mean square error of approximation) = .051, CFI (Comparative Fit Index) = .89, IFI (Incremental Fit Index) = .89

organization learning processes model. The results have demonstrated that there were only some minor differences found between the findings from the current study and Dixon's (1992) theoretical contentions about her information acquisition element, processes, and sub-processes. Table 7.7 and the following paragraphs delineate the validation of the new information acquisition measure and discuss these minor differences.

To assess external information acquisition, Dixon's (1992) reconceptualization contained four processes: *borrowing, searching, grafting,* and *collaborating.* The current study yielded three empirically derived

Table 7.7 Current Study Comparison with Dixon's (1992) Information Acquisition Processes and Sub-Processes

Dixon's (1992) information acquisition	Current study's information acquisition
External Acquisition	
1. *Borrowing* -Conferences -<u>Printed material</u>	1. *Borrowing* -Conferences
2. *Searching* -Reports, economic, technological, social -Customers -Competitors	2. *Searching* -Reports, economic, technological, social -Customers -Competitors
3. *Grafting* -New members -Acquisitions, mergers	3. *Grafting* -New members -Acquisitions, mergers -<u>Joint ventures</u> -<u>Consortiums</u>
4. *Collaborating* -<u>Joint ventures</u> -<u>Consortiums</u>	
Internal Acquisition	
1. *Congenital* -Founders -Prevailing technology	1. *Leadership on congenital learning* -Founders -Prevailing technology -<u>Emphasis on R&D</u>
2. *Experiential* -Success and mistakes	2. *Experiential* -Success and mistakes
3. *Experimenting* -<u>Emphasis on R&D</u> -Pilot projects	3. *Experimenting and improvement* -Pilot projects -Process improvement
4. Continuous process improvement -<u>Process improvement</u>	
5. Critical reflection -Dialogue -Questioning assumptions	4. Critical reflection -Dialogue -Questioning assumptions

processes: *borrowing, searching,* and *grafting.* Dixon's (1992) borrowing process contained two sub-processes: "conference" and "printed material". However, the current study only contained one sub-process with two items, "conference", in the borrowing process. Sub-processes associated with searching in the current study were the same as Dixon's searching sub-processes, which includes customers, competitors, and reports. In addition, Dixon's (1992) two processes of "grafting" and "collaborating" were combined as one factor after the factor analysis. In Huber's (1991) framework, the definition of "grafting" included not only an organization grafting in new members but also joint ventures or alliances, which were defined as "collaborating" in Dixon's (1992) study. Huber's "grafting" process contains both the concepts of grafting and collaborating. Since Dixon's (1992) model extended and modified Huber's (1991) model, the primary researcher labelled the empirically derived factor from Huber's concept as "grafting".

In terms of internal information acquisition, Dixon's (1992) reconceptualization contained five processes: *congenital, experiential, experimenting, continuous process improvement,* and *critical reflection.* The current study yielded four empirically derived processes: *leadership on congenital learning, experiential, experimenting and improvement,* and *critical reflection.* Dixon's (1992) congenital process contained two sub-processes: "founders" and "prevailing technology". However, the current study included one more sub-process, "emphasis on R&D", in the congenital process after the factor analysis. In Dixon's (1992) model, "emphasis on R&D" was defined and classified under the process of "experimenting". Huber (1991) has stated that congenital learning, the nature of the organization, is greatly influenced by the founders. The founders' vision and actions have an impact on both the organization's congenital knowledge and future learning. Therefore, the researchers inferred that founders put stress on R&D in determining the organization's initial knowledge and learning context in acquiring and interpreting information. This factor was labelled as "leadership on congenital learning". Second, the sub-process of experiential in the current study was the same as Dixon's experiential sub-process, "successes and mistakes". In addition, Dixon's (1992) two processes of "experimenting" and "continuous process improvement" were combined as one factor after the factor analysis. The researchers suspect that process improvement and experimenting are closely related in the high-technology industry. Hence, the researchers labelled the empirically derived factor as "experimenting and improvement". Finally, the sub-processes of critical reflection in the current study were the same as Dixon's critical reflection sub-processes, "dialogue", "action science", and "questioning assumptions". In summary, the minor differences that occurred in statistically grouping the items with similar theoretical meanings can be reasonably explained by some of the groupings in Huber's (1991) theoretical framework, which underpinned Dixon's (1992) reconceptualization.

CONCLUSIONS AND IMPLICATIONS
FOR RESEARCH AND PRACTICE

The primary purpose of this study was to validate a newly developed information acquisition measure. This measure was tested with a sample of product developers, designers, engineers, and marketing personnel. The findings resulted in the development of a measure that identifies a set of external (*borrowing, searching,* and *grafting*) and internal (*leadership on congenital learning, experiential, experimenting and improvement,* and *critical reflection*) information acquisition sub-processes that, for the most part, reflect Dixon's reconceptualization of the construct of information acquisition and also represent the approaches that may facilitate information acquisition by employees within organizations. These external and internal information acquisition strategies require both individual-level and organizational-level efforts to achieve information acquisition capability within an organization.

There are several contributions that this study makes to the organizational learning literature. A unique aspect of this study is that the researchers drew upon Dixon's (1992) theoretical reconceptualization of information acquisition to develop and validate a new information acquisition measure. While information acquisition has been positioned as an important construct associated with organizational learning processes in many conceptual models and frameworks (Dixon 1992; Gnyawali and Stewart 2003; Huber 1991; Lopez *et al.* 2005; Nevis, DiBella and Gould 1996), it does not appear that extensive testing of these models or components of these models has been done to advance the availability of instrumentation in the field.

Huber (1991) and Dixon's (1992) conceptions of the constructs associated with organizational learning processes have been influential in the literature, and the researchers have been unable to identify other studies that have operationalized Dixon's (1992) model. Although Templeton *et al.* (2002) have adopted Huber's (1991) organizational learning framework to develop an instrument to measure organizational learning, the constructs that emerged from their research considerably differed from Huber's (1991) framework. Huber's (1991) four main constructs of organizational learning were rearranged and renamed into eight constructs after instrument validation process in the Templeton et al. study. More recently, Lopez *et al.* (2005) have developed an organizational learning measure with four processes: knowledge acquisition, distribution, interpretation, and organizational memory, which were largely based upon Huber (1991) and Dixon's (1992) models. However, the operationalization of the knowledge acquisition construct was not theoretically comprehensive. In contrast to these few studies, the current study operationalized Dixon's (1992) information acquisition element and its two dimensions. Through the process of instrument validation, the findings from this study have demonstrated that the factors empirically derived from factor analysis mainly corresponded to Dixon's (1992) theoretical framework. The few minor differences in statistically grouping the items with similar theoretical meanings were reasonably explained by Huber's (1991) theoretical framework. In essence, all of Dixon's sub-processes were accounted for in the new measure. However, two were combined with other sub-processes that resulted in a seven-factor solution. The findings from the study also support the internal and external dimensionality of Dixon's information acquisition element. Since the organizational learning literature has been critiqued for lacking empirical evidence to support concepts and models that have been proposed, this study offers a contribution to the literature by documenting the existence of an underlying set of information acquisition process factors that should be recognized in promoting both internal and external learning activities at the workplace.

Although this newly developed measure represents the operationalization and testing of only one organizational learning process, given the limited instrumentation, the newly developed measure on information acquisition may be of high utility for future researchers interested in empirically examining information acquisition in the organizational learning process. However, additional research confirming the validity of the measure is recommended. It is also possible that this measure may have some practical utility for organizations who would like to assess the extent to which individuals select specific sources to acquire information that may be useful to the organization, as well as to consider organizational practices that may have utility for encouraging individuals to take a more proactive role in engaging in internal and external information acquisition activities.

Since individuals are at the heart of both organizational learning, which is intended to impact the whole organizational system, and workplace learning which may impact individual learners and their colleagues more specifically, there are also contributions that this measure may make to the workplace learning literature. Informal workplace learning is often conceived as learning that occurs naturally in the workplace as learners engage in their everyday work activities. Scholars have suggested that workplace learning of often social and highly contextual and research has provided some insights about factors that facilitate and inhibit informal workplace learning (Ellinger 2005; Ellinger and Cseh 2007). Often problems or challenges arise and become the triggers that initiate the informal learning cycle. Such triggers encourage learners to consider strategies that enable them to learn and problem solve. Since external environmental jolts or triggers for learning may occur that may necessitate that learners seek information-rich sources to aid in their learning, this new measure may be a useful tool for helping learners to consider different strategies to augment their learning.

The workplace learning literature has also been hampered with a lack of instrumentation to assess informal learning (Skule 2004). This newly developed information acquisition instrument may also have some utility for researchers who focus on workplace learning contexts. For example, some of the internal information acquisition strategies relate to the extent to which an individual's experiences may provide insights that influence learning. The critical reflection sub-process refers to the extent to which an individual questions organizational norms and assumptions, engages in dialogue with others to promote learning, or interacts with others to gain new information that may result in learning. Beyond the internal strategies, it is also possible that some of the external information acquisition strategies may be useful in promoting informal learning. For example, attending conferences, meeting with customers and competitors have been strategies that have been previously identified in the literature. Using this measurement tool to examine the extent to which these strategies are engaged may have some implications for the organization in terms of resource allocation in support of such learning activities.

Ultimately, for HRD professionals, the information acquisition measure may be useful as a diagnostic tool in helping organizational members to identify, access, and to more effectively manage internal and external information channels to increase the potential for obtaining information and insights that may promote learning at the individual, team, and organizational levels. It may also help to improve individuals' and the organization's information acquisition capabilities by identifying strategies that have not been sufficiently leveraged.

Limitations

The development and validation of the new information acquisition measure was done as a pilot study with a nonrandom sample of participants and therefore caution must be exercised about generalizing the findings. However, it was assumed that the collection of data within the 11 specific firms in the Taiwanese high-technology industry was an appropriate context to study this topic and that the respondents were appropriate participants to respond to the instrument. In addition, the study assumed that an instrument based on Western organizational learning literature could be tested in an Asian context through a rigorous cross-cultural instrument translation process. However, it may be possible that different results might be obtained if this study selected different industries or other countries as samples. Ultimately, despite the limitations associated with the sample and context, the results do generally support the theoretical contentions of Dixon (1992) and Huber (1991) and the robustness of the instrument suggests that it has utility that can be further tested in a variety of contexts in support of both the organizational learning and workplace learning literatures.

KEY LEARNING POINTS

- The newly developed information acquisition measure offers empirical support for Dixon's (1992) theoretical reconceptualization of one of Huber's (1991) organizational learning constructs and offers support for the internal and external dimensionality of information acquisition despite some minor differences in the statistical grouping process.
- Information acquisition is a critical component of organizational learning processes that may rely upon both individual-level and organizational-level endeavours to gather information internally and externally.
- The information acquisition measure may have utility as a self-diagnostic instrument for organizational members to further develop their information acquisition capability and also may provide the HRD professional with insights about the learning infrastructure for both the organization and its members to more effectively assess, engage, and manage information strategies and channels.

8   In Search of a Good Method for Measuring Learning from Errors at Work

Johannes Bauer and Regina H. Mulder

Research on expertise, case-based reasoning, and learning through work has indicated that errors at work can be significant sources for professional learning (e.g., Eraut *et al.* 1998; Gruber 2001). However, despite its relevance, the issue of individual and team learning from errors at work has received only marginal attention in empirical research (Bauer and Mulder 2008). Existing research on errors and learning from errors has mainly been conducted from an organizational perspective, for example, in studies on human error and safety management (Glendon *et al.* 2006; Reason 1990; Senders and Moray 1991; Zhao and Olivera 2006) or organizational learning (Argote and Todocara 2007; Sitkin 1992). By 'organizational perspective' we mean that errors, their prevention, or potential benefits of learning through them, are primarily analyzed from a macro perspective that focuses on the processes and characteristics of an organization as a system (e.g., Reason 1990). Because of their specific focus on the organization, the indicated lines of inquiry have made only minor contributions to explaining *individual* learning from errors at work (Ohlsson 1996). This is our area of interest: explaining individual learning from errors at work and providing instruments for its measurement. For this purpose, we employ a micro perspective on the behaviour, cognition, and learning of individuals and of individuals within teams (Bauer and Gruber 2007). Though a handful of studies exist that share this interest (e.g., Cannon and Edmondson 2001; Edmondson 1996; Meurier *et al.* 1997; Tjosvold *et al.* 2004; Tucker and Edmondson 2003), they vary substantially in their theoretical foundations as well as in their conceptualization and operationalization of learning from errors. Therefore, there is currently no coherent foundation for research in this area (for a review of existing approaches to individual and team learning from errors supporting this assertion, see Bauer and Mulder 2008).

The research question that guides our investigation is how individual learning from errors at work can be operationalized and measured. In order to contribute to answering this question, three steps are taken. Firstly, we will introduce a conceptualization of learning from errors at work that is based on theories of experiential learning at work and provides the basis for our operationalization. Secondly, based on this we propose (i) that the process of learning from errors at work can be conceptualized and operationalized in terms of the engagement in self-regulated experiential learning activities after an error episode and (ii) that the measurement of learning from errors should be grounded in concrete error cases. Thirdly, we present findings from a pilot study and from a larger study in nursing that aimed to test the feasibility of our approach and to improve it. Nursing was chosen because the highly standardized nature of nurses' work facilitates identifying errors and because learning from errors is an urgent issue in this profession regarding quality management and patient safety (Meurier *et al.* 1997; Tucker and Edmondson 2003).

The studies contribute to answering the research question by further development of an operationalization of learning from errors and by comparing modalities of measurement. The objectives of the pilot study were (i) to compare the viability of two measurement approaches in terms of the return quote and (ii) to provide initial information about the psychometric properties of the developed operationalization. Both approaches contain questions on learning from errors in concrete error episodes, but differ in that the first approach relies on asking the subjects to describe self-experienced errors (Critical Incident Technique; Flanagan 1954), while the second one relies on presenting vignettes of authentic error cases (Cases Approach). Based on these findings, a decision for the latter approach was made. In Study 2 we reapplied the Cases Approach in order to replicate findings from the pilot study, to gather further information about the psychometric properties of the developed scales, and to identify possibilities for improving the scales.

THEORETICAL BACKGROUND

In this section, we will discuss our conceptualization of learning from errors at work (please see Bauer and Mulder 2007, 2008, for a more in-depth elaboration). Our approach focuses on learning activities that individuals may engage in after an error, in order to learn from it. This represents a concrete instantiation of a problem-solving approach towards errors, instead of focussing on blame attribution and prosecution (e.g., Tjosvold *et al.* 2004; Zapf *et al.* 1999). From this discussion, we derive conclusions on how to operationalize and measure learning from errors.

Conceptualization of Learning from Errors

Conceptualizing learning from errors at work requires (i) the clarification of the concept of 'error' and (ii) an explanation of the learning process on the basis of relevant learning theories. Consistent with cognitive and action-oriented approaches to human error, we define errors to be individual actions or decisions that result in a deficient deviation from a desired goal and that endanger the attainment of higher order goals (e.g., Frese and Zapf 1994; Reason 1995; Senders and Moray 1991; Zhao and Olivera 2006). The deviation is attributed to the actions of an actor who is assumed to have sufficient skill and knowledge and occurs contrary to his or her expectations and intentions (Senders and Moray 1991). In our empirical studies we focus on knowledge- and rule-based errors that involve intentional decision processes and the application of declarative and procedural knowledge (Frese and Zapf 1994; Rasmussen 1987). The rationale for this is that these errors potentially enable individuals to deliberately revise their knowledge and practice through the engagement in learning activities (Keith and Frese 2005).

The case made here is to contextualize learning from errors in theories of experiential learning and learning through work (e.g., Billett 2004; Boshuizen *et al.* 2004; Eraut *et al.* 1998; Gruber 2001; Kolb 1984; Kolodner 1983; Schank 1999; Schön 1983). For this purpose, we draw upon and integrate two complementary perspectives that contribute to explaining learning from errors. Firstly, the cognitive perspective explains how schematic, action-oriented knowledge structures are extended and modified through reflection on errors and how this may lead to improved performance through drawing analogies to newly encountered episodes (Kolodner 1983; Schank 1999). Secondly, the activity perspective frames learning as a self-directed and self-organized effort to improve performance (Van de Wiel *et al.* 2004). It provides possibilities for operationalizing the learning process by identifying deliberate activities—both overt and cognitive—that assumedly lead to the learning processes and outcomes described by the cognitive perspective. Based on theories of experiential learning cycles (Gruber 2001; Kolb 1984; Schön 1983), we model learning from errors as the engagement in learning activities, involving (i) reflection on the causes of an error, (ii) the development of new or revised action strategies that aim to avoid the error in the future, and (iii) experimenting with and implementing the new or revised strategies. Each of these activities can be performed individually or in social cooperation with others at work (cf. Van Woerkom 2003).

In order to contextualize this framework of learning activities to the field of nursing, we conducted an interview study with expert nurses (i.e., nurses in a supervisory position with long-time work experience) and identified relevant learning activities after an error occurred (Bauer and Mulder 2007). Based on the findings from this study, we focus on socially performed learning activities in the form of joint cause analysis and joint development of new action strategies, following. This form of learning was emphasized by the experts as being important. Moreover, the role of social exchange has been stressed in theories on workplace learning and professional development (Billett 2004; Eraut *et al.* 1998) as well as in existing studies on learning from errors (Edmondson 2004). Communication and exchange foster the development of shared knowledge and understanding of errors as well as of solutions and strategies to handle them (Cannon and Edmondson 2001; Van Dyck *et al.* 2005; Meurier *et al.* 1997).

Because the engagement in social learning activities after an error involves admitting an error to others, it cannot be taken for granted. Initiating learning behaviour—like seeking feedback, asking for help, or talking about errors—in a team may be constrained by the fear of repercussions, disciplinary proceedings, and a potential loss of professional image (Edmondson 1999; Meurier *et al.* 1997). Thus, we expect the engagement in social learning activities to depend on two types of variables: (i) The first is the individual interpretation of the error situation as a learning situation versus a threat (Edmondson 2004; Rybowiak *et al.* 1999; Zhao and Olivera 2006). Rybowiak *et al.* (1999) proposed the construct of individual 'error orientation' as to consist of beliefs, attitudes, and behavioural intentions regarding errors. Taking their perspective, we focus more narrowly on the interpretation of a concrete error situation as a learning situation and on the motivational tendency to conceal or report an error. (ii) Moreover, the perception of a trustful and safe team climate, one that allows open discussion of an error in the social context of the team and alleviates fears of being punished, can be considered to be a determinant for engaging in learning after an error (Cannon and Edmondson 2001; Edmondson 1996, 1999; Tjosvold *et al.* 2004).

Conclusions for Measuring Learning from Errors at Work

Summing up the discussion up to this point, we formulate two propositions for the operationalization and measurement of learning from errors at work.

Firstly, we propose that learning from errors at work can be operationalized in terms of the engagement in experiential learning activities. We consider the learning activity approach to provide a fruitful perspective for several reasons: (i) it focuses on concrete and measurable behaviour in everyday work (Simons and Ruijters 2004); (ii) it is open for various research approaches by allowing the application of different data gathering techniques; (iii) it is derived systematically from theories of experiential learning and therefore fulfils prerequisites of content validity. Therefore, the learning activity approach can potentially provide a common conceptual basis for research on learning from errors that focus on specific types of errors in various fields of work. Following, we rely on this approach for developing an operationalization of learning from knowledge- and rule-based errors in nursing. In our empirical studies, we aim to develop questionnaire scales that measure the engagement in social learning activities regarding (i) the joint analysis of causes of an error and (ii) the joint development of new action strategies in order to avoid the error in the future.

Our second proposition is that the measurement of error-related learning activities should be grounded in concrete error episodes that represent a specific type of error. Asking questions on individuals' general engagement in learning activities after errors without referring to concrete situations is inappropriate, because this requires the subjects to generalize over a number of situations that may be incomparable. Errors differ in the underlying level of action regulation (Reason 1995) and in the learning potential they imply (Glendon *et al.* 2006; Keith and Frese 2005). Furthermore, it remains uncertain what kind of situations and errors participants refer to (Harteis *et al.* 2007) so that it is impossible to explain why they are relevant for learning, what can be learned from them, and what kind of learning activities are relevant. Both problems can be addressed by basing questions upon learning activities in concrete error episodes. This can be achieved by two approaches. Firstly, by applying the Critical Incident Technique (CIT) (Flanagan 1954), that is, asking subjects to describe a personal, actual error situation. Secondly, by presenting vignettes of error cases to the subjects and asking them to identify with these cases (Cases Approach).

Each approach has its particular strengths and weaknesses. Advantages of the CIT are that the participants' experience is directly involved and that real cases are used so that the participants can be asked how they actually reacted to the given incident. Problems are (i) that it is more demanding for the subjects and requires more disclosure, (ii) that the researcher depends on the participants' readiness and ability to provide relevant error examples, and (iii) that the incident may have happened a long time ago, making reconstruction difficult and leaving space for self-serving biases. Advantages of the Cases Approach are that it requires less disclosure from the participants and thus should facilitate their readiness to participate. In addition, the used cases are standardized. This ensures that the relevant type of error is included in the research. In addition, this standardization increases the comparability of the answers. Problems are (i) that valid cases have to be constructed, (ii) that the subjects need to be able to identify with the cases, and (iii) that it is unsure whether the answers about the engagement in learning activities are valid for actual behaviour. In light of this discussion, it seems inadvisable to decide for one approach only on the basis of theoretical reasoning. Therefore, we explored the viability of both approaches in practical application in a pilot study.

PILOT STUDY

Goals

The goal of this pilot study was to get information for the decision about how to anchor the measurement of the engagement in learning activities in concrete error situations and to provide initial evidence of the psychometric properties of the learning activity scales. Two criteria were set for the comparison.

The first criterion was the participation rate. Although this arguably does not yet provide evidence for the quality of the measurement, it has to be considered that errors are a delicate issue and that the readiness to participate cannot be taken for granted. Therefore, a method should be applied that reduces this problem.

The second criterion was whether the used scales worked in the intended way under each condition, that is, produced reliable scores and lead to a theoretically plausible pattern of results when testing for relationships with variables that have been argued to be related to learning form errors at work. This is supposed to be a preliminary indicator of construct validity (Cronbach and Meehl 1955). Specifically, we assumed that on the level of the individual interpretation of an error (i) perceiving the error as a chance for learning is positively related to the engagement in learning activities, whereas (ii) finding it advantageous to cover up the error is negatively related to the engagement in social learning activities (Edmondson 2004; Rybowiak *et al.* 1999; Zhao and Olivera 2006). On the level of the social context we assumed a safe team climate—in terms of (iii) a perceived trustworthiness of team members and (iv) a non-punitive orientation towards errors in the team—to be positively related to the engagement in social learning activities (Cannon and Edmondson 2001; Edmondson 1996, 1999; Tjosvold *et al.* 2004). The goal here is to examine the plausibility of the overall pattern of findings (e.g., consistent directions of correlations for both learning activity scales).

We emphasize that the conclusiveness of this study is limited in that it cannot clarify which approach is more valid. Answering this question would have required to have an established criterion—that is, an accepted measure of learning from errors at work—as well as known relationships between this criterion and given predictors at hand, in order to analyze which method is better capable to reproduce these relationships. Rather, the case made here is to explore the feasibility of two versions of a research instrument and to apply the more promising one in continuing research. This is a necessary condition for the establishment of more rigorous psychometric quality standards.

Method

Design and Sampling

The study followed a cross-sectional design with two randomized groups, one for the CIT, and another one for the Cases Approach. A sample of $N = 600$ nurses was selected randomly from one large hospital and assigned randomly to one of the two conditions ($n_{CIT} = 300$; $n_{Cases} = 300$). An occurring problem was that the study was conducted shortly after a long period of strikes in public service. It is hard to judge how this situation affected the participation. However, because the field access had been established and the strikes had already caused a considerable delay, we decided not to further postpone the data collection.

Instruments

Two questionnaires were developed, based on either the CIT or the Cases Approach. In the CIT condition the nurses were asked to provide a short description of an error situation that they had encountered at work. Subsequently, they rated their engagement in learning activities after this incident by indicating how much time they had spent with the activities described in the items after the error (six-point Likert scale: 1 = no time at all; 6 = very much time). In the Cases condition the subjects were presented vignettes of error cases. These cases had been constructed from examples for knowledge- and rule-based errors provided by expert nurses in the interview study mentioned earlier (Bauer and Mulder 2007). All of them comprised the misinterpretation of a situation and a subsequent inadequate decision. Vignette 1 concerned the application of an unnecessary emergency procedure based on the misinterpretation of values on a medical instrument. Vignette 2 concerned the misjudgement of complications, that is, administering an analgesic although the patient suffered from a thrombosis. Vignette 3 involved the misjudgement of a patient's risk of bedsore. The subjects were asked to identify with one of these examples, and to imagine the situation vividly. Subsequently, they were asked to answer questions about how likely they would engage in the given learning activities, after this situation (six-point Likert scale: 1 = very unlikely; 6 = very likely). The subjects judged the cases as authentic (Table 8.1; six-point Likert scale: 1 = low authenticity; 6 = high authenticity).

Learning activities after an error were operationalized by two scales. The items were constructed on the basis of the theoretical framework, examples of learning activities from the interviews, and some items on constructive versus defensive changes after an error provided by Meurier *et al.* (1997). The scale 'joint cause analysis' contains facets of analyzing possible causes for the error (e.g., own competence, interaction with the patient and colleagues, workplace conditions) either in informal discussions with team members or at formal team meetings (nine items, for example, 'Analyzing jointly with members of my team, what has lead to the error'). The scale 'joint development of new action strategies' contains aspects of considering and discussing new ways of behaviour or new guidelines (seven items, e.g., 'Initiating a discussion in a team meeting, how we could prevent similar errors in the future').

The interpretation of an error as a chance for learning and the tendency to cover it up were measured by two scales from the German version of the Error Orientation Questionnaire (Rybowiak *et al.* 1999). The perception of a safe team climate was operationalized by two scales regarding the perception of the trustworthiness of the team members (Bauer *et al.* 2007;

Büssing and Glaser 2002) and the perception how safe or precarious it is to admit an error within the team (Van Dyck *et al.* 2005; Tjosvold *et al.* 2004). Descriptive statistics and reliability estimates for these scales can be obtained from Table 8.1.

FINDINGS

Participation

Eight questionnaires in the CIT and 12 questionnaires in the Cases condition could not be delivered to the subjects, because the nurses no longer worked at their ward. Twenty-three of 292 correctly delivered questionnaires were returned from the CIT group (7.9 per cent). However, within this group only 10 subjects gave an error example, resulting in a rate of 3.4 per cent. From the Cases group, 45 of 288 delivered questionnaires were returned (15.6 per cent). Because of the low participation, the samples have to be regarded as being selective. Further analyses were conducted only for the Cases group, because of the particularly low participation in the CIT group. The planned factor analyses had to be postponed until Study 2.

Table 8.1 Descriptive Statistics and Reliability of the Scales; Authenticity of the Cases

Scale	Items	α	M	SD
1. Chance for learning	3	.65	4.05	1.04
2. Covering up errors	4	.82	2.22	0.91
3. Trust	5	.92	4.04	1.07
4. Non-punitive orientation	3	.80	4.16	1.06
5. Cause anaysis	5	.83	3.50	1.12
6. New Strategy	6	.84	3.80	0.98
Authenticity of error cases			M	SD
1. Values on a medical instrument			4.72	1.45
2. Misintrepreting complications			5.36	0.67
3. Misjudging the risk of bedsore			5.10	0.88

Note: Statistics for Cases-Condition (n = 45); 6-point Likert scale, higher numbers indicate higher intensity.

Scale Construction and Correlations

Despite the low participation, we analyzed the scales to obtain preliminary information. The scaling procedure was based on examining the items' discrimination and contribution to internal consistency. Items were excluded from a scale if the discrimination was below .5 or the exclusion would increase reliability. Table 8.1 shows the remaining number of items, reliability, and descriptive statistics of the scales.

The described procedure yielded sufficiently reliable scales, with the lowest reliability for the scale 'errors as chance for learning'. All other scales show good to very good internal consistency.

Correlations between the scales can be obtained from Table 8.2. Note that significance tests for effect sizes below .24 should not be interpreted because the power decreases below 50 per cent (Faul *et al.* 2007). Descriptive effect sizes and the directions of the correlations can be interpreted as preliminary information. From this perspective, the signs of the correlations among the learning activity scales and the other scales are in the expected directions and show a plausible overall pattern regarding the expectations presented earlier. However, it must be emphasized that it cannot be assumed that these insignificant correlations would have been significant in a larger sample. This matter can be settled only by replication with increased power.

DISCUSSION

Both approaches performed poorly on criterion one, the return quote, resulting in potentially selective samples. However, return quotes of 15

Table 8.2   Correlations Among the Scales

Scale	1	2	3	4	5	6
1. Chance for learning	—					
2. Covering up errors	-.12	—				
3. Trust	.18	-.40	—			
4. Non-punitive orientation	.05	-.57	.72	—		
5. Cause analysis	.22	-.20	.28	.12	—	
6. New strategy	.21	-.34	.40	.16	.64	—

Note: Statistics for Cases-Condition (n = 45); one-tailed test, correlations greater than ± .24 p<.05, greater than ± .34 p<.01

per cent and below are found frequently in postal survey in the social sciences (Diekmann 2007; Porst 2001). Further studies are needed in order to check whether the present findings replicate and to what extent they are biased. Beyond the mentioned strikes that may have had a negative effect on the overall willingness to participate, there is little information about possible reasons for the non-response. A possible reason for the particularly low participation in the CIT condition may be that the subjects could not give an example, for example, because they could not remember one. An alternative interpretation is that the subjects may have been unwilling to communicate an error example, for example, because they did not want to make the effort or did not trust the anonymity of the study.

These possibilities cannot be further explored with the current data. Anyhow, the finding of a low participation in the CIT condition is similar to the one of an interview study on learning from errors, in which employees from high-technology and service enterprises were asked to describe self-experienced error situations (Harteis *et al.* 2007). In the interviews, the subjects often experienced problems remembering an error case, or were reluctant to tell one. In contrast, Meurier *et al.* (1997) had successfully implemented the CIT in a study on errors, using anonymous questionnaires. Therefore, the failure of this method in the present study was not to be expected and should not be generalized to other applications of the CIT. Further research is required to check under which conditions the CIT can be applied effectively in research on learning from errors. In addition to the strike, the discrepant findings may also potentially be due to cultural differences between our and Meurier's samples (UK versus Germany; different local cultures at the hospitals). For our current purpose, we interpret the results to argue for the application of the Cases Approach in Study 2. Because the used cases are not directly related to the subjects, participation may seem less precarious. Additional efforts to increase the return quote involve reducing the amount of personal information requested in the questionnaire in order to mitigate potential fears of the subjects to be identifiable. The mentioned concern that the Cases Approach asks for hypothetical behaviour can be taken into account in the interpretation of the data.

Scrutinizing criterion two involved an examination of the relationships between the learning activities and supposedly related variables. Acknowledging the selective sample and the low statistical power, the findings deliver preliminary information that the scales worked in the intended way. Reliable scores could be established for the learning activity scales. The overall pattern of findings from the correlations indicates a plausible network of relationships (in terms of the direction of the correlations). A task for Study 2 is to test to what extent these results replicate in a larger sample.

Study 2

Goal

In Study 2 we applied the Cases Approach in a new sample in order to advance the developed operationalization of error-related learning activities in nursing and to check whether the preliminary correlative findings from the pilot study replicate.

Method

Design and sampling

The study was designed as a cross-sectional field study. Participants were full-time nurses from hospitals located in the German Federal State of Bavaria. The goal was to get a sample of $n = 300$. Nine out of 16 addressed hospitals agreed to participate in the study. These hospitals differ in size, location, supply, and sponsorship. A total of $n = 864$ nurses could be reached with the developed questionnaire. Unlike in the pilot study, no random sampling procedure could be applied because the hospitals did not allow access to their personnel data bases. The field access relied on the compliance of the hospitals' managers and therefore had to be executed according to their rules. The nurses were addressed via each hospital's CEO for nursing and their immediate supervisors. In order to increase the nurses' readiness to participate, hardly any personal information was asked for in the questionnaire that might have induced a feeling of being identifiable.

A total of $n = 276$ nurses participated in the study. The overall return quote is 33 per cent. Although not satisfactory, it is above an expectable rate for a postal survey (Porst 2001) and above both conditions in the pilot study.

Instrument

The instrument used was almost identical to the Cases Approach questionnaire in the pilot study. The following changes were made. Firstly, the direction of the Likert scale was inverted so that it reflects the German school-grade system (i.e., lower numbers indicate higher intensity). This should assist the subjects' comprehension of the answer format. Secondly, items from the pilot study that had not worked well in terms of discrimination or reliability were reformulated or replaced. The revised scale 'joint cause analysis' consisted of eight items, 'joint development of new strategies' of seven items (English translations of which are presented in Table 8.3).

Again, the subjects judged the cases as authentic (see Table 8.4). The engagement in learning activities was independent of the chosen case (MANOVA: $F (4, 550) = 2.30$, n.s.).

Table 8.3   Learning Activity Items from Study 2

Scale	Code	Items
Joint cause analysis		Discussing with my colleagues . . .
	CA1	why I made this error.
	CA2	what caused the error to happen.
	CA3	what was my part in making this error.
	CA4	whether there are gaps in my competence.
	CA5	whether something in our cooperation contributed to letting the error happen.
	CA6	whether something was wrong with the communication with the patient.
	CA7	how the work conditions contributed to that I made this error. (x)
	CA8	Bringing up the issue in a team meeting in order to analyze causes. (x)
Joint strategy development	ST1	Discussing the error with my colleagues so that the error will not happen again.
	ST2	Asking experienced colleagues what they would have done in my place.
	ST3	Asking my colleagues what I can do differently, next time.
	ST4	Initiating a discussion in a team meeting, how we could prevent similar errors in future.
	ST5	Discussion ideas for new guidelines with my supervisor.
	ST6	Making agreements about new standards and guidelines in a team meeting.
	ST7	Asking colleagues to control me in similar situations. (x)

Note: Items translated from German; x = sorted out in the item analyses.

Table 8.4   Descriptive Statistics and Reliability of the Scales; Authenticity of the Cases

Scale	Items	α	M	SD
1. Chance for learning	4	.91	2.38	1.15
2. Covering up errors	5	.81	5.05	0.89
3. Trust	5	.91	2.23	0.90
4. Non-punitive orientation	6	.87	2.23	0.97
5. General cause anaysis	3	.85	2.12	0.92
6. Specific cause analysis	3	.68	3.48	1.16
7. New Strategy	6	.87	2.82	1.07
Authenticity of error cases			M	SD
1. Values on a medical instrument			1.98	1.05
2. Misintrepreting complications			1.85	1.05
3. Misjudging the risk of bedsore			2.11	0.94

Note: n = 276; 6-point Likert scale, lower numbers indicate higher intensity.

Findings

Scale construction

The first step of the scaling procedure involved a screening of the items' discrimination and reliability, employing the same criteria as in the pilot study. From each of the learning activity scales, one item had to be removed because of their low discrimination (UA8; ST7).

In a second step, exploratory factor analyses with oblique rotation were applied in order to check the dimensionality of the scales (Principal Axis, Direct Oblimin rotation with delta = 0). We expected single factor solutions because each scale was supposed to measure one underlying construct.

For the cause analysis scale, a KMO coefficient at .75 and a significant Barlett's test of sphericity ($p < .001$) indicated appropriate conditions for conducting a factor analysis. In contrast to the expectation, the analysis indicated a two-factor solution, as judged by the Kaiser criterion, the scree test, and Velicner's MAP test (O'Connor 2000). After removing one item that loaded badly on both factors, an interpretable solution with two correlated factors ($r = .38$) and substantial factor loadings (Table 8.5) could be obtained that explains 71 per cent variance. Factor 1 contains items that indicate a general readiness to address other team members in order to communicate about the error and to analyze it (cf. Table 8.3). The factor therefore is interpreted as 'general cause analysis' (48 per cent explained variance). The items of the second factor address joint discussions about how specific causes may have contributed to the error. It is therefore interpreted as 'specific cause analysis' (23 per cent explained variance). A point of concern is the cross-loading of item CA3 that would indicate to remove it. However, it is kept for further analyses in order to not further diminish the number of items.

For the scale 'joint strategy development', the KMO coefficient (.83) and Barlett's test ($p < .001$) indicated a good factorability. As judged by the Kaiser criterion, the scree test, and the MAP test, a single-factor solution was most appropriate. The common factor explains 60 per cent variance. Table 8.6 provides the factor matrix.

Descriptive statistics and reliabilities for the scales constructed from the factor analyses as well as of the other used scales can be obtained from Table 8.4. The learning activity scales had sufficient to good internal consistencies.

Construct Validity

For the examination of construct validity, Table 8.7 depicts the correlations between the three learning activity scales and the scales regarding the interpretation of the error situation and a safe team climate. The pattern of findings is plausible and similar to the pilot study. (i) The interpretation of errors as a chance for learning is positively correlated to the three learning activity scales. (ii) Covering up errors is negatively correlated with general cause

Table 8.5 Rotated Pattern Matrix for the Scale 'Joint Cause Analysis'

Item	Factor loadings	
	1	2
CA2	.96	
CA1	.81	
CA3	.66	.23
CA5		.76
CA4	.12	.67
CA6		.52

Note: Loadings < .1 omitted

Table 8.6 Factor Matrix for the Scale 'Joint Strategy Development'

Item	Factor loadings
ST4	.83
ST5	.79
ST6	.77
ST3	.67
ST2	.66
ST1	.61

analysis and the development of new strategies, however not significant with specific cause analysis. (iii) Trust in the team members is positively correlated with all learning activity scales, and (iv) a non-punitive orientation towards errors in the team positively with general cause analysis and strategy development (n.s. with specific cause analysis). Finally, the three learning activity scales are interrelated positively. A higher order factor analysis on the aggregate scales, employing the same criteria as used earlier, indicates that they load on a single common factor (loadings: general cause analysis $\lambda = .52$; specific cause analysis $\lambda = .64$; new strategy $\lambda = .67$).

Table 8.7 Correlations between the Scales

Scale	1	2	3	4	5	6	7
1. Chance for learning	—						
2. Covering up errors	-.03	—					
3. Trust	.18	-.24	—				
4. Non-punitive orientation	.03	-.43	.66	—			
5. General cause analysis	.21	-.43	.20	.18	—		
6. Specific cause analysis	.27	-.09	.14	.05	.33	—	
7. New strategy	.24	-.20	.28	.12	.35	.43	—

Note: n = 276; one-tailed test, correlations greater than ± .10 p<.05, greater than ± .14 p<.01

DISCUSSION

In Study 2 we reapplied the Cases Approach to a new sample and conducted further analyses on the scales, measuring the engagement in social learning activities. The findings provide information about further revision requirements.

In contrast to our intention, the factor analysis revealed a two-dimensional structure of the original scale 'joint cause analysis'. This underlying two-dimensionality may be a reason why in the pilot study several items had to be excluded from this scale. We interpret Factor 1 as a global readiness or decision to approach others in order to discuss and analyze an error (e.g., 'Discussing with my colleagues what caused the error to happen'). In contrast, Factor 2 contains items that refer to examining specific assumptions about underlying causes of an error ('. . . whether there are gaps in my competence'). The items had substantial loadings on their factors and the scales that were built on the basis of the factors proved to be reliable. The problem that the scales consist only of few items should be addressed in a revision. However, for many applications it is preferable to have a few good indicators than many items that are actually paraphrases of one question (e.g., Schumacker and Lomax 2004). In terms of content validity, the scale 'general cause analysis' has a narrow construct scope (i.e., an initial readiness to communicate about an error). Hence, with one or two additional items the scale should represent this construct adequately. The scale 'specific cause analysis' should be extended in a way that it reflects more relevant reasons that underlie the present error cases. For this purpose, it may be adequate to present only one error vignette, so that the error case and the learning activities can be better adjusted to each other.

The factor analysis on the scale 'joint development of new action strategies' yielded the expected single-factor structure. A reliable scale could be established on basis of this factor. Hence, the current data do not indicate a requirement to revise this scale.

The higher order factor analysis of the three learning activity scales provides preliminary evidence that the scales measure a common underlying construct. We interpret this factor as 'engagement in social learning activities'. A next step would imply the application of confirmatory factor analysis in order to test the assumed hierarchical factor structure.

The correlative findings largely replicated the findings from the pilot study and indicate that the developed scales worked in the intended way. The observed correlations were in the expected directions and statistically significant, with the two mentioned exceptions. The overall smaller correlation coefficients for specific cause analysis may be due to the lower reliability of this scale.

CONCLUSION

In our contribution, we aimed to contribute to answering the question how individual learning from errors at work can be operationalized and measured. We developed an exemplary operationalization of learning from errors in terms of learning activities that start a process of inquiry into root causes and aim at changing the underlying causes. This activity perspective on learning from errors is systematically derived from experiential learning theory (e.g., Gruber 2001; Kolb 1984; Kolodner 1983; Schank 1999). This is a prerequisite for content validity. The developed operationalization is limited (i) to the field of nursing, (ii) to a specific type of error (i.e., misjudging a situation and subsequently making a wrong decision), and (iii) to the special case of learning activities that are performed in social exchange. This degree of specificity is necessary, because asking for activities taken after errors in general neglects the variability of errors (Reason 1990) as well as the incidental and situated nature of work-related learning (Billett 2004). Nevertheless the proposed learning activity perspective can potentially be applied flexibly. Combining the introduced learning activity framework with error taxonomies allows to systematically construct new operationalizations of learning activities for given errors in given fields of work.

From our studies we obtained initial evidence about the psychometric properties of the learning activity scales, especially regarding internal consistency and construct validity. Although the conclusiveness of the findings is limited due to the selective samples, the results are encouraging in that reliable scales could be built and that we were able to find a theoretically plausible pattern of correlations with the interpretation of an error situation and the perception of a safe team climate in both studies. This provides initial evidence of construct validity. The findings legitimate further efforts to advance and validate our operationalization of learning from errors.

KEY LEARNING POINTS

Our paper delivers the following propositions on how to measure learning from errors at work:

- Learning from errors can be measured by asking workers about activities that they engage in after an error in order to analyze causes and to develop strategies for preventing similar errors in the future. This approach is based on research on experiential and workplace learning.
- Questions about the engagement in error-related learning activities should be based upon concrete error cases that represent a specific type of error, because different types of errors offer a different potential for learning. Therefore, specific errors may require specific learning activities that do not generalize to other types of error.

Part III

Learning in Various Workplace Settings

9 Learning from Differences

The Relationships between Team Expertise Diversity, Team Learning, Team Performance, and Team Innovation

Marloes Van Engen and Marianne Van Woerkom

In many organizations, teams are being held responsible for important products or services (McDermott 1998). Teams are expected to stimulate the necessary innovation and flexibility in organizations, because they can offer space for creativity and problem solving of team members (Anderson and West 1996; Lambert and Peppard 1993). In recent years especially there has been an increase in the use of multidisciplinary teams (Van der Vegt and Bunderson 2005), in which the expertise of team members from different functional backgrounds is combined. Expertise diversity refers to the differences in knowledge and skills among group members as a result of their work experience and education (Van der Vegt and Bunderson 2005). One big advantage of these teams is that the different work-related experiences of team members represent important resources from which a team can draw when solving problems and making decisions (Bunderson 2003). When relevant expertise is brought together, this may enhance the quality of decisions and actions. Creating diverse teams is therefore believed to be an attractive option for organizations (Van der Vegt and Bunderson 2005). However, the literature about the relationship between expertise diversity and team performance is ambiguous. Differences among team members may also complicate information exchange and coordination within teams (Milliken and Martins 1996; Van der Vegt et al. 2006; Van Knippenberg and Schippers 2007). Many studies confirmed a positive relationship between expertise diversity and performance (Bantel and Jackson 1989; Barsade et al. 2000; Eisenhardt and Tabrizi 1995; Jehn and Bezrukova 2004; Jung et al. 2002; Katzenbach and Smith 1993; Sosik and Jung 2002). Other studies, however, found negative or no relationships between those concepts (Bunderson and Sutcliffe 2002; Cummings 2004; Hambrick et al. 1996; Jackson et al. 1991; O'Reilly et al. 1993; Pearce and Ravlin 1987; Pegels et al. 2000; Pelled et al. 1999; Simons et al. 1999; Van der Vegt and Bunderson 2005; Wagner et al. 1984). It is as yet unclear how these contradictory results can be explained.

Since little is known about the team processes that result from expertise diversity and that may eventually lead to team performance (Lawrence 1997; Van der Vegt and Bunderson 2005), in this study we focus on the relationships between expertise diversity, team learning, and team performance. Team learning may be enhanced when different areas of expertise are combined to generate novel insights (Van der Vegt *et al.* 2006), leading teams to perform better. The results of this study may therefore be used for opening the black box between expertise diversity and team performance.

TEAM LEARNING

Many teams need to deal with a changing environment and changing needs of customers. To remain effective in such a changing environment and to improve internal processes within the team, teams need to be able to learn (Edmondson 1999). Team learning refers to the processing of information and knowledge between team members, resulting in a change in the range of the team's potential behaviour. When team members share their knowledge and experiences with each other, this may result in new knowledge structures or routines (Clark *et al.* 2002). In this chapter, we conceptualize team learning in three team-learning activities (Huber 1991; Van Offenbeek 2001; Van Woerkom and Van Engen 2009), namely information acquisition, information processing and information storage and retrieval. By information acquisition, teams obtain information by passive scanning or actively initiating inquiries in the internal and external environment. Information processing refers to the process by which team members distribute information to other team members and engage in a dialogue in which the distributed information is given interpretations that are commonly understood by the team. The process of information storage and retrieval refers to the storage of common information and locating and using information in the future.

Engaging in learning processes enables teams to adapt to changing circumstances, to improve their way of working, and to solve new problems, which will finally result in a better team performance (Bunderson and Sutcliffe 2003; Edmondson 1999; Edmondson *et al.* 2001a; Van der Vegt and Bunderson 2005; Zellmer-Bruhn and Gibson 2006). In the following, we will outline that team learning may especially pay off when team members are diverse in their expertise.

Expertise Diversity

Team members often differ in the domain of their task-related knowledge and expertise. Expertise diversity refers to the differences in the types of knowledge, skills, and capabilities team members possess as a result of education, experience, and natural ability (Van der Vegt *et al.* 2006). In our study we define expertise diversity as the amount of diversity that team members personally experience. We consider diversity in team members' expertise at the level of the team member's individual experience rather than as an aggregated group-level variable. In many studies, researchers instead of team members define whether a team is considered diverse in expertise, for instance, by assigning different codes to different professions and calculating the index of homogeneity/heterogeneity of that particular variable in the team (see, e.g., Barsade *et al.* 2000; Bunderson and Sutcliffe 2002; Jehn and Bezrukova 2004). However, diversity in expertise may have consequences only when the diversity is actually experienced by an individual rather than assigned by a researcher (Garcia-Prieto *et al.* 2003; Van Knippenberg *et al.* 2004). Expertise diversity exists in the eye of the beholder: People of different professions, educational, or functional background may experience little differences in their team members' expertise. Reversely, team members with the same professional and educational background may experience differences in expertise. Therefore, we argue that team expertise diversity becomes important when it is considered as such by the individuals it concerns.

According to the information/decision-making perspective (see Van Knippenberg *et al.* 2004; Williams and O'Reilly 1998), diverse teams should perform better than homogeneous groups because they possess a broader range of task-relevant knowledge, skills, and abilities, giving the group a larger pool of resources that when combined may generate new insights. When team members differ in their expertise, they might have different perceptions of what the problem exactly is. According to De Dreu and Weingart (2003), these different perceptions may force team members to think more deeply and more creatively about the problem they have to solve, making the group more effective and innovative. Uncritical agreement within the team, on the other hand, can have a negative impact on problem solving (Aldag and Fuller 1993; Janis 1985). Especially in creative tasks or in situations characterized by a high information load and ambiguity, diversity in attitude towards the task is important to learning (Fiol 1994) and offers a significant contribution to team performance (Agrell and Gustafson 1994; Jackson 1996). Also, Van Offenbeek (2001) found that the more divergent the ideas about the task at the start, the more the team experienced to have learned. Thus, we expect that expertise diversity in a team relates to more information acquisition, more information processing, and more storage and retrieval of information. Consequently, we hypothesize that:

Expertise diversity is positively related to team learning (Hypothesis 1).

TEAM LEARNING AND TEAM PERFORMANCE

Since many teams operate in a dynamic environment, teams must engage in learning processes to understand their environment and to coordinate members' actions effectively (Edmondson 1999). By learning, teams can make relatively permanent changes in their collective level of competence produced by the shared experience of the team members. This enables teams to adapt to changing circumstances, to improve their work routines, and to solve new problems, which will eventually result in a better team performance. However, research has only begun to examine the empirical relationship between team learning and team performance (Druskat and Kayes 2000).

In this chapter we define team performance in terms of the ability of a team to be effective, efficient, and realize a good quality. Where effectiveness refers to an absolute level of attainment of goals (Hoegl and Gemuenden 2001), the efficiency of a team refers to an input-output ratio or comparison (Ostroff and Schmitt 1993) and relates to, for example, the team's adherence to schedules and budgets (Hoegl and Gemuenden 2001). The quality that a team has realized depends on the degree that work products or processes are free from errors or defects (Janz 1999) and to the satisfaction of internal or external customers with the value of the products or services that are provided by the team (Spencer 1994).

Furthermore, we also see innovation as a crucial performance factor which provides key competitive advantage in high-value-added industries and the service sector (Dunphy and Bryant 1996). In the context of teams, innovation refers to the intentional introduction and application of ideas, processes, products, or procedures that are new to the team, and designed to improve the team performance (Anderson and West 1996).

Several studies (Edmondson 1999; Edmondson *et al.* 2001a; Van der Vegt and Bunderson 2005; Zellmer-Bruhn and Gibson 2006) have demonstrated a positive link between team learning behaviour and team performance. Team learning has also been found to be positively related to innovation (Bunderson and Sutcliffe 2002, 2003; Edmondson *et al.* 2001b). Teams that underemphasize learning may persevere with inferior alternatives that become inadequate for the current situation. In line with the findings in the studies mentioned earlier, we formulate our second hypothesis as follows:

Team learning is positively related to team performance (Hypothesis 2a).

Team learning is positively related to innovation (Hypothesis 2b).

Expertise Diversity, Team Learning, and Team Performance

The relationship between team diversity and team performance has been the topic of a large flurry of studies in the past decades (see for reviews Harrison and Klein 2007; Horwitz and Horwitz 2007; Milliken and Martins 1996; Van Dijk *et al.* in preparation; Van Knippenberg and Schippers 2007). Earlier theorizing (Milliken and Martins 1996; Pelled *et al.* 1999; Williams and O'Reilly 1998) suggested that diversity related to social categories (i.e., gender, age, ethnicity) may impair the performance of a team, whereas diversity related to the task (i.e., expertise diversity, functional diversity, educational diversity) may improve the performance of the team. The growing body of empirical evidence suggests, however, that for both dimensions of diversity the relationship with performance is inconsistent (Bowers *et al.* 2000; Van Knippenberg *et al.* 2004; Van Knippenberg and Schippers 2007). On the one hand, differences in the expertise of team members can complicate information exchange and coordination within teams. Expertise diversity may result in an overflow of information or a lack of understanding between team members, making group information processing more difficult (Ancona and Caldwell 1992; Milliken and Martins 1996). As Van Knippenberg *et al.* (2004) argue, differences in expertise may also trigger social categorization processes. Group members may make a distinction between others in the team as similar to themselves— in-group, 'us'—and others different from themselves—out-group, 'them'. Social categorization theories (e.g., social identity theory, self-categorization theory [see Tajfel and Turner 1986; Turner *et al.* 1987]) and similarity/attraction theory (Berscheid and Reis 1998; Byrne 1971) suggest that people respond more favourably to similar others. These categorization/ attraction processes may hamper group information processing (Earley and Mosakowski 2000) and consequently team performance.

On the other hand, the information/decision-making perspective suggests that teams diverse in expertise should perform better than homogeneous groups because they possess a broader range of task-relevant knowledge, skills, and abilities, giving the group a larger pool of resources (Van Knippenberg *et al.* 2004) that when combined may generate new insights. These different perceptions may force team members to think more deeply and more creatively about the problem they have to solve, making the group more effective and innovative (De Dreu and Weingart 2003).

The consensus amongst diversity theorists is growing that all types of diversity may trigger both social categorization processes and group information elaboration processes. However, a recent meta-analysis by Horwitz and Horwitz (2007) shows that overall diversity related to the task (including expertise diversity) in general relates to better performance and innovation. Apparently, expertise diversity may trigger functional processes (performance and innovation) more than dysfunctional processes (social categorization). Therefore, we argue that:

> *Expertise diversity is positively related to team performance (Hypothesis 3a).*

> *Expertise diversity is positively related to team innovation (Hypothesis 3b).*

As we have argued earlier, team learning may be the process by which expertise diversity leads to a better team performance. As teams become more diverse in their knowledge, skills, and abilities, they may use their greater informational resources, engage in more discussion and integration of their diverse expertise, and reach a more in-depth understanding of the task. In other words, they learn more as a team. This increased team learning, as is previously argued, in turn leads to improved team performance. Consequently, we argue that:

> *The positive relationship between expertise diversity and team performance is mediated by team learning (Hypothesis 4a).*

> *The positive relationship between expertise diversity and team innovation is mediated by team learning (Hypothesis 4b).*

The hypotheses are summarized in the conceptual model (see Figure 9.1).

METHODS

Participants and Design

We employed a cross-sectional design in which we sampled teams from seven different organizations both in the public sector and in the private sector. Our sample consists of a diversity of teams, but all respondents were participants in ongoing teams with a long task duration (Bradley *et al.* 2003) where team members are interdependent for some common purpose, work together regularly for an extended period of time, and also expect to work together in the future. Information about these team characteristics was provided to us by our contact person in the organization (usually a manager or a HR manager).

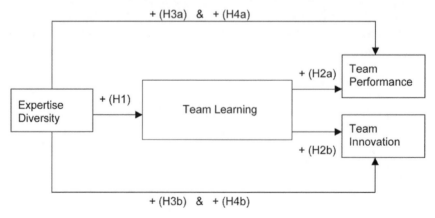

Figure 9.1 Conceptual model.

Table 9.1 Descriptives and Correlations Between Variables (individual level)

Variables	Mean	SD	1	2	3	4	5	6	7	8	9	10
1. Team performance	5.15	.88										
2. Team innovation	4.85	1.06	.52***									
3. Expertise diversity	5.32	.92	.34***	.23***								
4. Team learning	5.02	.78	.62***	.56***	.48***							
5. Gender[a]			.06	.10*	-.07	.09*						
6. Age	39.40	11.48	.004	.04	-.03	.07	-.08*					
7. Education[b]	3.31	.70	-.08*	.01	.04	-.03	.12**	-.07				
8. Years in team	6.49	7.55	.11**	.05	-.08	.08	.13***	.43***	-.05			
9. Team stability/boundedness	5.22	1.04	.38***	.21***	.18***	.34***	.01	.11**	.04	.09*		
10. Team size	15.25	8.18	.03	.05	-.07	-.03	.37***	-.05	-.05	.23***	-.04	

Note: N between 606–624; all scales measured on 7 point scale (1 low, 7 high); [a] 0 = male, 1 = female; [b] 1 = primary school, 5 = academic; *** $p < .001$, ** $p < .01$, * $p < .05$

Questionnaires were distributed to a total of 1,107 respondents. The overall response rate was 56.4 per cent. The final sample consisted of 624 respondents, working in 88 teams in seven different organizations. Health care teams were overrepresented with 43 teams (nine hospital units and 34 teams from nursing institutions). Apart from the health care teams, there were teacher teams (secondary vocational education) (8 teams), production teams in the food industry (15 teams), retail (10 teams) and 12 teams in an engineering and construction teams company. There were 41.6 per cent men and 58.4 per cent women in our sample; the average age was 39.4 years old (SD = 11.48). Of our respondents, 36.5 per cent held a bachelor's degree or higher, 56.6 per cent held a vocational education degree, and 6.8 per cent had low educational levels. Team size varied from four to 35 members with an average of 12.21 members in a team.

Instruments

Team members were asked to indicate their perceptions of the expertise diversity in the team, team learning processes, and how well their team performed. Unless otherwise stated, we assessed all variables by questionnaire items with a response scale ranging from 1, 'strongly disagree', to 7, 'strongly agree'. Random missing data on items of each scale were replaced by imputation of regression estimates with added error components, controlled for team, organization, gender, age, and educational level (Little and Rubin 1990). Means and standard deviations at a between-teams level are presented in Table 9.1.

Expertise Diversity

We measured expertise diversity using an adapted scale of Campion *et al.* (1993), resulting in five items. Examples of items are 'The members of my team vary in their areas of expertise' and 'The members of my team vary in their educational background'. Cronbach's alpha for this scale was .79.

Team Learning

We measured team learning using 26 items from the team-learning scale developed by Van Offenbeek (2001). Furthermore, we elaborated this scale with items adapted from Van Woerkom and Croon (2008) concerning critically reflective work behaviour and from Tjosvold (2004) concerning team problem-solving behaviour. A principal components analysis with oblique rotation on all team learning items showed a three-factor model, explaining 47.59 per cent of the variance. The first factor consisted of 31 items measuring information processing (alpha = .96), the second factor consisted of seven items measuring information storage and retrieval (alpha = .84), and the third factor consisted of nine items measuring information acquisition (alpha = .86).

Information acquisition measures the extent to which team members bring in information that is collected outside the team or is generated inside the team. Examples of items are 'In my team we retrieve information from outside the team by collaborating with others outside the team' and 'In my team, we experiment with different ways of working'.

Team information processing assesses the way the team deals with the distribution of information amongst all team members and the process of collective sense making. Examples of items are 'In my team members help each other to make sense of information' and 'In my team we listen to each other's ideas'.

Information storage and retrieval measures whether team information is systematically stored, retrieved, and utilized (e.g., 'In my team reports are made of team meetings', 'My team refers to documents made previously').

The three team-learning activities are correlated (between .35 and .48). A second-order principal components analysis on the three team-learning activities dimensions showed one underlying factor explaining 71 per cent of the variance (alpha = .80). Consequently, we will test our hypotheses with the overall team learning scale.

Team Performance

We measured team performance using five items adapted from Zellmer-Bruhn and Gibson (2006) concerning team effectiveness (e.g., 'Our team achieves its goals'), four self-developed items concerning efficiency (e.g., 'Our team spends the available time well'), and items adapted from Lai *et al.* (2004) concerning quality (e.g., 'The clients [internal or external] of our team are satisfied'). Innovativeness consisted of four self-developed items. Examples of the items are 'Our team develops new and improved ways of working' and 'Our team develops new products or services'. Principal component analyses showed that two underlying dimensions can be distinguished (together explaining 55 per cent of the variance): *Performance* (consisting of the items of concerning efficiency, effectiveness, and quality, alpha = .92) and *Innovation* (alpha = .85).

Control Variables

We controlled in our analysis for gender, age, educational level, and team tenure. We also asked the manager of the team of how many team members the team contained (team size). Furthermore, we wanted to control for the extent to which the team was bounded and stable. To measure to what extent the teams in our sample were bounded and stable, we used a scale from Wageman *et al.* (2005). Example items of this scale are 'Team membership is quite clear—everybody knows exactly who is and who isn't on this team' and 'This team is quite stable, with few changes in membership'. We aggregated this control variable to the team level as we wanted to have a measure of the team's stability and boundedness (as the intra-class correlation [ICC1] for this variable was as high as .32 aggregation is allowed).

Analysis

The present study demonstrates a hierarchical data structure with three levels. Employees are nested within teams and teams are nested within organizations. The nesting of data is likely to cause dependency among the data, that is, employees have their working context (a particular team and organization) in common. The data structure of the individual ratings by employees of team performance, expertise diversity, and team learning was clearly hierarchically nested (i.e., dependency between individual ratings). For perceived team performance, the intra-class correlation (the proportion of the total amount of variance in the data that is between the teams [ρ or ICC]) is .25, which implies that 25 per cent of the total variance in employee ratings of their team's performance is variance that is between the teams. For team innovation, the ICC was .12. The intra-class correlations for expertise diversity and team learning were .10 and .15, respectively. Although most researchers studying teams prefer aggregation of data to the team level, aggregation of data is problematic for a number of reasons. First of all, one consequence of aggregating the data is that one loses most variance between the variables of interest (in this study not less than 75.5 per cent and 91 per cent of the variance of the [in]dependent variables). The most important threat of treating these data at the aggregated level, however, is that the interpretation of findings runs the risks of the ecological fallacy (see, e.g., Bryk and Raudenbush 1992; Nezlek and Zyzniewski 1998; Snijders and Bosker 1999). Consequently, all our hypotheses are tested at the individual level, while controlling for the dependency that is inherent in the nesting of the data. The use of multilevel random coefficient modelling models this dependency by simultaneously estimating effects at the within- and between-subunit level and is therefore the most appropriate instrument for data analyses. As there were only seven organizations, we did not model the third (organizational) level, but tested all the hypotheses with two-level multilevel random coefficient models (see Bryk and Raudenbush 1992; Nezlek and Zyzniewski 1998; Snijders and Bosker 1999). We used the statistical package MLWIN V 2.02 to analyze the data.

To test the mediating role of team learning, three sets of analyses were conducted according to the procedure suggested by MacKinnon *et al.* (2007). A mediating effect exists if (1) the independent variable (expertise diversity) has a significant effect on the mediating variable (team learning) and (2) the mediating variable has a significant effect on the dependent variable (performance and innovation) in a regression analysis of the independent and mediating variable on the dependent variable. If in this analysis the independent variable has no significant effect on the dependent variable, we have a case of pure mediation. If the independent variable (in addition to the mediating variable) does have a significant effect on the dependent variable, we have a case of partial mediation. The Sobel test for mediation is also reported (Krull *et al.* 2001). Significance of subsequent multilevel models (i.e., the mediation) is tested by means of the improvement of the model fit by means of the deviance test (deviance in the −2 log likelihood ratio) following a χ^2 distribution with the number of added parameters as degrees of freedom.

RESULTS

Table 9.1 reports the correlations between (in)dependent variables and control variables at the individual level. Women report more team learning than men do ($F = 3.12$, $p < .03$), and also report more team innovation than men ($t = 6.08$, $p < .02$). Therefore, respondent sex is controlled for in the analyses testing the hypotheses. At the aggregated level (sex composition of team), no significant relations were found with the (in)dependent variables. Respondent age and respondent team tenure are highly correlated (.43). As the latter also positively relates to team performance, we decided to include team tenure rather than age as a control variable in the analyses.

The first hypothesis was tested by means of a multilevel random coefficient model (MRCM) with team learning as dependent variable, expertise diversity as independent variable, and controlled for gender and years in team at the individual level and team size and team stability and boundedness at the team level. We tested this model (Table 9.2, model 2) against a baseline model without the independent variable expertise diversity to see whether the model showed an increase in fit (−2 log likelihood). This baseline model (Table 9.2, model 1) shows a significant relationship between employee gender and team learning (women report more team learning) and a positive relationship between team stability and boundedness and learning. As can be seen in Table 9.2, model 2, our hypothesis was confirmed: expertise diversity is positively related to team learning ($\beta = .39$, $z = 10.78$, $p < .001$).

Next, we tested whether team learning is positively related to team performance. Two separate MRCMs, one for team performance and one for team innovation, were run with team learning as independent variable and gender, team tenure, team size, team boundedness, and team stability as control variables. This model is tested against the baseline model predicting team performance and team innovation from the control variables. The results are presented in Table 9.3. As predicted, team learning is positively related to team performance ($\beta = .58$, $z = 11.98$, $p < .001$, model 2), confirming hypothesis 2a. For team innovation the pattern was very similar: Team learning is positively related to team innovation ($\beta = .74$, $z = 15.16$, $p < .001$, model 4), confirming hypothesis 2b.

Table 9.2   Results of Regression Analyses Predicting Team Learning From Expertise Diversity (Multilevel Analyses)

	Team Learning	
	Model 1	Model 2
Fixed parameters		
Constant	4.990(.087)**	4.947(.078)
Gender	.155(.070)*	.159(.061)*
Years in team	.004(.004)	.007(.004)
Team stability and bounded-ness	.260(.030)***	.190(.027)***
Team size	-.007(.006)	-.006(.005)
Expertise diversity		
Variance components		.388(.036)**
Individual level	.476	.340
Team level	.063	.089
Model fit (-2 log likelihood)	1303.965	1141.076 $\chi^2 = 162.89, p<.001$

Note: All predictors are measured at the individual level (nested in teams), except for team size and team boundedness and stability, which are measured at the team level; N = 597; a 0 = male, 1 = female; *** p <.001, ** p <.01, * p <.05

Hypothesis 3, suggesting a positive relationship between expertise diversity and team performance, was tested with two separate MRCMs, one for team performance and one for team innovation. This model is tested against the baseline model predicting team performance and team innovation from the control variables. The results are presented in Table 9.3. As predicted, expertise diversity is positively related to team performance (β = .30, z = 6.91, p < .001), confirming hypothesis 3a. In a next step, the mediator variable team learning was added to the analysis (Table 9.3, model 3). As hypothesized (hypothesis 4a), team learning fully mediated the relationship between expertise diversity and team performance.

Again, the results for team innovation mirror the results of the MRCM for team performance: Expertise diversity is positively related to team innovation (β = .25, z = 5.21, p < .001, confirming hypothesis 3b), and this relationship is fully mediated by team learning (confirming hypothesis 4b).

CONCLUSION AND DISCUSSION

Many organizations see multidisciplinary teams as Columbus' egg to a better performance. They are unaware, however, of the processes that lead diverse teams to a better performance. Our study shows that perceived team learning mediates the relationship between expertise diversity experienced by team members and their perceptions of the performance and innovation of the team. Since there is a lack of empirical attention to the processes that are presumed to underlie the effects of diversity (Van Knippenberg and Schippers 2007), our study contributes to the literature by shedding a light on the processes underlying the diversity-performance relationship. As suggested by the information/decision-making perspective, our study shows that if team members report that they see differences in expertise in their team, they perceive their team to learn more, to perform better, and to be more innovative. Team members who experience more expertise diversity in their team report more information acquisition, more information processing, and more storage and retrieval of information than team members who experience low expertise diversity.

We have looked at the relationship between expertise diversity and performance from the perspective of individual team members. Thus, our conclusions are based on diversity in expertise as it is experienced in the eye of the beholder. This is in contrast with most studies on the diversity performance relationship that base their conclusion on an aggregate measure of diversity, mostly assigned by the researcher and some team level indicator of performance. Although the latter procedure obviously has the advantage of seeing the team as an entity and of measuring the team's performance and innovation with other than perception measures, it is blind to the option that a certain assigned diversity is not experienced as such by the individuals in a team. It is possible that the inconsistent findings that are reported in reviews and meta-analyses (Horwitz and Horwitz 2007; Van Knippenberg *et al.* 2004; Van Knippenberg and Schippers 2007) are a consequence of discarding the individual perceptions of diversity in the team. In addition to the perception of diversity of individual team members, it is also possible that reactions to diversity may be informed by individuals' beliefs about the value of diversity (vs. homogeneity) for their team (cf. Van Knippenberg *et al.* 2007). Future research should therefore study not only whether individuals actually experience expertise diversity in their team but also their evaluation of this diversity. This evaluation may be just as decisive in whether individuals in the team are ready to learn from each other and profit from the differences in knowledge, skills, and abilities.

Table 9.3   Results of Regression Analyses Predicting Team Performance and Team Innovation From Team Learning (Model 2), Expertise Diversity Mediated by Team Learning Model 3a and 3b (Multilevel Analyses)

	Team Performance			
	Model 1	Model 2	Model 3a	Model 3b
Fixed parameters				
Constant	5.072 (.117)***	5.111 (.090)***	5.054 (.107)***	5.101 (.089)***
Gender	.069 (.077)	-.048 (.060)	.040 (.070)	-.039 (.060)
Years in team	.010 (.005)	.007 (.004)	.010 (.004)*	.007 (.004)
Team stability/ boundedness	.276 (.033)***	.113 (.028)***	.222 (.031)***	.115 (.028)***
Team size	-.002 (.008)	.002 (.006)	-.001 (.007)	.005 (.006)
Expertise diversity			.304 (.044)***	.064 (.035)
Team learning		.575 (.048)***		.539 (.051)***
Variance components				
Individual leve	.499	.300	.398	.295
Team level	.174	.188	.215	.196
Model fit (-2 log likelihood)	1378.937	1118.842***	1288.380***	1114.649***
Sobel test				7.546***

(continued)

Limitations

Since our data are cross-sectional we cannot draw conclusions about the causality between our variables. Longitudinal designs that study the sequence of expertise diversity, team learning, and team performance and innovation are called for.

Table 9.3 (continued)

	Team Innovation			
	Model 1	Model 2	Model 3a	Model 3b
Fixed parameters				
Constant	4.673 (.116)***	4.695 (.096)***	4.641 (.112)***	4.653 (.094)***
Gender	.190 (.099)	.072 (.083)	.209 (.096)*	.091 (.082)
Years in team	.003 (.006)	.001 (.005)	.004 (.006)	.001 (.005)
Team stability/ boundedness	.278 (.081)***	.099 (.068)	.233 (.078)	.105 (.067)
Team size	.001 (.008)	.006 (.006)	.002 (.007)	.009 (.006)
Expertise diversity			.262 (.046)***	-.062 (.055)
Team learning		.743 (.049)***		.763 (.059)***
Variance components				
Individual leve	1.021	.729	.974	.699
Team level	.086	.057	.077	.172
Model fit (-2 log likelihood)	1744.592***	1540.641***	1713.579***	1530.370***
Sobel test				8.279***

Note: All predictors are measured at the individual level (nested in teams), except for team size and team boundedness and stability, which are measured at the team level; N = 597; a 0 = male, 1 = female; *** p <.001, ** p <.01, * p <.05

A potential limitation to the large diversity in type of teams included in our sample was that we could not control for specific organization and team characteristics. Therefore, further research should include moderators concerning the circumstances under which diverse teams are able to profit from their diverse expertise. For instance, task routineness, task complexity, and task interdependency may moderate the relationship between expertise diversity on the one hand and team learning and performance on the other hand. Teams that need to perform challenging tasks that require a lot of coordination among team members are likely to profit more from expertise diversity than other teams. Furthermore, since expertise diversity may also result in social categorization processes or in similarity attraction processes leading to professional rivalry, emotional conflict, and other dysfunctional affective processes in the team, future research should include both the processes related to social categorization processes and information/decision-making processes simultaneously.

Another constraint of our study is our self-reported performance and innovation measures. The percept-percept bias may result in halo effects, such that team members who are happy in the team value the different contributions of team members, perceive more team learning, and perceive their team to perform better. Future studies should therefore include more objective performance measures, or use observation methods to study team learning processes.

Practical Relevance

One important lesson that practitioners may take from our study is that team performance and innovativeness can be enhanced by stimulating team learning. One way to do this is by composing teams of members who differ in their expertise. It might be especially important for team and organizational leaders to make expertise diversity explicit, and to stress a positive interpretation of differences in team member attributes since both team expertise diversity and the evaluation of this diversity is something experienced by individuals. Furthermore, our study also shows that diverse teams benefit from team learning when the team's boundaries are clearly defined and the team is stable over time. Although project teams and job rotation are popular concepts in theories concerning employee motivation, too much dynamics may be dysfunctional when it comes to teams.

KEY LEARNING POINTS

- Teams that are diverse in terms of the knowledge and skills of the team members display more team learning behaviour and are more positive about their team performance and innovation.
- Teams that are actively engaged in team learning are more positive about their team performance and innovation.

- Team learning mediates the relationship between expertise diversity and performance and between expertise diversity and innovation.

10 The Relationship between Central Actors and Level of Reflection in Project-Based Learning
Dutch and US Data and Theory Compared

Rob Poell, Victoria Marsick, and Lyle Yorks

Many organizations are updating their learning systems to favour learner-driven strategies integrated with work, in the context of an emerging knowledge economy (Tsang 1997; Tjepkema *et al.* 2002; Berends *et al.* 2003; Scarbrough *et al.* 2004a). Such learning is triggered by performance needs of individuals, groups, or the organization as a whole. Project-based learning is one learner-driven strategy increasingly applied to encourage both individual and organizational development (Keegan and Turner 2001; Ayas and Zeniuk 2001; Arthur *et al.* 2001). Employees learn from real-life experiences based around common interests, normally within a particular context and time, and usually within groups (DeFillippi 2001). Project-based learning can be defined as the creation and acquisition of knowledge within projects and the subsequent transfer of such knowledge to other parts of the organization (Scarbrough *et al.* 2004b). Project-based learning is one way of organizing workplace learning and the focus of this exploratory study.

PROJECT-BASED LEARNING IN WORK CONTEXTS

The evidence that employers are beginning to see project-based learning in the workplace more as an investment rather than a cost is expanding (Van Buren 2002; Zuber-Skerritt 2002). One type of project-based learning in the workplace is action learning, as developed by the physicist Revans (1982)—often considered the "father" of action learning—who suggested that relevant knowledge comes from action, not just through the study of books. Revans described action learning as learning from and with peers by solving real problems. Action learning has been variously interpreted and applied. One application is action reflection learning, which emphasizes, among other things, learning through reflection (Rimanoczy and Turner 2008). Marsick *et al.* (1992) describe action reflection learning as problem solving by a small group of participants, who because of this learn and attempt to increase their critical potential.

Another type of project-based learning in the workplace is engaging in a work-related learning project (Poell 1998). The work-related learning project is a set of coherent learning activities based in the work context, which is conducted by a group of employees. They may be directed and/or supported by a supervisor and/or a facilitator but they can also be entirely self-directing. This notion of a work-related learning project as a small network of organizational actors is based in the learning-network theory as developed by Van der Krogt (1998, 2007; see also Poell and Van der Krogt 2008). This is a theoretical framework about workplace learning that puts networks of actors at the centre of attention.

Thus we have introduced two perspectives on project-based learning in work contexts; the first will be referred to as the critical-pragmatist perspective and the second as the actor-network perspective. These two perspectives share a number of similarities. Both of them focus on workplace learning. In both cases the learning process is conceptualized as a project, with a preliminary decided start and end point. And finally, the assumption in both concepts is that, by working with other group members, each member learns from one another. Because of the conceptual overlap between the two perspectives, the question arises as to whether it is possible to relate the two theoretical frameworks to each other.

Actor-Network Perspective

Within this perspective the organization of a learning project is central. The assumption is that there is always an actor (workers, managers, HRD professionals, trade unions, workers' associations, and external training providers) who plays a central role within the learning project. The actor-network perspective derives from the learning-network theory developed by Van der Krogt (1998, 2007; see also Poell and Van der Krogt 2008). This theory describes how learning is organized in the context of an organization. As Figure 10.1 indicates, there are three central components within this theory, namely, the learning actors, the learning processes that they organize, and the learning structures that come into being over time. The

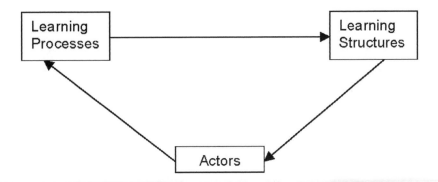

Figure 10.1 The learning project as a network (Van der Krogt 1995; Poell 1998).

basic assumption is that employees are capable actors who interact with each other on the basis of their own theories and premises. Over time, as their interactions start occurring along more permanent patterns, actors thus develop learning structures (e.g., learning programs and the tasks and responsibilities associated with them). These learning structures in turn influence the opinions, interests, and strategies of the actors, as they enable but also limit the possible actions that actors can undertake.

While Van der Krogt (1995) throws light upon learning networks on the organizational level, the notion of a learning project described by Poell (1998) is based on the team and individual level. The learning project enables employees to combine work improvement with their own development. It mainly consists of three phases, namely, orientation, learning and optimizing, and continuation. The intention of the orientation phase is involving all interested parties, determining the learning theme, placing the program in the context of the organization, and setting up a learning contract. In the learning and optimizing phase the actual learning takes place and there will be a connection with the daily learning activities. While the learning is taking place, adjustments can be made to optimize the process. During the continuation phase the individual participants resume their daily learning activities and the learning system of the organization will be updated with the knowledge that is received during the program.

The organization of these three learning phases can occur in different ways. Poell (1998) presents four ideal types. These are referred as the liberal-contractual learning project, the vertical-regulated learning project, the horizontal-organic learning project, and the external-collegiate learning project.

In the *liberal-contractual* learning project, the individual is the central actor and is responsible for his or her own learning activities. The organization plays a minimal role; and therefore, individuals must be highly independent. They are still a project team, as they have entered into a (psychological) contract to use each other for furthering their individual learning. An example of this project type would be four car salespeople working for different vendors, who at their own initiative meet informally each month to exchange ideas about selling techniques and customer profiles.

In the *vertical-regulated* learning project the management is the central actor and there is a learning policy present. The HRD staff translates this learning policy into learning activities. Then the learning program that they have designed is delivered to the employees. This whole process is governed by rules and regulations and the learning climate can be described as regulated. This kind of organized learning occurs frequently in large organizations. An example of this project type is a two-week intensive induction program in a large multinational, which new hires are obliged to attend to learn about the mission, culture, and communication channels characteristic for the company by engaging in games, assignments, and other practical socialization activities.

In the *horizontal-organic* learning project the solution of a problem is central. The team is the central actor and works on complex work-related problems, in other words, problems without a standard solution. The learning project group, which is relatively autonomous, is dominant. An example of this project type would be a multidisciplinary group of professionals from the same department who decide to sit together a number of times over several months to find out why their job satisfaction has gone down so dramatically since the introduction of a set of new work methods some time ago (and to change that situation).

The *external-collegiate* learning project starts outside the organization, by a professional association. The new learning projects are built around new developments within the profession of the employees. The central actor is the professional association. An example of this project type is a group of medical doctors from different academic hospitals participating in a continuing professional development program offered by their medical association, who set up a number of inter-collegial consultation sessions to help each other apply their new knowledge and skills with clients in their respective workplaces.

Having introduced the actor-network perspective, we will now turn to an overview of the critical-pragmatist perspective on workplace learning.

Critical-Pragmatist Perspective

The critical-pragmatist perspective is a lens for theorizing about adult learning that combines elements of both critical theory and pragmatism. More specifically, this perspective has been significantly influenced by Mezirow's (1991, 2000) writing on the transformative dimensions of adult learning. Mezirow draws on elements of John Dewey's (1925) pragmatism, especially the emphasis on learning from experience, through testing the validity of ideas and principles through reflection on their consequences in action. Mezirow also uses elements from the critical social theory of Jürgen Habermas (1984), particularly the concepts of instrumental and communicative action. He recasts the latter as requiring learning domains and the role played by critical reflection on premises for emancipatory learning (Poell *et al.* 2009).

The critical-pragmatist perspective has been used to classify different kinds of action-learning programs into ideal types. This classification is based, first, on the nature of the learning that occurs in the program. Second, it looks at the relative degree to which the program is used to support experimentation and change. From this perspective, such change should go beyond the individual learner in ways that change how groups or the organization learns and works. Based on O'Neil (1999), this framework distinguishes four schools of practice—keeping in mind that actual practice may combine several of these types: tacit, scientific, experiential, and critical reflection (O'Neil and Marsick 2007).

In the *tacit* school, people work on real problems and they are expected to learn from this. These programs focus primarily on task accomplishment; learning is incidental and does not involve much personal reflection to learn from experience. If learning coaches are used, they are often process consultants who manage the learning process on behalf of participants (Marsick and O'Neil 1999). The existing culture within a company is usually reinforced and the strategic thinking of participants is stimulated without questioning organizational norms (Yorks *et al.* 1999).

Revans (1982) is illustrative of the *scientific* school. Central to Revans' learning theory is finding the right question to ask, which is formulated as Learning = Programmed knowledge from the past + Questioning insight (L = P + Q). Programmed knowledge is expert knowledge and knowledge in books. Revans believed managers need more Q learning by wrestling with live problems, asking "fresh questions", and reflecting on results. The focus is gathering data to solve the problem, although Revans also encouraged managers to look at themselves and the larger system as part of the solution. Revans eschewed learning coaches, and instead urged managers to be self-directed learners. Coaches, if used, primarily support learners in organizing themselves in the early stages of the program, and then remove themselves from active engagement in the group. The emphasis on rigorous data collection and the minimal role of the learning coach distinguish this school from the experiential and the critical-reflection school (Yorks *et al.* 1999).

Action learning based on Kolb's *experiential* learning cycle is illustrative of the experiential school. According to Kolb (1984), four steps are taken. The learner first *has* an experience; in the next step the learner *reflects* on this experience; in the third step the learner devises new ideas; and in the fourth step the learner experiments with the new idea. Bunning (1992) showed that action learning can help learning in each stage of the experiential learning cycle. Problem reframing and problem solving are central to this school. What differentiates the experiential from the scientific school is the intentional focus on personal development through reflection on their experience (Yorks *et al.* 1999). In this school a learning coach makes sure reflection on learning from the action or process takes place.

According to the *critical-reflection* school of action learning, the kind of reflection in the experiential school is useful, but not sufficient. The proponents of this school believe participants need to reflect on underlying norms and values, which is closely related to the concept of double-loop learning (Argyris 1991). Critical reflection can be used in different ways: a reformulation of a problem when people uncover misunderstandings, or it can lead to the investigation of personal, group, or organizational norms (O'Neil and Marsick 1994). In this school of practice the learning coach creates a climate in which participants feel comfortable in examining their beliefs, practices, and norms. The goals of this school are personal and organizational transformation (Yorks *et al.* 1999). Another goal is creating trans-situational learning (Cell 1984); this is learning how to learn.

The four schools can be depicted as a pyramid, as illustrated in Figure 10.2, in which, in general, each progression upwards requires more systematic and intensive processes of reflection that are facilitated by a learning coach (Yorks *et al.* 1999). Noise (i.e., organizational turmoil) increases as one moves up the pyramid due to the critical nature of reflection and the fact that participants look both at themselves and the organization as a system. This means the learning outcomes at the top of the pyramid are more complex and critical as opposed to the learning outcomes at the bottom.

Problem Statement and Research Question

The problem that this exploratory study addresses is whether or not, and how, the actor-network and critical-pragmatist perspectives can be combined in ways that are both conceptually and empirically valid, and that are practically more powerful as a framework for describing and improving project-based learning.

Increasingly, actor perceptions have been used to explain learning effectiveness (Kwakman 1999; Straka 1999). Marsick and Watkins (1990) additionally point out the significance of critical reflection, noticing "people learned best when they were able to ask questions about why they saw the world as they did, whether their thinking was correct, or how they came to believe a perceived truth that they held sacred". Van Woerkom *et al.* (2003) further concluded that good employees can be characterized as critically reflective employees. In view of the relevance of actor perceptions

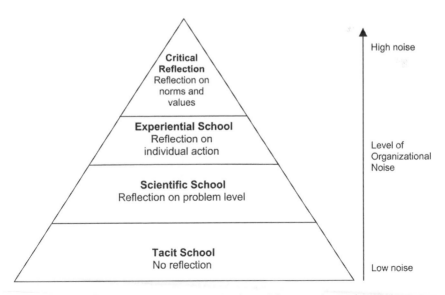

Figure 10.2 The action learning pyramid (adapted from Yorks et al. 1999).

and critical reflection, the question arises as to whether it is possible to combine the actor-network perspective and the critical-pragmatist perspective to both achieve greater conceptual clarification and to offer a more robust framework for understanding project-based learning. Furthermore, research could help guide focused action learning design: can various levels of reflection be achieved best using specific types of learning projects? Finally, if a relationship between the two frameworks is found, actors in organizations would seem more capable of directing the form of reflection they choose to use in their learning programs.

As Poell *et al.* (2005, 2009) have pointed out elsewhere, there are some conceptual commonalties between the two perspectives, in particular: 1) both of them implicitly or explicitly distinguish various stages in learning projects, which can be described using the orientation, learning and optimizing, and continuation phases described earlier; 2) both of them acknowledge explicitly that much learning is informal and characterized by both action and/or reflection; 3) both of them take into account the work climate and organizational supports or barriers that affect both the learning and its continuation beyond the learning project.

Poell *et al.* (2005, 2009) have also identified some important differences between the two perspectives, in particular: 1) the relative strength of the actor-network perspective with respect to task-related individual and instrumental learning that can be applied immediately at work versus the critical-pragmatist perspective's attention to both individual and organizational learning that surfaces and challenges assumptions and practices (except in the tacit school), which may make changes difficult to implement; 2) although power is central to theory underlying the critical-pragmatist perspective, power remains unproblematized when viewed through that lens; and the learning-network perspective focuses so strongly on particular interests that it does not keep in mind the bigger organizational picture (which is not really its major concern in the first place).

The aforementioned commonalties between the two perspectives make it plausible that there may be some kind of relationship between them; due to their differences, however, it is not so clear what exactly that relationship might look like. The two perspectives are based on different classifications; the dominant actor is what differentiates learning projects in the actor-network perspective, whilst in the critical-pragmatist perspective the learning projects differ in their level of reflection. Hence, our research question for this exploratory study is as follows: *What is the relationship between the dominant actor and the level of reflection in organizing work-related learning projects?* Our purpose in the study is to formulate expectations to guide future research in the area of project-based learning. The intended outcome is an idea of whether a more integrated framework of project-based learning based on both perspectives would make sense and, if so, what it could look like.

Linking the Two Perspectives

To our knowledge, there are no previous studies that have looked into our research question (with one exception described following, Marcelis 2006). This implies that we have had to bring together different literatures to shed some initial light on the possible relationships between the two perspectives.

Tillema (1997) showed that people in teams care about making different opinions explicit and see confronting those opinions as a way to get to new ideas. Van Woerkom (2003) further asserts that teams can only be successful if they do what Tillema describes. These observations could be interpreted as pointing to a possible relationship between horizontal-organic learning projects, in which the team is the central actor, and learning projects from the critical-reflection school, where there is reflection on norms and values. On the other hand, Van Woerkom (2003) pointed out a necessary precondition only, the presence of which does not imply automatically that critical reflection will occur. Moreover, teams have also been known to succumb to the dangers of groupthink (Aldag and Fuller 1993), which would make it implausible for critical reflection to occur.

Confessore and Kops (1998) suggested that self-directed learners constantly seek new challenges by setting goals, selecting learning resources, and managing time. They asserted that learners do not necessarily take in information unquestioningly but also assess and evaluate what they hear and reflect upon. This could be understood as pointing to a possible relationship between learning projects from the experiential school, where reflection is on individual action, and liberal-contractual learning projects, where individual learners take the forefront in organizing their learning processes. The fact that self-directed learners are responsible for their own learning processes makes it probable that reflection on individual action does take place in this project type.

Argyris (1991) claimed that highly skilled professionals are often very good at single-loop learning, because they have spent a lot of time acquiring academic skills and using those skills to work on real-world problems. Professionals (who have come to value expertise and success very highly) are often, however, taken aback when they fail, may become defensive, and may not learn as effectively as they otherwise could (Argyris 1991). Perhaps this is an indication of a possible relationship between external-collegiate learning projects, where the professional organization is the dominant actor, and learning projects from the scientific school, where the level of reflection is on the problem level. On the other hand, there are indications that most employees find it very difficult to go beyond single-loop learning (Argyris and Schön 1996); therefore, this may not be true just for higher skilled professionals. And the question could also be raised if even professionals with a high level of professional autonomy are not able to reach the level of critical reflection, who else will?

Marcelis (2006) has so far been the only author to test the relationships between the two theoretical perspectives empirically. She found that management was the central actor in the (one) case she studied. She expected the tacit level of reflection to dominate, because the emphasis is on the task and on problem solving, and therefore, learning would more likely be incidental. This was not what she found, however, perhaps because—as she pointed out—her sample consisted exclusively of high potentials and she only used one company case. Marcelis' expectation was for vertical-regulated learning projects, where management is the central actor, to be related to learning projects from the tacit school, where there is little or no reflection. The reasoning behind this expectation was that learners may be less committed when they do not have a real say in what or how they learn, and therefore they will only reflect incidentally, if at all. There are also arguments to undermine this expectation, however; very often the learning project participants are managers themselves, which confounds the initial expectation, and very often learning facilitators are brought in by higher management to organize at least a certain level of reflection.

Summarizing the literature we have used to shed some initial light on the possible relationships between the two theoretical perspectives, it is very hard to draw any definite conclusions. There seem to be no convincing arguments to state any specific expectations and we will, therefore, let the data speak first and attempt to make sense of the empirical findings using some of the literature we have referred to in the current section.

METHODS

Context of the Research

This research utilized a multiple case study design. The goal of these case studies was to determine the level of reflection engaged in by each central actor in a learning project. The research question was examined on the basis of content analyses of semi-structured interviews from eight work-related learning projects. This method makes it possible to make statements on the basis of a systematic analysis of interviews.

Cases

The interviews have roots in different branches of organizations and often respondents from multiple levels of the organization were interviewed; thus in this research multiple embedded data are used. The four cases selected from the actor-network perspective were chosen because Poell (1998) had established earlier that these four cases best approached the four theoretical ideal types. From the critical-pragmatist perspective, Marsick and Yorks selected four cases that were closest to the four ideal action-learning types.

By selecting cases with the four various dominant actors, the expectation was to test for varied levels of reflection. By choosing four cases with different levels of reflection, the researchers hoped to look at what happens with various dominant actors. This method is known as theoretical replication. Swanborn (1996) indicates this method as useful to examine a theoretical model.

The interviews from the actor-network perspective were conducted in the Netherlands and are taken from Poell (1998). The Dutch data are cross-sectional, and the respondents were interviewed once after the learning project. The interviews of external-collegiate (n = 3) and liberal-contractual learning projects (n = 4) were from a collaboration between two consultancy firms with the learning organization as a theme. The cases of horizontal-organic (n = 5) and vertical-regulated learning programs (n = 5) took place at a hospital where a new technology for helping with heart and lung flaws was introduced. All interviews were held with participants in the learning projects. The interviews from the actor-network perspective were examined to establish the level of reflection that took place.

The interviews from the critical-pragmatist perspective were conducted in organizations headquartered in the United States. The US-based data are longitudinal; respondents have been interviewed before, during, and after the action-learning projects were completed. Most interviews were conducted with participants in the action-learning projects, while some were held with non-participants. The interviews for the critical-reflection case took place at a large-scale multinational chocolate company that aimed for a transformation into a global company with one culture (n = 8). The interviews for the experiential case, where reflection focused on individual action, were conducted in a division of a global pharmaceutical organization (n = 5). The goal of this program was the development of high-potential leaders within the organization. The scientific case interviews were conducted in the Department of Veteran Affairs, where it was expected that reflection took place on the problem level. The intention of this initiative was to reduce aggressive behaviour at the workplace (n = 8). In the tacit case, an insurance company set up an action-learning program intended to help growth leaders think differently about the business (n = 3). The interviews from the critical-pragmatist perspective were examined to establish which actor was dominant. The cases are described in Table 10.1.

Coding Process

Because this was a secondary analysis, it was not possible to simply search for keywords. Therefore, two research assistants (hereafter referred to as 'the researchers') analyzed the interviews independently from each other and extracted relevant quotes in order to identify which actor was dominant or which type of reflection occurred. A possibility taken into account was that either the type of reflection or the dominant actor was not explicitly

Table 10.1 Description of the Cases

Company	Closest ideal type	Country	Goal of the program
Clinical-chemical laboratory of teaching hospital	Horizontal learning project	The Netherlands	Logistic process improvement
Consultancy A	Liberal learning project	The Netherlands	Learn more about the subject 'Learning Organization' and collaborate with another consultancy company
Consultancy B	External learning project	The Netherlands	Learn more about the subject 'Learning Organization' and collaborate with another consultancy company
Academic hospital	Vertical learning project	The Netherlands	Implementation of a new machine in a hospital for heart and lung flaws
Multi-national chocolate company	Critical reflection school	United States	Transform the divided company into a company with one culture
Division of a Glbal pharmaceutical company	Experiential school	United States	Develop a "bench" of qualified leaders within the organization
Department of Veteran Affairs	Scientific school	United States	Reduce aggression in the workplace
Global insurance company	Tacit school	United States	Develope future leaders and enable them to "think differently" about the business

noted. In these cases the researchers agreed to base the analysis on relevant quotes. In case of disagreement, discussion took place to draw conclusions. By identifying the type of reflection that occurred and/or which actor was dominant, the researchers agreed on coding rules.

To determine the level of reflection in the Dutch data, the following rules were used:

- The highest level of reflection within an interview is decisive for typifying the person;
- The risk of "counting quotes" is that highly articulate respondents provide more useful quotes and therefore would dominate in the analysis. To prevent this we identified level of reflection for each respondent separately;
- The level of reflection of the majority of respondents within one learning project is decisive for typifying the case;
- If there is no clear majority, it is called a hybrid form.

To determine which actor is dominant in the US-based data, the researchers searched for answers to the following questions:

- Who took the initiative for the learning project and who was responsible for the design of each learning project?
- In what form (team, individual) did the participants work on the assignments that were an integral part of each learning project?

All relevant quotations and discussions between the two researchers were registered in memos; those memos are available for other researchers to examine. During the research, the research assistants held various interviews with the original researchers (Yorks, Marsick, and Poell), where the final data interpretations were discussed. Since the original researchers were familiar with the data, a valuable discussion about the interpretations of the research assistants was possible. The outcomes of these discussions are also available in the memos.

RESULTS

Dutch Case 1: The Liberal-Contractual Learning Project

In the consultancy firm (B) that provided the context for a liberal learning project, a collaboration was formed with another consultancy firm around the theme of the learning organization. The method of working in this small firm was pragmatic and individualistic. Three out of four respondents from the Consultancy B stated there was hardly any reflection, as these quotations illustrate:

"In the eyes of Consultancy A, the return was very low. We learned, but there was no systematic reflection." (tacit)

"Participants kept asking the learning coach for answers. She kept saying there was no clear cut response. Participants seemed to be annoyed by this, but no one levelled this with the group." (tacit)

Dutch Case 2: The Vertical-Regulated Learning Project

In the academic hospital that served as the context for a vertical learning project, nurses needed to learn about the workings of a new machine to avoid heart and lung failures in newborn babies. Management decided to have the nurses taught by introducing theory in combination with group practice, performing a number of experimental treatments. In these sessions, four of the five participants indicated being able to reflect on their individual actions. This is illustrated by the following quotations:

"The activities in the lab were very helpful. Doing tricks and finding out what was going on." (experiential)

"The experimental sessions in the lab were very important. Doing this refreshes your knowledge." (experiential)

Dutch Case 3: The Horizontal-Organic Learning Project

In the Dutch chemical laboratory of a teaching hospital that represented the context for a horizontal learning project, the goal of the participants was to redesign its logistical system. In this case three out of five respondents provided examples of a level close to critical reflection. Some quotations from the interviews included the following:

"There are other ways to see the department than only from a logistic view." (critical reflection)

"At first the analysts were opposed to the changes, which they perceived as a dictate from management. When it became clear that they could decide on many aspects themselves, they did get involved and came up with some good new ideas." (critical reflection)

Dutch Case 4: The External-Collegiate Learning Project

In the consultancy firm (A) that provided the context for an external learning project, most of the interest was focused on the founding theories and publications around the learning organization (in a collaboration with consultancy firm B). This case saw several forms of reflection, making it into a hybrid: reflection on norms and values, individual action, as well as the problem level. This is illustrated by the following quotations:

> *"As I already had some practical experience, I could place the presented vision in a broader perspective." (experiential)*

> *"I gained some more theoretical insights about the learning organization." (scientific)*

> *"Through reading Senge and discussing with the other participants I realized that the learning organization is actually more than just a hype. And also that, if you want to market it, you will need to come up with a much more commercial term." (critical reflection)*

US-Based Case 1: The Tacit School

In the insurance company that represented the tacit school, an action-learning program was offered to participants on an invitation-only basis. Prior to launching the program, management played an important role in its design. Therefore, management was the dominant actor in this case. One quote from an interview with a manager that is vital for this case is the following:

> *"If I could redo the program, I would go through a more deliberate process of selection of the candidates. There were candidates who participated in this program who either didn't want to be there, who viewed it as something that they were compelled or forced to do, who were not committed to the development and . . . I think that they were distracting and distracted." (vertical)*

US-Based Case 2: The Scientific School

In the department of veteran affairs (VA) that represented the scientific school, an action-learning program was designed to reduce aggression in this workplace. The project team consisted of three academics from three different universities, several HR professionals, and several VA professionals. A learning coach introduced many tools for reflection and learning, including a learning window as a method for surfacing and reflecting on the experiences of the groups. In this case the team was the dominant actor. Consistent with the horizontal actor network, teams were working on practice-focused questions; reflection also took place in groups and on group performance, as these quotations illustrate:

> *"The learning practices have seeped into the common language of the team without being viewed as a formal event." (horizontal)*

"The introduction of the learning piece helped us to be able to talk to another." (horizontal)

US-Based Case 3: The Experiential School

In the pharmaceutical company that represented the experiential school, the CEO and several members of the executive committee were involved in the design and the selection of participants in the action-learning program. Each participant came into the program with a personal learning goal based on feedback through a multi-rater assessment and discussions with their manager and learning coach. The learning coach helped participants reflect on their thinking and actions through the use of questions. This case was a hybrid form of a liberal and vertical learning program. It was liberal because participants focused on individual learning goals and a learning coach helped them reflect on their individual learning process. It was vertical because management designed the project and selected the participants. This is illustrated by the following quotations:

"Each participant came into the program with a personal learning goal developed from a multi-rater assessment and discussions with their manager and learning coach." (liberal)

"[The executive committee HR director] collaborated with the project manager to co-design the program to fit the needs of the organization." (vertical)

US-Based Case 4: The Critical-Reflection School

In the multinational chocolate company that represented the critical-reflection school, the action reflection learning program was recommended by a task force that consisted of a few managers. Twenty employees who were regarded as the future leaders of the organization participated in this program. In teams they worked on strategically important assignments. The chocolate company case was, as shown in Figure 10.4, a hybrid form of a horizontal and a vertical learning project. It was horizontal because the participants worked in teams on their problems; it was vertical because management took the initiative in setting up and running the action reflection learning program. This is illustrated by the following quotations:

"We have these different teams. All of these teams come up with very good ideas and they want to implement these ideas when they're finished. Then they want to form other teams to go out and do things." (horizontal)

"We continue to function as traditional teams in all organizations.
You put five people together and tell them to work." (vertical)

The findings are summarized in Figure 10.3. No clear-cut pattern emerged
from these results in terms of relating dominant actors to levels of reflection
in the various learning projects.

	Critical Reflection school: Reflection on norms and values	Experiential school: Reflection on individual action	Scientific school: Reflection on problem level	Tacit school: Little or no reflection
Horizontal learning project: Team is the dominant actor	OX		O	
Liberal learning project: Individual is the dominant actor		O		X
External learning project: Professional organization is the dominant actor	X	X	X	
Vertical learning project: Management is the dominant actor	O	OX		O

Figure 10.3 Results of the case analysis.
Note: X = Dutch data, look at rows for match with U.S.-based data.
O = U.S. - based data, look at columns for match with Dutch data.

DISCUSSION

The aim of this exploratory study is to examine to what extent the actor-network and critical-pragmatist perspectives can be combined. The research question focuses on two key dimensions that vary in the two perspectives: *What is the relationship between the dominant actor and the form of reflection in organizing work-related learning projects?* Eight learning-project cases from the Netherlands and the United States were analyzed to answer the research question.

Many cases turned out to be hybrid forms rather than resembling their proposed ideal types, which is one reason why it was difficult to see any patterns in the relationships between the two perspectives. There were two relationships for which evidence was found both in the Dutch and the US-based cases (labelled OX in Figure 10.4): first, the relationship between horizontal-organic learning projects and learning projects from the critical-reflection school; and, second, the relationship between vertical-regulated learning projects and learning projects from the tacit school. In both cases (actually in most cases), however, also other relationships emerged as a result of hybrid project types being involved, which makes the two relationships mentioned earlier not quite as clear cut as to warrant any definite statements.

One key observation from the analysis concerns the strong role of management across most critical-pragmatist (US-based) cases. Actually, three of the four US-based cases were leadership-development projects paid for by management, which makes it seem natural that management would be a dominant actor in the design of such corporate oversight programs. This is similar to what Marcelis (2006) found in her single case study of an American company. The very fact that management was found to be a dominant actor in virtually all critical-pragmatist cases (except for the scientific school), however, makes it difficult to find any meaningful relationship with other variables. Perhaps action-learning projects at the shop floor level would show more variation, increasing the chances of finding relationships. The dominance of management also possibly points to cultural differences between American and continental European companies as well as fundamentally different theoretical frameworks on both sides of the Atlantic (Poell *et al.* 2005, 2009). This factor should be taken into account in conducting further research in this area.

The focus in this study was on type of reflection and the dominant actor as primary forces shaping learning processes and outcomes. The inconclusive results from this study lead us to think that other factors may also need to be examined. For example, it is possible that changes in the way in which organizations now organize learning may also be shifting the extent to which control over learning is shared in organizations, such that vertical (management-dominated) forms of organizing learning may often be hybrids with other types. We may need to consider the cognitive capabilities of the learners and their ability to engage in reflection, no matter what type of learning project they are involved in. The culture of the organization may impinge on ways that actors prefer to organize their learning, for example, the extent to which the organization is centralized versus decentralized or collaborative versus silo'd. Barriers and supports to learning, regardless of type, may be organizational variables such as supervisory support; the nature and flow of communication across boundaries; and/or the nature of the reward/incentive system.

Our limited number of cases and respondents, however, made it problematic to introduce many other variables in the analysis, whilst at the same time increasing the chances of finding idiosyncratic results tied solely to the respondents that ended up in our relatively small data set. As a matter of fact, the role of individual agency may also be a crucial factor in shaping work-related learning projects (Poell and Van der Krogt 2009). Further research in this area should look more explicitly, therefore, at the ways in which individual employees organize their own learning processes in various work and organizational contexts.

HRD specialists could benefit from this study by paying attention to the questions of who are the dominant actors and which levels of reflection are intended in organizing work-related learning projects, without necessarily assuming any linear relationships between those two. They should also ask themselves how individual agency plays out in these projects and how they may facilitate this. Further research in this should also look more closely at the roles played by facilitators in learning projects. Most US-based cases employed facilitators, whereas most Dutch cases did not. Their involvement may be related to the questions of who is the dominant actor as well as which level of reflection occurs in a learning project. Whether this holds true empirically is an issue for further investigation.

CONCLUSION

Although building on prior work (Poell *et al.* 2005, 2009), this was an exploratory study. Differences in the kinds of data available in the various cases, cross-cultural differences, and the relatively small Ns are among the limitations of the data. Although the findings remain largely inconclusive in terms of our original research question, we believe they do provide support for embarking on more systematic and extensive research including several other variables. The present study has added to insights into the relationship between the actor-network and critical-pragmatist perspectives; however, more investigation is still needed to support the development of a robust framework encompassing several types of work-related learning projects with empirical support. Confronting the two theoretical perspectives through applying them to mutual data sets can be regarded as an addition to the validity of the theoretical concepts. According to Poell *et al.* (2005, 2009), this way of data interpretation does not very often occur this explicitly. Looking at the data through the lens of the other perspective, however, generates better insights in the strengths and limitations of each perspective (Poell *et al.* 2005, 2009).

KEY LEARNING POINTS

- Both the dominant actor and the intended level of reflection are relevant questions to consider in organizing work-related learning projects.
- No clear-cut patterns emerged from a multiple case study relating these two variables to each other. Findings were therefore inconclusive and other variables will have to be included in further research investigating differences among work-related learning projects.
- Looking at data through the lens of more than one perspective, however, generates better insights in the strengths and limitations of each separate one.

ACKNOWLEDGEMENT

The authors would like to thank Thomas Eussen, MSc, and Sander Veldhoen, MSc, for initially cross-analyzing the data and reporting their findings based on the eight cases.

11 A Call for Learning!

The Challenge of Realizing Learning in Call Centres

Eira Andersson and Berg Anna Jansson

Call centre work is described as one of the most rapidly growing forms of employment in Europe (Kinnie *et al.* 2000; Deery and Kinnie 2004) and the Swedish Institute for Working Life (2003) defines call centres as one of the most expansive businesses in Sweden. Call centres deal with customer relations using sophisticated telephone and computer-based systems (Tengblad *et al.* 2002; Norman 2005). In part, the expansion of this business is due to the development of modern information and communication technology. The connection between call centres and modern technology is one reason why this kind of service work has been discussed as a symbol for 'the work of the future' (Thompson and Warhurst 1998). Information and communication technology enables new industries and occupations associated with high-qualified jobs, yet this new technology enables both positive and negative changes in work organizations. Consequently, the use of technology to centralize and control the work process negatively affects the working environment (Sandgren 2000; Le Grand *et al.* 2002) in terms of time pressure, low variation, and high levels of control (Kinnie *et al.* 2000; Tengblad *et al.* 2002; Norman 2005). In addition, call centres have been criticized for being too Tayloristic and routine, work that includes high levels of control and surveillance developed by management (Fernie and Metcalf 1998; Thompson and Warhurst 1998; Richardson and Belt 2001).

Academic interest in call centres springs largely from the labour process debate. In his book *Labour and Monopoly Capital*, Harry Braverman (1974) presented a Marxist analysis of the labour process for the twentieth century, in which he argued that work is undergoing a process of debasement and deskilling. Braverman argued that there is an intensification of the division of labour, the tendency towards a specialization of tasks and the systematic, rational, and scientific application of managerial methods. The most important catalyst for such a management approach, according to Braverman, was to be found in F. W. Taylor's book *The Principle of Scientific Management*, first published in 1911.

In the labour process debate, call centre work has been described as 'electronic sweatshops', 'satanic mills', and 'twentieth-century panopticons'

(Thompson and Warhurst 1998). Thompson and Warhurst (1998) describe how service work can be governed by Tayloristic principles and call this phenomena 'McDonaldization', characterized by a highly standardized and controlled work process. Although the foregoing discussion is mainly based on international literature, the same problems and conflicts are identified in Swedish call centres. However, Sandgren (2000) argues that compared to other countries, call centres in Sweden are characterized by lower levels of formalization, standardization, and workload, implying lower levels of emotional pressure and control and higher levels of participation and discretion. To sum up, research shows that the principles of management in call centres generate poor and problematic working conditions, such as monotonous work, high demands, low control, limited social support, and few opportunities for participation and learning (Houlihan 2000; Lindgren and Sederblad 2001; Norman 2005).

These expressions of neo-Taylorism can be discussed in contrast to more current theories about management, such as total quality management and business process reengineering, where a core is learning and 'the learning organization'. All of these concepts are based on the idea that the key to corporate survival and success depends on multi-skilled and involved workers and a flexible organization with 'space' for learning (Abrahamsson 2000; Jacobsen and Thorsvik 2002). A 'learning organization' (Senge 1990) encourages employees to develop their competencies, a strategy that looks for ways to encourage personal development to achieve sustainable working conditions (Ekberg and Barajas 2000; Ellström 2002).

The present discussion about learning as an integrated aspect of human activity (e.g., Säljö 2000; Wertsch 1998; Engeström 1987) connects work and learning and defines learning as an integrated process of working life. This perspective focuses on learning as a process where knowledge is created through collaboration between individuals in their daily work activities rather than the traditional form of knowledge transmission. Therefore, participation is seen as an important condition and the link between working life and learning (Ellström 1992, 2002). However, establishing 'learning organizations' is hard because many organizations rely on conventional management strategies that result in organizational inertia and barriers (Lowe 2000). Indeed, the conditions for learning in call centres have been criticized regarding the possibilities for employees to develop new knowledge (McPhail 2000). Houlihan (2000) discusses how systems that establish routines and supervision strategies often lead to few possibilities for the call centre agents to learn from their experiences and use what they learn to improve the organization. This lack of institutionalized learning is a barrier to an organization's ability to identify, build, and maintain the knowledge that ensures success (Houlihan 2000).

In this chapter, we address the question: How can learning strategies be implemented in these companies? To do this, we examine an interactive project to test and develop outlines for learning in a call centre. In addition, we will identify and examine principles of learning in call centres.

TO ORGANIZE FOR LEARNING

The theoretical framework presented next describes the relationship between learning and development, different levels of learning, and how learning processes can be implemented.

The Interrelation between Learning and Development

Learning in organizations can be discussed from different perspectives. In this chapter, we use an interdisciplinary perspective of learning and view learning as a force for improvement and development. As mentioned in the introduction, literature discussing organization and management emphasizes the changeability of the surrounding world and that an organization, in its struggle for survival, must master learning, renewal, and change (Jacobsen and Thorsvik 2002). These concerns mean that an organization must consider and prioritize learning and competence development. To survive a turbulent and changing surrounding world, organizations should develop and implement effective learning strategies and skills, competencies that will enable them to adapt and innovate as new challenges present themselves (Docherty 1996).

Dilschmann (2000) illustrates the dynamic interrelation between learning and change by describing how learning both leads to and demands change. Continuous development and change are achieved when the connection between learning and change is considered and stimulated. Employees must be given opportunities to learn and be given opportunities to use what is learned in their physical and social work environment. Therefore, such possibilities must be part of the daily organization or included in specific change projects. The learning organization comprises both an internal and an external aspect. The way in which the organization adjusts to and answers the surrounding world is part of the external aspect, and the processes 'within' the organization are part of the internal aspect. These processes should be moulded so that they make it possible for the organization to continuously change and adjust to the surrounding world. Therefore, learning processes should not be regarded as something 'extra' and time consuming. Rather, they should be viewed as part of the natural features in work and activities. Traditionally, learning was mainly regarded as a way to correct errors or mistakes; this is also goal of any learning organization, but the learning organization should above all be committed to finding new possibilities, new conditions, new opportunities, and new methods (Dilschmann 2000).

Individual, Collective, and Organizational Learning

The preceding discussion highlights an interesting question about how individual, collective, and organizational learning are connected. By itself, individual learning will not lead to organizational learning, as this assumes that the organization must 'learn' through the experiences and actions of the collective. The competence of individuals and groups constitutes the ground/base for the competence of the organization, and a strengthening of this requires an organizational support that integrates the developing competence with ongoing activities. In this way, individual learning is necessary for collective and organizational learning, but it is not sufficient. Individual learning must be supplemented with collective learning, implying that individuals/employees develop joint knowledge, policies, attitudes, and values. From these 'mental models', one can begin to discuss and solve problems, a process that in turn leads to a development of a joint idea, an idea that both the organization as a whole and the employee as an individual can own. When this notion spreads between employees and different groups at the workplace, a collective learning process has begun. However, individual and collective learning do not automatically lead to organizational learning. Organizational learning is hindered if, for example, information about imperfections in the organization is not disseminated, making it impossible for learning to continue. Organizational learning processes require that organizational routines, practices, individual learning, and collective learning develop ways to share experiences, ideas, notions, and policies. Therefore, it is crucial that organizational structures and systems facilitate the spread and circulation of this knowledge in different places and in different ways (Dilschmann 2000).

Learning as Adjustment or Development

Ellström (1992, 2002) defines two types or levels of learning from an organizational perspective: one focuses on adjustment and one focuses on development. This distinction points out how the relationship between the individual and the context in which learning takes place affects the outcome of the learning process. Traditionally, the debate about learning has dealt with how individuals acquire knowledge, solve problems, and act in situations with given tasks, goals, and other predetermined circumstances. This perspective emphasizes individual adaptation to given conditions without any critical consideration, and Ellström calls this 'adjustmental learning'. In contrast, Ellström's definition of 'developmental learning' focuses on development, creativity, and possibilities for the individual to reflect and improve on the work process. Such learning encourages problem identification and management of complex situations instead of only solving already given problems.

Ellström notes that both kinds of learning are necessary and not mutually exclusive. That is, they complement each other and can ideally be interchanged. Depending on the given organizational conditions, one or the other will dominate: 'Learning with the aim to adapt is needed to handle the routine actions, and thus provide security and stability to both individuals and organizations. Learning with the aim to develop comes from surprises, the need for change, and visions, and builds on the ability to distance, call into question, reinterpretations and critical analysis' (2002: 340). Argyris (1993) emphasizes the same line of argument using the metaphor of single-loop and double-loop learning within an organization. He defines single-loop learning as characterized by correcting a given problem without further consideration about the cause of the problem. Double-loop learning, however, is characterized by a reflective problem-solving strategy and assures that there will be another day in the organization, that is, that the organization will 'survive'.

How can an organization simultaneously create good conditions for both production and learning? Demands of efficiency, flexibility, and rationalization increase simultaneously as demands of integrating learning are emphasized. Ellström (2002) views this as an expression of two different logics of activity and learning, specifically the logic of development and the logic of production. The logic of development builds on developmental learning, thought, reflection, tolerance, and alternative thinking. The logic of production builds on adjustmental learning, effective action, standardization, routines and rules, stability, and safety. This logic is a prerequisite for an effective production and focuses on action, doing, planning, and management. This is a way for the organization to handle events, problems, and requirements, while attaining security and stability. The logic of production, therefore, is very important for an organization and is in many cases dominant in an organization's strategic planning, but it is important that it does not eliminate the logic of development, which is space for reflection and alternative thinking. An organization must strive to create space for both logics and a constant 'variation' between the two. One way to do this is to employ different types of activities for learning.

Implementation of Learning

Different types of methods can be used to integrate developmental learning into an organization. Dilschmann (2000) describes the core of such methods as creating organizational arenas for discussion, that is, space to share experiences and ideas about work. Such arenas stimulate collective interpretation and understanding, which in turn encourages problem solving and organizational development. These processes result in good conditions for developmental learning and can consist of identification and problem solving, different types of mapping or summaries of the workplace, and so forth (Dilschmann 2000). Even more traditional and formal working-life education can offer good opportunities for developmental learning if it is based on the experiences of employees, and the work process is just as important as the content of the education (Ellström 1992). Developmental learning implies processes of reflective problem solving, participation, and creativity. The creation of a 'learning organization', therefore, implies bigger space for developmental processes to reach sustainable conditions for the individual and the organization.

LEARNING ENVIRONMENT IN CALL CENTRES

The interactive project discussed in this chapter was part of a research project, 'A Model for Sustainable Competence Development in Call Centers', carried out between 2003 and 2005. The aim of the research project was to study the conditions for learning, competence development, and organizational development in call centres. The research project was initiated with a pilot study based on nine qualitative interviews with local managers at nine call centres, aiming to describe the working and learning environments in this specific context (see Jansson 2006). Although there were differences among the studied companies, they were all characterized by similar and problematic conditions for learning. When discussing the work environment, managers describe the physical factors in detail and stress the importance of a 'good' working environment as well as the many activities that aim to improve this area. Regarding the physiological and social dimensions of the working environment, the managers repeatedly expressed that variation in work is needed because call centre work is monotonous. The managers who tried to find new ways to bring variation in to the work felt that this was a difficult job. Participation and motivation are pointed out as important factors to experience job satisfaction, but was defined as a problematic area in this context. The ongoing learning activities in the nine call centres can be described as 'adjustmental', focusing mainly on production and efficiency. What the managers expressed as 'learning' was in fact a kind of updating of competence related to the daily work that aimed at correction and safe production.

The pilot study also showed that systems for information and communication, both decisive for implementation of learning and a 'learning organization', were top-down, leaving little space for discussion and reflection. The subject of information was mainly related to the companies' economic result or information about new customers. The managers also described how the production to a certain level 'controls' information and communication, illustrated by the fact that meetings are cancelled during intensive periods. Furthermore, the organizations are characterized by structures for control and measures of employee performance, implying that the individual performs his/her tasks according to the routine and standard defined by management. Although the managers stressed that they do not strive to 'control' or 'chase' the agent, these systems potentially delimit organizational learning as they encourage the agent to carry out the work tasks in strict order following current rules/routines. This implies delimited freedom of action and a risk that the agent does not reflect or pay attention to previously experienced problems or that they reflect but do not share what they learned.

In conclusion, when analyzing the results from the perspective of organizational conditions that encourage learning and development, the pilot study shows the following: To create the necessary conditions for development and learning, these companies should provide more space for reflection and discussion about working tasks and working conditions, strategies that will increase and improve processes that encourage sharing ideas and information, processes that may also improve job satisfaction.

AN INTERACTIVE APPROACH

Previous research (see, e.g., Houlihan 2000; Belt *et al.* 2002) and the findings from the pilot study describe learning in call centres as focusing mainly on training and updating of daily tasks and can be discussed in terms of adjustmental learning. Organizational learning aiming towards development, on the other hand, does not seem to be fully implemented in these organizations. With this as a departure, we wanted to develop and actually test outlines for developmental learning in a call centre context. To do this, such processes had to be 'created' for research purposes in a given company. Consequently, a local project focusing on learning was formulated in collaboration with one call centre. The interactive project intended to initiate learning processes, introduce new tools, and support positive ongoing learning activities in this specific company. Then as the project progressed, we evaluated the process and the result to make concluding remarks on the conditions and identify possible ways to improve learning in this environment.

The company (named ProPhone in this chapter) was one of the companies in the pilot study and was chosen because it was one of Sweden's largest and most well-established call centres. Receiving 20,000 calls a day from different clients, ProPhone's more than 150 employees offers answering services—'switchboard at a distance' services. Due to its previous activities with respect to working environment and competence development, ProPhone can be described as a 'good example' in this line of business. The interactive project was based on the idea that personnel at ProPhone, especially the call centre agents, took an active part in a project concerning organizational development with guidance of a researcher. The activities were based on theories about implementing learning described previously, highlighting active participation, interaction with others, time for reflection, and problem solving.

The choice of an interactive research approach was based on the idea of knowledge exchange between academia and society. Interactive research is not a distinct method or theory, but more a perspective on how to conduct research. However, an action component is central and the research should support a normative change (in problem solving or developmental work and so forth), while at the same time produce new knowledge (Nielsen and Svensson 2006). An interactive approach also focuses on the usefulness for the parties involved, often practitioners from a company, and stresses participation and the opportunity to influence the research process. The truth about the organization is established in dialogue between practitioners and researchers; that is, it is not based only in theory (Gustavsen 1990; Toulmin and Gustavsen 1996; Räftegård 1998). Interactive research is sometimes criticized for a lack of general theory and too much focus on a specific context. To reach a sustainable theory, Nielsen and Svensson (2006) argue that an understanding of the adapted situation can be a starting point, but needs to be combined with an explained approach that shows the fundamental mechanisms and relationships at work. In an attempt to draw conclusions from the interactive project, we combine the results from the project with a more general description and explanation from the pilot study and previous research.

A PROJECT FOCUSING ON LEARNING IN CALL CENTRES

Below is a summary of the interactive project at ProPhone presented in terms of groundwork, the project management tool, and realization (see Andersson 2005). This is followed by an evaluation of the learning process.

Groundwork

The collaboration with the call centre started with an open dialogue between the research team and the management group at ProPhone. The executives described a problematic working situation for the call centre agents, such as static seating positions or lack of variation in the monotonous routines while answering the phone. Consequently, they had invested in the physical working environment: they renovated the premises, purchased adjustable chairs/desks, and promoted headsets. Health and exercise were also emphasized in the working environment policy. However, when discussing learning activities and development for the personnel, the executives repeatedly stated the limitations in the hectic production: 'A call center agent must be constantly aware to keep important customers. Even though some employees share their time as operators with administrative work in the reception, they are still in some way tied to the telephone', said one senior manager.

Initially, the executives saw few possibilities to naturally integrate learning in the daily activities at the call centre. An important mission for the researchers was to explain how processes of learning could contribute to the organization, especially in terms of positive effects for the personnel, but also to support strategic company development. With this as a departure, attention was drawn to one escalating problem at ProPhone, namely conflicts between departments. The executives thought that 'lack of understanding' about the work in or between departments could be the cause of these conflicts, especially among the isolated call centre agents. They stressed a need for a comprehensive approach in the company and an overall view of important work processes and economic key factors. Based on this problem, the outlines for the interactive project were put together. The project was called *'Projekt Helhetssyn'*, 'A Comprehensive Approach', dealing with organizational improvements through processes of developmental learning for the personnel.

Next, the company assembled a project group from different divisions. Finally, the group consisted of nine participants: three call centre agents, two operating managers, and employees from the departments of administration, economics, technology, and customer service. At ProPhone, as expected, most call centre agents were women and most of the technology support staff and mangers were men. The participants, excluding the two operating managers, mostly dealt with routine tasks and had no or little activities in their daily work that can be described as developmental learning. The call centre agents and the employees from customer service were usually busy all day answering the telephone and had little interaction with others. The call centre agents, in particular, had few opportunities to get a comprehensive view of the company and to influence their own work situation. In general, the participants in the upcoming project were not used to teamwork to solve complex problems or deal with overall company improvements. Only one of the operating managers had some experience with project work.

Project Management Tool

Before the interactive project took off, a project management tool was formulated by the researcher to support the activities in the project. The tool was based on general knowledge for project management, inspired by a concept used in the manufacturing industry to support developmental work and change management (Ranhagen 1995). The tool was based on six significant steps to simplify the complex tasks in project management and to give a hint in what order to deal with upcoming problems. Each step consisted of systematic activities that were designed to push the process forward. Methods and exercises were defined, but the interactive project was also designed to develop and modify the project management tool as the work progressed and circumstances in the organization changed. Following is a short summary of the steps in the project management tool.

1. *Projecting.* In this step, the participants learned about each other and defined common grounds, aims, and goals for the project. The work in the project is organized and areas of responsibility are defined.
2. *The present situation.* This step included collecting facts about the organization and analyzing the given situation. Problem areas and examples of ways to address these areas were identified.
3. *Demands.* This step formulated specific demands: What will the organization achieve and how can the project contribute? The demands provide a concrete form to the overarching goals in the first step of projecting.
4. *Solutions.* This step implies searching for solutions in a creative and open environment. The solutions are then valued according to the given demands.
5. *Develop solutions.* In this step, the solutions were defined and modified for implementation in the organization.
6. *Implementation and evaluation.* The new solutions were implemented in the organization and then, after a short while, evaluated to find out if they had given the expected effect.

Realization

The interactive project was carried out between September 2004 and May 2005, including ten half-day workshops at ProPhone. The researcher guided the project group during the workshops and in between the project group worked on their own. The activities in the project were also supported with the project management tool, pushing the process forward, step by step. Most of the project members participated in every project meeting and seemed excited to work with broader issues in the company, but one of the operating managers had difficulties making the meetings. In the beginning, the group was quite insecure and dependent on the guidance of the researcher. However, they slowly became more independent and found their own ways to solve problems and work as a team. The project management tool helped to organize the activities at first, but became redundant by the end of the project.

To start, the project group defined their ambition and goal with the project using the executive's objectives as a point of departure. They agreed on the importance of consciousness and knowledge about the company and a comprehensive approach in the daily routines. They discussed that a lack of communication and poor knowledge about their colleagues' work often resulted in misunderstandings and conflicts. The project group decided to work especially with improving communication and to focus on upgrading the information system between departments and between different occupational groups in the company. A set of demands was formulated:

- Better knowledge of the most important processes, activities, and routines to gain a comprehensive view of the company.
- Better communication and collaboration between different departments to counter conflicts and misunderstandings.
- Better routines for information, both inside and outside the given departments.
- Better explanation of economical key factors to understand common goals and follow-up reports.

The project group decided to do an overarching 'mapping study' of all departments to gain knowledge about the work, routines, and different kinds of difficulties. The mapping study was conducted by observing the work routines in all departments and interviewing key persons from every occupational group. The project group documented all their findings and gathered the new information in joint files; for instance, they compiled a list of problem areas concerning a lack of information. The final step was to come up with new solutions to the existing problems or to highlight the importance of forgotten routines. All suggestions for organizational improvements were gathered in a document called 'Plan of Action'.

The outcome of the project, such as organizational improvements, can be summarized in three main results. First, the project updated the 'schematic view of the organization' to describe clearly the activities of every department and all employees. Second, the project provided a summary of problem areas in each department concerning communication and routines for information sharing. A 'Plan of Action' was assembled that included the applicable suggestions for improvement, such as new arenas and routines for information sharing, new uses of the internal Web site, and a checklist for newcomers. Third, in the 'Plan of Action' the project group suggested ways to improve economic follow-up reports. The results of the project were officially communicated to all personnel at ProPhone during a large company gathering. The new organizational chart and the 'Plan of Action' were also communicated through the company's internal Web site.

Evaluation

At the end of the interactive project, the participants and managers involved had the opportunity to express their opinions about the outcome. Both managers and members of the project group believed the project was successful. The success was described both in terms of organizational improvements and new knowledge for the employees. One executive commented on the results: 'I think that we have come a long way in this project. Some of the results are already implemented and all solutions and recommendations are realizable. I am very satisfied with the outcome'. The members of the project group expressed that they, due to the project, had the opportunity to work with new and 'broader' tasks that lead to new experiences and learning. One call centre agent expressed her feelings this way: 'Investigating the working routines in all departments was really fun and instructive for me; solving problems was like riding a bike in the end'. Another experience was that the project had encouraged new arenas for meetings and relations as personnel from different departments and levels of the organization worked together towards a common goal. One member in the group put it this way: 'One outcome of the project was a closer fellowship among the employees and a possibility to participate in the overarching processes in the company'. One operating manager explained her new awareness of the positive effects of learning: 'The project was a reminder to me how important it is for all people to participate in learning activities to grow as a person. There are individuals in this group who matured enormously, thanks to the work in the project. New skills and better self-confidence open up for personal advancement in the company'. Indeed, one of the call centre agents was promoted because of her personal development and dedicated work in the project.

Nine months after closure of the project, six follow-up interviews were carried out. Some of the participants in the project expressed a disappointment over the fact that the project had not been discussed much since the end, and though numerous improvements were implemented, several ideas and proposals formulated during the project have crumbled for the production. One of the participants described how other more urgent and prioritized tasks tend to take over. However, some of the call centre agents expressed that they still use new knowledge and experiences derived from their project work in their daily work.

REALIZING LEARNING IN CALL CENTRES

The results of the interactive project, that is, the attempt to 'create' learning, illustrate that it is possible to implement learning activities in a call centre environment. When analyzing the results of the project using Ellström's (1992, 2002) description of the characteristics of 'developmental' learning and Dilschmann's (2000) description of the individual, collective, and organizational learning and how this type of learning can be implemented, the following emerges. The project can be described as successful in many ways, especially in terms of individual learning for the project members. The members of the group had little or no experience in project work, but gradually progressed due to their work in the project. The activities gave them possibilities to plan, problem solving, dialogue, and reflection, all skills that are considered important for developmental learning.

Additionally, the project illustrated how learning processes among employees can be beneficial for the organization in terms of a safe and efficient production. The outcome of the project was new knowledge about work operations in different departments, new routines for information sharing, and new understanding of key economic factors. The participants described how the project resulted in an improved knowledge about 'each other' (e.g., different departments and their respective work tasks). Interestingly, during the evaluation (nine months after the closure of the project), this new knowledge still lived on and was seen as a way to improve work.

Furthermore, the project illustrated how learning activities can function as a counter towards the negative aspects of the call centre environment, illustrated in both the pilot study and previous research, for example, by providing opportunities for variation and participation. The project provided an opportunity to escape the limiting logic of the production 'to escape the telephone', especially for the call centre agents. Finally, the interest by the executives at ProPhone to take part in the research project, their investment of both time and resources, illustrates a desire and need to improve the call centre agent's daily work situation. That is, the executives understood that the organization lacked the tools and knowledge to start up such processes of learning.

At the same time, the interactive project and the learning processes previously described mostly affected the members of the project group and were conducted during a limited period. The project, however, seem to have resulted mostly in learning on a individual level or in the small collective of the project group, which can be explained by the fact that the activities in the project were detached from the daily production. Therefore, positive effects in terms of learning on a more organizational level are negligible. The evaluation of the project also indicates that management had not developed or fully used the experiences from the project; that is, some of the 'positive' processes that took place were not maintained and supported. This lack of institutional follow-up prevented the complete success, a goal that included integrating what was learned into the organizational life at ProPhone. Without effort to maintain and provide good conditions for learning, these effects can be described as temporary and not fully implemented. Therefore, determination to support positive processes of learning and development can be defined as an important requirement for building more sustainable organizations that improve the companies and their employees.

On the other hand, the heterogeneous composition of the project group challenged the existing organizational structure and hierarchies. In many ways, this implied a more open working climate and the members gained respect for their individual competencies. This also implies that the existing hierarchy and power structures at times became more visible. For example, managers sometimes neglected project meetings. In similar ways, the gender segregation at ProPhone became visible as persistent conflicts between men and women dominated departments and were difficult to solve. These findings can be discussed in terms of difficulties in implementing organizational learning and that the production logic, discussed earlier, can be hard to break. These difficulties confirm previous research and the description of the call centre context as characterized by problematic conditions for learning.

1. *A detached project.* The environment in call centres is characterized by a 'hectic' production that ties the agent to routine work tasks, providing little space for learning. Working with overriding issues outside the daily routines, in the form of a detached project, creates possibilities to escape the limiting logic of production. This offers variation, compared to monotonous working tasks, and new opportunities to influence one's own work situation as well as the organization's comprehensive strategies and goals.
2. *Active participation.* Participation is described as an 'immature' process in call centres, yet this is an important condition for developmental learning. The result of the interactive project shows that active participation, that is, to take an active part in all phases within a development process (planning, problem solving, and realization), is both achievable and rewarding. However, one important condition is that the participants should be given actual possibilities to gain a relevant understanding of the issues and should be given enough time to take part in solving these issues.
3. *Interaction.* The daily work in call centres offers little space for dialogue and cooperation between members in the organization. Providing space for interaction, such as meetings, discussions, and relationships, both horizontally and vertically, challenges present organizational boundaries and hierarchies. Cooperation between different competences also implies an understanding of the organization as a whole, motivating collective interpretation and understanding of work.
4. *Usefulness.* Finally, usefulness, to point out how learning processes assure practical results, is important to motivate management and employees. To start from the needs, concerns, and problems of both organization and employees assures that learning processes result in a win-win situation, supporting further development work.

To sum up, the principles (a detached project, active participation, interaction, and usefulness) can be used as a point of departure to realize developmental learning in call centres. Learning processes counteract the problematic work situation in these companies and provide space for development and improvement, and can be described as both a tool and a decisive condition for more sustainable organizations.

KEY LEARNING POINTS

- Call centres are characterized by a problematic work situation, routine tasks, and limited ways to influence one's work situation.
- Learning processes can counter a problematic work situation by encouraging active participation and interaction.

12 Work-Based Learning Programmes in English Universities
Government Policy and Organizational Practice

Paul Smith and David Preece

The chapter compares and contrasts government policy towards work-based (especially postgraduate) learning in higher education with policies and practices at the local, that is, university, level. It is informed by human capital theory, but also the recognition that relevant actors shape and configure practice within wider outer- and inner-organizational contexts, subject to a range of constraints and opportunities. Such a perspective would expect to find both some variation in practice and in views about practice between actors and across organizations in the same broad institutional (that is, university) context. We were particularly interested in the extent to which policy gets translated into practice, and, if this happens only partially (or not at all), what the key inhibitors are at the university level.

The first main section of the chapter outlines and discusses human capital theory in relation to work-based learning (WBL) programmes in an attempt to tease out key aspects of the underlying philosophy informing UK government policy towards such programmes. We then move on to provide some definitions of and clarify what is understood by WBL in the higher education (HE) context. The third section examines governmental policy and strategy relating to work-based learning programmes in HE in England, informed by a review of the main policy documents, interviews with government policy advisors, and the relevant literature. There follows a brief outline of our research methodology and the three universities which formed our case studies. They were selected because they had a national reputation for running WBL programmes, and in particular bespoke partnership programmes designed by the university, employer, and student. In a Higher Education Funding Council for England (HEFCE) report (HEFCE 2006a) and in a report of a study on workplace learning in the northeast of England (HEFCE 2006b), such programmes are called 'Type D', 'learner in the workplace' programmes, where the focus is upon the learner's/student's work role and links to HE. Documentary materials, including policy and strategy statements, were collected from the universities and interviews were conducted with a range of people engaged in postgraduate WBL programmes. The penultimate section presents and discusses our research findings under the two broad headings of 'Benefits of WBL Programmes' and 'Challenges and Contexts for WBL Programmes'. The chapter finishes with a concluding discussion.

HUMAN CAPITAL THEORY AND HIGHER EDUCATION

> Instrumental rationality in its capitalist form relegates everything to its use-value for capital itself, and as capitalism is the dominant ideology in contemporary society it has colonised not only our language but our thinking.
>
> (Jarvis 2007: 121)

As Garrick has noted, human capital theory involves 'thinking in terms of human value (and performance) as a return on investment in a cost-to-benefit ratio . . . a way of viewing the preparation of workers to meet the labour requirements of a market economy.' (1999: 217). In the formal education context, it sees a correlation between quantities of education and training, economic development and competitiveness; however, providing evidence for causal relationships is extremely difficult. King (2004) claims it is not easy to prove conclusively that investment in education is a cause of economic development, but argues rather that it is empirically plausible that increased investment on higher education follows economic growth rather than causes it. It can be argued that the development of a flexible workforce has become essential to organizations which 'have to keep adapting to the pressures that global capitalism exercises' (Jarvis 2007: 115) and universities are no exception as they too attempt to come to terms with global and national developments. A human capital vision of higher education has come to dominate government policy in the UK, as will be seen when we review recent HEFCE strategies.

A human capital orientation towards higher education is now a global phenomenon, with, according to Scott (1998), a possible future being a few 'world universities' and networks of existing universities that trade in the global marketplace. Global policymaking organizations are embracing this vision of higher education:

> This thrust towards a human capital vision of higher education was based on the assumption that good though higher education was, its students were inadequately prepared for the workplace and were unable to put into practice what they had learnt at university . . . the same thrust had also come from global policymaking bodies such as the OECD [Organisation for Economic Co-operation and Development], which recognized the need for their membership states to invest in human capital if they were to take advantage of the knowledge-based economies which were beginning to emerge in the 1980s (Symes 2001: 205).

Universities face some significant challenges if they are to meet this agenda, as King (2004: 131) has pointed out: 'Doubts have continued about the ability of the universities to reform their curricula and research orientations to more explicitly facilitate economic growth and to deliver what employers want and, in part at least, this helps to explain the growth of private and corporate universities in the 1990s.'

The main thrust of UK government policy towards HE since the 1980s has been to emphasize the economic importance of education, and how universities should and can work with industry and a market model of educational planning. Williamson and Coffield (1997) argue that this has meant that universities have lost autonomy and are compelled to compete in a marketplace, potentially undermining their core ethos.

The literature points to a number of consequences resulting from the drive for vocational education in a mass higher education system, such as the development of a new vocabulary for higher educational curricula. Terms such as 'transferable skills', 'enterprise', 'outcomes', 'capability', and 'work-based learning' have emerged (Barnett 1997), along with an ideology that represents the perspectives of corporate capital (Barnett 1994).

At the same time, WBL programmes in higher education have emerged to some extent from a demand by students and employers for this type of programme, and we have seen the emergence of more vocationally based provision within many universities and a wider policy agenda, whereby universities have been encouraged by government to forge alliances with business in the name of economic reform. Symes (2001) argues that this has meant that the instrumental has now become more favoured than the liberal in universities, and that the changes have been profound:

> The recent changes to higher education, arguably as dramatic as any that have occurred in the whole history of the university, have led to a repositioning of higher education in society. Much of this repositioning has been policy driven, with governments in the Western world, particularly in the UK and Australia, demanding that higher education modernize itself and align itself to the economic needs of the contemporary nation state. Roderick West in Australia . . . and Lord Dearing in the UK produced reports on higher education that articulated the need for more work-oriented universities.
>
> (Symes 2001: 205)

The shift of many universities towards becoming more 'business/work-oriented' has meant that the differentiation between the university and the workplace in terms of (formal) learning has become increasingly narrow.

DEFINING WORK-BASED LEARNING IN HIGHER EDUCATION

Major (2002) argues that WBL is a planned programme of accredited learning in a higher education context, which can include undergraduate placements, distance learning programmes, and sandwich courses. Sandwich degree courses are usually courses which include an extra year of work experience (or language training) 'sandwiched' between two or three years of concentrated study. During the extra year the student usually goes on work experience with an employer, organization, or department in their subject field.

Boud *et al.* (2001: 4) observe the term 'being used to describe a class of university programmes that bring together universities and work organizations to create new learning opportunities in workplaces'. They see WBL programmes as sharing the following six features: a partnership between an external organization and an educational institution is specifically established to foster learning; learners involved are employees of, or are in some contractual relationship with, an external organization; the programme derives from the needs of the workplace and the learner rather than being controlled by the disciplinary curriculum because work is the curriculum; the start of the programme and educational level is established after learners have engaged in a process of recognition of competencies and identification of learning needs rather than relying on educational qualifications; learning projects are undertaken in the workplace; and the educational institution assesses the learning outcomes of the negotiated programmes with reference to a framework of standards and levels which are transdisciplinary. Thus, for 'WBL degrees, work is quite literally the foundation of the curriculum . . . the activity from which learning arises and by which learning is defined' (Boud and Symes 2000: 21).

Thus WBL creates significant challenges for HE institutions as it offers an alternative vision to the traditional approaches to teaching and learning. As Boud and Solomon (2001) have noted:

> Work-based Learning as a pedagogical site challenges most of our conventional assumptions about teaching, learning, knowledge and curriculum. It is a disturbing practice—one that disturbs our understandings about our academic identity and its location. Indeed, work-based learning in higher education institutions disturbs most of the conventional binaries that have framed our academic work, including: organizational learning and university learning; performance outcomes and learning outcomes; organizational discourses and academic discourses; theory and practice; and disciplinary knowledge and workplace knowledge.
>
> (Boud and Solomon 2001: 225)

The research project reported upon here focused on one particular form of WBL, that which places the workplace at the centre of the individual's programme of study; the WBL programmes were bespoke partnership programmes negotiated between the university, employer, and student:

> The aspect that distinguishes WBL from other processes of learning is the part that negotiation between individual, employer and higher education institution plays: negotiation between these three stakeholders in identifying achievable learning outcomes which are meaningful and challenging to the individual, are relevant to the employer and have

academic credibility; establishing, through negotiation, appropriate methods of and criteria for, assessment acceptable to all parties; establishing and maintaining, through negotiation, a supportive learning environment (based primarily in the workplace).

(Brennan and Little 1996: 7)

Let us now move on to outline and review the HE policy framework for England in the light of the preceding discussion of human capital theory and conceptualization of work-based learning.

THE NATIONAL POLICY FRAMEWORK

In order to provide an overview of the English national policy framework for work-based learning programmes it is necessary to explore two key policy documents on higher education in England: the white paper 'The Future of Higher Education' (DfES 2003) and the 'HEFCE Strategic Plan 2003–08'(HEFCE 2003). The strategy for higher education in England (DfES 2003) made public a number of key developments relating to the future of higher education (HE) which were intended to shape the growing relationship between business and HE institutions and, in particular, the future provision of WBL in HE. The following extract from the white paper highlights the importance that was attached to forging relations between higher education and business:

> Higher education in the UK generates over £34 billion for our economy and supports more than half a million jobs. But less than one in five businesses taps into universities' skills and knowledge. Universities and colleges can play a bigger role in creating jobs and prosperity.
>
> (DfES 2003: 6)

The white paper identified a number of priorities, including building stronger links between universities and business through 'third stream funding', and the rapid expansion of the number of foundation degrees on offer, which in turn would increase the number of employer and university partnerships.

The HEFCE Strategic Plan (HEFCE 2003) also reflected the government's view on HE and the economy in stressing the importance of human capital and meeting the needs of employers:

> Human capital, and the generation and application of new knowledge, are as important at the start of the 21st century as the fixed capital or machine power of the industrial revolution. In the modern global economy, employers increasingly look to universities and colleges to deliver the well-educated workforce they need to stay competitive. Employers want the HE system to produce rounded, readily employable graduates.
>
> (HEFCE 2003: 5)

The strategic plan has four core strategic aims: widening participation and fair access; enhancing excellence in learning and teaching; enhancing excellence in research; and enhancing the contribution of higher education to the economy and society. The aim of 'enhancing the contribution of HE to the economy and society' reflects the importance attached to the so-called 'knowledge economy' and the role that HE is expected to play in developing it.

The Higher Education Innovation Fund (HEIF) is a third stream of funding alongside those for teaching and research. It is designed to provide incentives for the less research-intensive universities to forge a closer working relationship with business at a local and regional level. The government's strategy for HE (DfES 2003) emphasizes the importance of knowledge and skill transfer between business and higher education and the boost that this can give the regional economies.

The development of foundation degrees is a key priority within the white paper, as the government wants to make them the main work-focussed qualification in higher education. The drive for a two-year sub-degree qualification negotiated and designed in conjunction with employers comes from an anticipated skill shortage at the 'associate professional' and 'higher technician' levels. The government hopes that its provision of financial incentives for universities and colleges to develop vocational programmes such as foundation degrees would act as a stimuli to change in employer's traditional patterns of demand.

The emphasis, then, on forming partnerships between HE and companies is expressive of the government's drive to grow the knowledge-based economy, which, it argues, is dependent on the effective sharing of knowledge between business and higher education and leads to improvements in economic competitiveness and quality of life. The HEFCE strategy recognizes that one of the key risks of this approach is that universities do not respond effectively by developing approaches which respond sufficiently to the needs of business and the community.

Given, then, this government policy framework for HE, we wanted to know whether, and if so the extent, to which it was being translated into practice at the 'local' (that is, university) level, with respect to collaborative work-based learning programmes, and also how WBL programmes were being received by the relevant local actors. Before we report our findings it is necessary to outline the research methodology we adopted.

RESEARCH METHODOLOGY

A qualitative research methodology was employed, deploying semi-structured interviews with national senior policy advisors and documentary analysis of policy papers, along with case studies based upon three English universities which were operating postgraduate WBL programmes. The national-level policy research elaborated the context of and objectives for the development of WBL programmes within HE, and the interviewees were two policy advisors at the Higher Education Funding Council for England (HEFCE), one policy advisor at the Department for Education and Skills (DfES), and the director of the National Centre for Work-based Learning Partnerships (NCWBLP) based at Middlesex University.

The 'stratified purposeful sampling' strategy (Patton 1990) involved selecting a particular sector (i.e., universities) and purposefully choosing cases in each. In the case of two of the universities, interviewees were drawn from postgraduate WBL programmes based within the business school, whilst the interviewees from the third university were from the School of Lifelong Learning and Education, which has a centre specializing in WBL programmes. The rationale for choosing these three cases was that a wide range of innovative work-based learning programmes were available to choose from, and the logistics of conducting field research at a number of geographical locations with one researcher within a relatively tight time frame necessitated research in one country. The academics selected for interview at each university were a senior manager within the school/ university with responsibility for WBL; the dean or deputy dean or their equivalent within each school; the WBL programme leader; and a WBL academic with teaching and management responsibilities related to WBL programmes. A total of 11 interviews were undertaken for the second stage with one senior academic at the School of Lifelong Learning and Education interviewed in relation to two roles that she carried out. Analysis of the data was undertaken on a within-case (comparing the findings from the relevant actors involved in each university's postgraduate WBL programmes) and across-case basis, with the latter facilitating the analysis of the influence of different 'micro' contexts, histories, and programmes.

The Case Study Universities

University A

University A is a post-1992 university in the north of England and has a history of involvement in widening access initiatives. WBL programmes are translated into learning across the university via a 'negotiated learning' framework, which is an accredited framework allowing individuals to study a tailored programme drawing on core modules from the Centre for Lifelong Learning and from across the university and in-company programmes. This framework was adopted in order to follow the widening participation agenda, which had proved to be successful in terms of student recruitment. Students on WBL programmes typically enter on the basis of their work experience, rather than more traditional qualifications such as A-levels.

Historically, the business school had been involved in a number of programmes with a strong WBL element, such as a master's in management practice (MMP), certificate in management, and NVQ level 4/5 in management. The MMP is indicative of the type of WBL programmes which had been offered, and, along with the MBA (public management) programme which superseded it, was the focus of our empirical research at university A. The WBL programmes have proved particularly attractive to supervisors and middle managers, whose entry qualifications are usually management or other professional programme certificates, rather than a first degree. Many of the participants have a number of years of management experience and use the Accreditation of Prior Learning (APEL) process to help them enter directly onto a later stage of the programme. The MMP programme had some distinctive features, as outlined in the course document:

> The key differences between this model and the traditional approach to learning is that the organisation or individual takes greater responsibility for identifying learning and assessment opportunities; the learning takes place at a time, location and speed that is different from traditional courses; and there is more flexibility available to design specific learning outcomes that reflect the overall outcomes appropriate to the programme.

A number of students on the MMP programme came from the local authority, and received named awards at the postgraduate certificate and postgraduate diploma levels. The award was replaced by the MBA (public management) in 2001—a qualification designed for public sector staff, but with a stronger emphasis on taught modules. This was developed following feedback from the local authority to the effect that they wanted a modular programme which incorporated recent changes such as the 'modernization agenda' within local government.

University B

University B is another post-1992 university, based in the southeast of England. The focus of the programmes is on pedagogies that centre on the creativity and reflexivity of individuals within a work-based context with WBL as a field of study. The corporate plan for 2004–08 places a strong emphasis on the expansion of WBL, as illustrated in the following extract:

> While we shall maintain our commitment to widening participation and to serving the higher education needs of our local communities, we shall build on our emerging strengths by expanding substantially places for postgraduate, international and work-based students in London and, increasingly, around the world.

The WBL programmes offered by the centre at university B are built around three stages: learning review and planning, project design, and project implementation. The first stage involves an evaluation of prior learning. This is followed by the design of a personal WBL programme in negotiation with the student's employer and the university, and leads to an individual learning agreement containing the proposed study plan; this second stage centres around the design of a proposal for a real-life work-based project. The third stage involves the implementation of the project in the workplace.

This partnership approach to WBL is usually triggered by university accreditation activity, which involves an exploration of the forms of learning to be found in the organization, and how they might be systematically quantified and used within the programme. The aim here is to explore how an existing valuation framework can be used to build a customized programme, rather than forcing change on the employer.

The study focused on the public sector MA programme, where the majority of participants are middle managers or above, and most of them have previously studied for academic qualifications such as a management certificate or first degree, and have relevant prior learning.

University C

University C is another ex-polytechnic, based in the south of England, and has a long history of providing WBL programmes. The university has a cross-school 'Partnership Programme', which is offered on a part-time basis to individuals in employment, and was described by the business school's business development director as 'design your own degree'. Following an accreditation of prior learning assessment, the programme is developed as a partnership between the learner, the employer, and the university. Typically, the programme leads to an undergraduate or postgraduate degree and learning is largely geared to the employer's espoused needs. The university's strategic plan for 2004–2008 places emphasis on it being

> the first choice provider of skills development, enterprise, innovation, knowledge transfer and support for private, public and voluntary sector organizations of all sizes in our region and more widely in appropriate sectors of the economy.

Our case study research was based in the business school, and the focus of the research was the MSc Contracts Management, which was said to be 'typical' of the school's corporate WBL programme. The programme is targeted at junior and middle managers. The participating company owns the programme for three years, when it reverts back to the university, which can then develop it as it wishes. The MSc Contracts Management is an example of the business school's fast-track 'Integrated Flexible Masters Programme', involving an 'employee learning contract', that is, a formalized agreement between the employee, the university, and company mentor setting out the programme plan. The business school's programmes, such as those previously outlined, are primarily designed for corporate clients, whereas the university-wide Partnership Programme is aimed at individuals in employment.

The learning process on WBL programmes is managed via a learning contract with each student, which focuses upon work-based assignments. The contract is the vehicle for managing the quality of the learning process, and is agreed between the three parties involved: the student, their workplace mentor, and the course tutor. The contract, according to the associate dean at the school,

> is a measurable tool, which can be used to see whether the programme is meeting the needs of the student. The learning contract is viewed as a living document because things can change rapidly and the contract needs to be dynamic so it can meet changed priorities at work.

The learning contract acts, then, as a tracking document for the whole WBL process.

THE CASE STUDY FINDINGS

Involvement in WBL programmes was generally found to be associated with a positive view of them, whilst 'distance' seemed to breed contempt or indifference. Those members of university staff who had a direct involvement in postgraduate WBL programmes generally talked about them in positive terms, whilst in the wider academic community there was a lack of awareness and/or interest in them and, in some cases, outright resistance. The resistance took three main forms: the perception that WBL was taking students from other disciplines; the view that WBL involved a 'watering down' of intellect and standards; and an unwillingness to get involved in WBL programmes because of a lack of incentives. A form of 'self-selection' process might well be at work here. In addition, constraints on the potential spread of WBL programmes were also identified.

Benefits of WBL Programmes

A number of benefits from WBL programmes were identified by the university staff we interviewed, and they can be summarized as: financial returns to the university; flexibility; career development for students; enhanced influence over the learning process and content for students.

Financial gains were said to have accrued at universities A and C through the extra revenue brought in by the students enrolling onto WBL programmes. Whether this represented a net gain after staffing and other resource and overhead costs are taken into account, we do not know as we were not provided with this information.

In terms of flexibility, the programmes at university C were seen as helping partnership working with local employers, and triggering the development of alternative approaches to teaching and learning. The 'learning contract' (see earlier) for WBL programmes allowed all parties to reflect upon whether the programme was meeting the needs of the student at any given point in time. In a sense, it acts as a monitoring device which tracks the built-in flexibility of the programme, not least in relation to changing organizational priorities and contexts.

At university B, the postgraduate curriculum leader emphasized how the employer can vary the programme to meet their organization's needs, whilst the head of research pointed out that WBL offers customized programmes to a diverse range of clients, and is not simply there to meet the vocational needs of particular employers:

> A heck of a lot of them [the students] are just individuals who belong to an organization, or who are doing a project in the public sphere. It is not just about employers, and I think we need to steer work-based learning away from the idea that it just has a vocational focus.

The latter observation was echoed by a WBL academic at university A, who commented that, based upon feedback from students and employers, there was general satisfaction with the WBL programmes—this overall positive feedback being in terms of the quality of the teaching, relevance to the workplace, and the encouragement given to students to be reflective practitioners.

With regard to career development for students, the programme leader at university A commented that a number of the students who completed the former MMP programme had gained promotion as a result. At university B, research had been carried out into the effectiveness of WBL programmes from the students' and employers' perspectives. The head of research noted that the feedback had been positive: ' . . . it has given them self confidence, it has progressed their career.' She also pointed out that the final work-based project helped experienced practitioners on the programme ' . . . in a work situation using evidence-based practice and informed knowledge about how to make decisions about change.'

Also, students were said to be able to take control of their own learning and link it to their professional development, whilst generating/obtaining knowledge of value in the workplace. The following observation of the director of the centre at university B is indicative:

> I think the lasting benefit is making them a more effective work based learner so that they are better able to cope with the changing demands of the workplace. They are able to be, in their own right, knowledge workers, to be knowledge creators, users and they are far better equipped in that role from the work based learning programme.

Many of the university staff we interviewed were of the view that the learning experience on WBL programmes had acted to transform the careers of many students and enhance their personal development and learning in a variety of ways.

Whilst many of our interviewees had positive things to say about the 'returns' from engagement in WBL programmes for all three main parties, they also offered some more critical reflections upon practice (or, rather, lack of practice in many cases) in their host institutions, and it is to a consideration of these that we now turn.

Contexts and Challenges of WBL Programmes

A key message to emerge from our case study universities is the general lack of awareness of WBL developments amongst academic staff. At university C, the business development director said that 'two thirds of the Business School staff would not know much about the WBL programmes the School offers'. Even at university B, which, as we noted earlier, has a centre specializing in WBL programmes, the head of research commented that 'it had taken ten years for people to start to notice that the Centre exists'.

WBL programmes within English HE form a minority of the overall provision, with only a few academics contributing to them. One reason for this may be that 'learner in the workplace' programmes demand a particular set of skills which may be in short supply in HE. As the CHERI/KPMG report (HEFCE 2006a: 33) noted:

> ... the nature and extent of negotiation needed between the higher education provider, the learner and the employer to create an acceptable programme requires a set of skills which 'traditional' academics may not possess. The complex brokerage skills required to establish an agreed programme of activities and provide ongoing support to the learner provide but one example.

It should be noted that the previous comments came from staff at universities which have an established reputation for WBL provision, implying that there may well be even less awareness and interest at other universities which have not devoted the same level of attention and resources to establishing and operating such programmes. Our findings concur with those of Reeve and Gallacher (2003), who argued in their study of WBL partnership programmes:

> It would appear that WBL developments within universities in the UK are still limited and marginal. There are clearly some examples of UK institutions where WBL has become a significant form of provision, and Middlesex University and Portsmouth University are often quoted in this context. However elsewhere in the UK, even in the new post '92

university sector which emerged out of the more vocationally oriented polytechnics, there is little evidence that WBL has become a major form of provision in many universities.

(Reeve and Gallacher 2003: 202)

The Higher Education Academy study of work-based learning practices in UK HE found that:

> Perceptions of work-based learning show that it is still seen by some as belonging to more vocationally oriented institutions. It is very much a contested area felt by many to be the preserve of particular disciplines and outside this it tends to be a bit of a 'cottage industry' supported by enthusiasts.
>
> (Higher Education Academy Report 2006: 16)

This lack of awareness of and interest in WBL would seem to imply that it has failed to have any significant impact other than in highly localized, circumscribed cases.

Even in those universities where postgraduate WBL programmes have been adopted, however, such as in our case studies, resistance to such programmes was reported in our interviews at all the universities, and took three main forms: WBL being seen as taking students from other disciplines; WBL involving a 'watering down' of intellect and standards; and an unwillingness to get involved in WBL programmes because of a lack of incentives.

In university A, resistance appears to be linked to the weak relationship which exists between the Centre for Lifelong Learning and the university schools, and the limited degree of communication emanating from the centre has fuelled a fear and resentment in the university that the CLL is 'taking their students and thus their resources'. The head of research at university B drew attention to what she described as 'the current economic situation in Higher Education', and accepted that WBL could be seen as poaching students from other academic disciplines and acting as a threat to academic standards:

> Another form of resistance is where other academics see work-based learning in its transdisciplinary mode being a watering down of intellect, standards and of what higher education should stand for, and I think this university encounters that as much as anyone.

A contrasting view was provided by the director of the centre at this university, who argued that WBL does not take students away from the academic disciplines 'because it is a very different path to go down'.

At university C, the lack of financial incentive for academic staff to get involved in WBL programmes was highlighted; this was attributed to the changes which had occurred in the method of calculating workloads, which were seen as no longer encouraging involvement. As a WBL lecturer commented:

> Well without being too political, there is internal resistance at the moment because we do have differences of opinion, and a lot of this is down to work constraints and work load issues.

A number of the staff commented on quality issues in relation to WBL programmes. At university B, for example, the director of the centre pointed out that the quality assurance procedures are more stringent for WBL than for many other university programmes, as they have many unique characteristics which lead them to be put under the spotlight. This can, of course, be seen as both a strength and a drawback of such programmes, depending upon one's orientation to these sort of matters.

Other constraints on the further development of such programmes identified by our interviewees included: government funding not taking account of WBL; WBL programmes being labour intensive and expensive to run; difficulties experienced in providing the flexibility needed by WBL students; lack of management support. With regard to government funding, the business development director at university C commented that it does not take account of WBL and, what is more, 'the government assumes that what all academics do is teach, and therefore all the funding is geared to students, teaching, teaching hours and full-time equivalent students'. At the same time, the demand for postgraduate WBL programmes, according to her, was outstripping supply, and therefore additional resources were needed if the area was to grow. A programme leader at the same university said that involvement in WBL programmes was 'pushing the boundaries', yet the institutional context offered little support: 'We don't see HEFCE and QAA [Quality Assurance Agency] as our friends, we see them reinforcing and ossifying the current system.' Thus, for the staff we interviewed at university C, the lack of flexibility in the funding system was hindering developments in WBL programmes.

Another challenge to the spread of WBL programmes was said to be their labour intensiveness and resultant relatively higher 'running' costs. The programme manager at university A observed that when the Centre for Lifelong Learning offered work to a school it would expect funding to follow; otherwise it would not want the work because of its resource intensity. On the other hand, if schools did provide more WBL modules, then this could create resource problems for them because they were not always able to recruit the additional staff members they needed. The argument was that 'seed corn' funding is required in order to have the staff available to deliver the programmes, and it is easy to see how one can get into the classic 'chicken and egg' situation. The Higher Education Academy Report (2006) would seem to recognize that WBL is typically more resource intensive than many other modes of learning:

More flexible and improved public funding models aligned to the increased use of co-financing arrangements (the State, employer and individual) in funding higher level (work-based) learning will need to be worked through to ensure that the benefits can be realised on all sides.

(Higher Education Academy Report 2006: 56)

The challenges posed in providing the flexibility required by WBL students was seen as another constraint on the expansion of WBL programmes. The director of the centre at university B said that the major problems in managing WBL programmes were structural, in that the students who registered at the centre differed from the general student population in that they were studying at distance, often only visiting the centre once a semester: 'It is providing that flexibility that is not driven on the same scale as the undergraduate which is sometimes difficult, given that the university is still dominated by the concept of students coming onto campus'.

Thus our findings point to the challenges and resistance to the spread of WBL programmes taking many different forms, ranging from practical issues impacting on the motivation of academics to get involved (such as a lack of financial incentives) to more fundamental issues, such as political opposition to what has been called 'academic capitalism' (Taylor *et al.* 2002: 137). For WBL to move from being a minority provision to a mainstream activity will clearly require a significant step change at the level of practice, and government policy needs to be seen in this context.

CONCLUSIONS

It was noted at the beginning of the chapter that a key priority of the government's strategy for HE, as set out in the white paper 'The Future of Higher Education' (DfES 2003) and the 'HEFCE Strategic Plan 2003–08' (HEFCE 2003), is the expansion of WBL. The interviews with national senior policy advisors and documentary analysis of policy chapters clearly point to the government strategy for higher education having an explicit vocational agenda. The HEFCE policy advisor commented that WBL is becoming more important and that it 'is moving up on the list of priorities'.

Whilst the main parties concerned have undoubtedly gained benefits from WBL programmes, as outlined and discussed in an earlier section, these have been localized even within the particular universities studied, bearing in mind that these universities have made concerted efforts on the WBL front. Thus we suspect that the picture elsewhere is unlikely to be any better, in the sense of being more widespread within those universities. The CHERI/KPMG Report to HEFCE (2006a: 78) noted that 'learner in the workplace' programmes have 'yet to achieve widespread take-up' (whilst this project was focussed upon employer views of WBL, and often the report conflates sub-degree, undergraduate, and postgraduate programmes in its narrative, the findings are nonetheless indicative in relation to postgraduate programmes, and the report does explicitly refer to them at various points). To understand why this is the case, one needs to situate WBL programmes in their wider institutional contexts of a lack of awareness and interest on the behalf of academic staff, resistance, and constraints to implementation. This clearly presents a fundamental challenge to the government agenda for reform. What is more, whilst the government has made partnership working between industry and HE a priority, it takes time for funding arrangements to filter down to the local level, and delays in lead-in times are adversely affecting developments in the field; the funding arrangements in place do not appear to be currently gaining widespread management support for WBL developments.

Thus we find a disjuncture between government policy and practice. This is due in particular to apathy and resistance to WBL on the behalf of university academic staff who are not involved in WBL (the majority)—the 'non-converts'—and the range of constraints which operate at the local university level. Government policy towards HE since the 1980s has emphasized the employability of graduate students and HE's contribution to economic competitiveness. Combined with the developing role of central government in HE through directing funding, an enhanced inspection/ quality assurance regime, and a stronger managerial orientation, it can be argued that British universities have been through some of the most dramatic changes that have occurred in the history of higher education (Symes 2001). The result appears to be that many academics have been pushed into a corner where they feel that the only way to deal with such challenges to their autonomy and professional ethics is to resist developments such as WBL.

What is more, government initiatives such as WBL, particularly at the postgraduate level, do not fit readily into HEFCE funding streams. This discourages their pursuit, as HE institutions focus on where the funding is concentrated, and winning over senior management becomes more difficult. The introduction of new initiatives, such as Higher Education Innovation Fund (HEIF) under permanent third stream funding arrangements, means that WBL programmes will need to compete for funding in HE institutions. In addition, they may lose out to other initiatives, such as the development of new spin-off businesses or consultancy contracts. In order for WBL to gain a higher profile and wider dissemination across universities, government funding arrangements need to be more flexible, so that, for example, ring-fenced funding is available for innovative WBL developments.

Consecutive UK governments have continued with policies supporting closer ties between education and the business sector, which Coffield (2000: 28) has described as 'a skills growth model allied to a learning market'. Recent policy initiatives have reinforced these messages in, for example, the government strategy for higher education (DfES 2003), which places emphasis on building links between business and higher education through funding mechanisms and employment-based qualifications such as foundation degrees. The government objectives that underpin these developments are part of a wider political discourse that justifies developments in education in narrow economic terms, informed by human capital theory. These objectives will ultimately force universities to make strategic choices in respect of their relations with commerce and industry.

These programmes are in many ways unique and at the leading edge of developments in knowledge production, yet remain at the periphery of developments within higher education. If WBL programmes at the postgraduate level are not taking hold within HE, then this raises serious doubts about policy and practice across the whole HE sector, as it is arguably at the postgraduate level that there is the best chance of this occurring. It is worth noting that HEFCE recognizes (HEFCE 2006c) that more needs to be done: reference is made in this strategy document to the need to explore incentives for employer-funded HE in order to address the 'employer engagement agenda', and to strengthen the links between HE and employers, and promote opportunities for WBL and lifelong learning. It has set a target for the proportion of Higher Education Institutions (HEIs) reporting high levels of employer engagement to increase to 80 per cent by 2009.

Our research, then, points to a lack of organizational fit for WBL programmes in areas such as standard teaching delivery patterns, workload models, and government funding. These factors, combined with organizational constraints and non-awareness and resistance on the behalf of academics, go some way to explaining why innovative WBL programmes still represent a minority of the overall provision.

WBL is an area of study which is growing in significance through, inter alia, an increased numbers of publications, research projects, and conferences. An area which needs further development is international research based on current practice (as Gilhooly *et al.* 2004 have also identified), particularly in Australasia and Western Europe. It is intended that the present research study will not only contribute to the latter, but also help develop our understanding of the issues involved in implementing WBL within higher education.

KEY LEARNING POINTS

- In-depth case study research is needed to understand why there are gaps between government policy towards WBL and organizational practice.
- WBL does offer something new/different to both HE and non-HE organizations and staff, but the realization of this offer in practice is by no means guaranteed.

- Those university staff directly engaged in HE WBL programmes tend to see them in a positive light, but they operate in a form of enclave, often semi-detached from the rest of the university—where one is more likely to find apathy and resistance to such programmes.

13 The Relation between Broad Professional Identity, Self-Directed Professional Development, and Broad Coaching Style of Teacher Educators

Marianne Van Woerkom

Teachers no longer work in stable contexts but are being confronted with many changes in societal values, family conditions, educational and professional structures, and new opportunities of technologies (Niemi 2002). Increasingly, the role of the teacher shifts from someone who transfers knowledge to someone who coaches students (Geijsel and Meijers 2005; Korthagen 2004a). Whereas in the past teachers had a relatively autonomous position within their classroom and their school organization, pedagogical changes ask for more collaboration between teachers (Seezink and Van der Sanden 2005). More and more, the learning process of pupils is not just the responsibility of one teacher but of all teachers (Van Veen *et al.* 1999). In many countries a need is felt to build collaborative structures inside schools to reverse the isolation felt by many teachers (Lieberman 2000). Furthermore, instead of being objects in the design of school organization, teachers are more and more seen as agents of change and active decision makers (Geijsel and Meijers 2005).

To deal with these changes, teachers will need a greater readiness to work and learn collaboratively in the school community and will therefore, in addition to skills related to working with children, also need skills to work together in multiprofessional teams (Niemi 2002). Moreover, teachers need to become able to learn creatively, as opposed to reproductively (Geijsel and Meijers 2005). These changes have important implications for teacher education. Student teachers should not only be prepared for their didactical and pedagogical role, but also for the role they can play in the development of their school organization. Since teacher educators have an important task in the guidance of processes of competency development of student teachers, they should also play a role in preparing student teachers for this new role. As teacher educators tend to regard themselves as role models (Egan 1978), however, it is likely that teacher educators will differ in the way they carry out this task, depending on their own professional identity, their subjectively experienced professional image of the teacher educator. Therefore, it can be expected that teacher educators with a broad professional identity (Hoyle and John 1995) and who see a role for themselves in the innovation of schools are more likely to coach student teachers for their future tasks in the school organization than teacher educators with a restricted professional identity. Furthermore, it can be expected that teachers with a broad professional identity employ more professionalization activities themselves, which on its turn will also affect their coaching style.

Although there is a growing interest in the professionalization of teacher educators (Lunenberg *et al.* 2000), research into the profession of teacher educators is still scarce (Lunenberg and Korthagen 2003; Buchberger *et al.* 2000; Ducharme 1993, 2003). Although the concepts of professional identity and professional development have been investigated in samples of teachers, they have hardly been studied in a sample of teacher educators. Also, whereas most research on beginning teachers has focused on issues directly related to classroom teaching, didactical competence, and classroom management, much less attention has been given to the fact that beginning teachers also become members of an organization (Kelchtermans and Ballet 2002). Therefore, the objective of this study was to explore the relationships between a broad professional identity of teacher educators, their involvement in professional development, and the extent to which they coach student teachers to play an active role in the school development.

THEORETICAL FRAMEWORK

Professional Identity

How teacher educators perceive their role is closely related to their professional identity. A differentiation can be made between a social and a personal professional identity (Klaassen and Sleegers, in Klaassen *et al.* 1999). Social identity refers to the professional image that the outside world has of teacher educators. In this study we speak about professional identity as a personal identity; the subjectively experienced professional image of the teacher educator. Professional identity is formed by a process of self-reflection in which the perspective of others, of the outside world, is also taken into account (Klaassen *et al.* 1999). Hoyle (1980) and Jongmans and Beijaard (1997) distinguish between a restricted and an extended professional identity of teachers regarding their role in the school organization. The notion of a restricted professional identity refers to a dominant orientation on pedagogical issues, subject content, or one's own teaching activities. Teachers with a restricted professional identity share the opinion that the responsibility of the individual teacher is limited to one's own classroom. Teachers with a broader professional identity are more focused on the school organization, consider professional cooperation of high importance, see their functioning as a team member as a prerequisite of adequately performing teaching tasks, and find it therefore important that their class practice is in harmony with the goals and policy of the school.

Although professional identity has never been studied in relation to teacher educators, it is likely that the same distinction also applies to teacher educators. Teacher educators with a broad professional identity may see it as part of their role to participate in research projects, support schools in processes of development and innovation, and to participate in activities relating to retraining and the professional development of teachers. Those with a less broad professional identity, on the other hand, are likely to stick to those tasks that result directly from teaching and guiding student teachers.

Self-Directed Professional Development

Despite the discussion on the professional status of the occupation of teachers and teacher educators, there is strong agreement about one characteristic of the profession, that is, the need for further professionalization (Kwakman 2004). Professional development activities can have the character of following courses, training, or attending conferences (Kwakman 2003). However, since teachers and therefore also teacher educators have to learn new conceptions of content and pedagogy and have to take on new roles, traditional ways of learning characterized by transmission of knowledge are bound to miss the mark (Kwakman 2003). Ideally, professional development has to take place in practice or in various types of communities of professionals, and should be seen as a process, not as separate events (Guskey 2002), and should have the character of 'self-directed learning' (Brookfield 1995). Self-directed learning refers to self-initiated learning processes that are related to work, and for which there is no formal frame of organized education. Self-directed learning activities are, for example, reading professional and scientific journals to refresh and update one's knowledge and skills, or developing new methods or learning materials together with colleagues. Also participation in research projects or other forms of practitioner inquiry that involve systematic, intentional, and self-critical inquiry about one's work (Cochran-Smith and Lytle 1999) can be seen as important forms of self-directed learning.

Since behaviour is a function of self-concept (Korthagen 2004b) and perceptions of professional identity are of great influence on the way teacher educators behave in practice (Beijaard and Verloop 1999), we expect that teacher educators who have a broad professional identity, and who have a focus on processes of school development, also employ more self-directed professionalization activities. According to Hoyle (1980) and Hoyle and John (1995), teachers with a broad professional identity are more concerned with theory and current educational developments and therefore read more educational books and journals, are more involved in various professional activities, and are more concerned with their further professional development, including small-scale research projects. Teachers with extended professional identities value professional collaboration and are more active in their professional development. We therefore hypothesize that:

A broad professional identity is positively related to self-directed professional development (Hypothesis 1).

Broad Coaching Style

An adequate guidance of student teachers during their education is of high importance for their future functioning in practice. In the Netherlands, this guidance should be in line with the minimum competency requirements as stated in the Law on Professions in Education. The minimum competency requirements are related to dealing with students, with colleagues, with the surroundings of the school, and with oneself. All basic requirements are focused on the functioning of the individual teacher. However, beginning teachers do not only face problems of an educational, didactical nature, but also problems related to their socialization in the school as an organization (Kelchtermans and Ballet 2002). Teacher educators can opt for a way of coaching that emphasizes the development of didactical and pedagogical skills. On the other hand, teacher educators may also emphasize the role of the teacher in the process of school development and pay attention to participating in learning processes at team and school level, and contributing to school innovation processes.

Teacher educators regard themselves as role models (Egan 1978) and will often want to create a spitting image of themselves while forming student teachers. Therefore it can be expected that teacher educators with a broad professional identity and who are themselves actively involved in professional development activities such as signalling new trends and developments, participating in research projects, or developing new learning materials with colleagues will want to prepare their students for a similar active role. Also, teacher educators that are actively engaging in professional development will have more knowledge of recent trends and developments in the profession of educators and will therefore be better able to prepare student teachers for the role they can play in school development. Therefore, the following hypotheses can be formulated:

Self-directed professional development is positively related to a broad coaching style (Hypothesis 2).
A broad professional identity is positively related to a broad coaching style (Hypothesis 3).

Professional Identity and Coaching Style

We expect that the relationship between a broad professional identity and a broad coaching style is partially mediated by self-directed professional development. Mediation analysis is a key part of what has been called process analysis. A mediating variable transmits the effect of an independent variable on a dependent variable (MacKinnon *et al.* 2007). A broad professional identity will determine teacher educators' activities regarding their own professional development, and this behaviour will in turn influence how they coach student teachers for their development. Consequently, the following hypothesis was formulated:

Self-directed professional development has a mediating effect in the relationship between a broad professional identity and a broad coaching style (Hypothesis 4).

Figure 13.1 presents a summary of our conceptual model and the hypotheses that were formulated.

METHODS

Participants and Design

The profession of teacher educators is very broad. In the Netherlands, some teacher educators work in a school for primary or secondary education, and are allowed to spend a considerable part of their time on educating novice teachers, whereas other teacher educators work in institutions for teacher education. We employed a cross-sectional design in which we used a database with members of the Association of Teacher Educators in the Netherlands (VELON). This database consisted of 1,000 registered teacher educators, of whom 650 e-mail addresses were known. These 650 e-mail addresses were used to invite the teacher educators to participate in the research. Respondents received the questionnaire by e-mail with an accompanying letter. In this letter, the importance of the research to schools, teacher education, and science was stipulated, to motivate as many people as possible to fill out the questionnaire. For this same reason, the guarantee of anonymity was emphasized. After two weeks, a reminder to fill out the questionnaire was sent to all possible respondents. In total, the respondents had four weeks to respond to the request of cooperation.

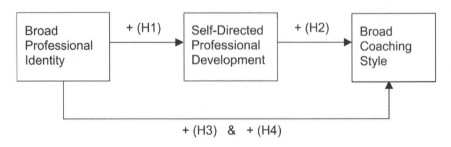

Figure 13.1 Conceptual model.

Table 13.1   Respondents' Gender, Educational Level, Organization, Age, and Years of Work Experience in Education

Gender	Education level	School/institute	Age	Number of years working in education
4% male	27% HPE	37% school	5% < 30	3% < 30
54% female	73% University	63% institute	22% 30–40 69% 40–50 34% > 50	7% 3–5 10% 5–10 16% 10–15 18% 15–20 47% > 20

Of the 650 addresses, 90 were not in use. The final sample consisted of 146 respondents, which makes for a response rate of 26 per cent. As Table 13.1 shows, 54 per cent of the respondents were women. In terms of age, 22 per cent of the respondents were between 30 and 40 years old, 39 per cent were between 40 and 50 years old, and 34 per cent of the respondents were older than 50. Only 5 per cent of the respondents were younger than 30. Almost half of the respondents (47 per cent) had worked in education for over 20 years. With respect to their educational level, 73 per cent had a university grade and 27 per cent had successfully finished higher vocational education. Sixty-three percent of the respondents worked in an institute for teacher education, whereas 37 per cent worked in a school for primary or secondary education.

Instruments

Since there were no validated scales available for measuring our variables, we used scales that we developed ourselves on the basis of interviews that were held with six teacher educators and a pilot of the questionnaire among four VELON members. In the questionnaire, participants were asked to indicate the extent to which they experienced having a broad professional identity, being active in professional development, and having a broad coaching style.

Broad Professional Identity

For this concept, a scale including 11 items with answering categories ranging from 1 = completely disagree to 5 = completely agree was constructed. Examples of items are 'I find it important that a teacher educator participates in school innovation projects', 'I find it important that a teacher educator advises schools related to school development', and 'I find it important that a teacher educator participates in a team that aims to improve the quality of teacher education'. In a principal component analysis on the items we found one underlying component (eigenvalue 4.40) that explained 40 per cent of the variance. Reliability analyses showed an alpha of .84.

Self-Directed Professional Development

Six items on general professional development activities were developed on the basis of the interviews and the pilot version of the survey. Examples of items are 'I conduct research in the field of education', 'I develop new teaching materials together with colleagues', and 'I signal new developments in the field of teacher education'. In a principal component analysis on the items we found one underlying component (eigenvalue 2.21) that explained 36.79 per cent of the variance. Reliability analysis on the items showed an alpha of .65.

Broad Coaching Style

For the measurement of broad coaching style, a 10-item scale with five Likert answering options (ranging from 1 = hardly attention to 5 = a lot of attention) was constructed on the basis of the interviews with teacher educators. The final scale consists of items such as 'How much attention do you pay to coaching students in learning to function in a team?' and 'How much attention do you pay to guiding students in participating in school innovations?' In a PCA on the items we found one underlying component (eigenvalue 4.80) that explained 48 per cent of the variance. Reliability analyses showed an alpha of .88.

Control Variables

Since we wanted to explore to what extent the concepts in our conceptual model were affected by both personal characteristics and characteristics of the work context of teacher educators, respondents were asked to indicate their gender (male is 0, female = 1), age (1 < 30, 2 = 30–40, 3 = 40–50 and 4 > 50), years of work experience in education and as a teacher educator (1 = 0–3, 2 = 3–5, 3 = 5–10, 4 = 10–15, 5 = 15–20 and 6 > 20), educational level (0 = professional education, 1 = university), hours a week working as a teacher educator (1 = < 1 day, 2 = 1 day, 3 = 2 days, 4 = 3 days, 5 = 4 days and 6 = 5 days) and affiliation (0 = school, 1 = institute).

RESULTS

Table 13.2 reports the correlations between the independent, mediating, dependent, and control variables.

Table 13.2 Descriptive Statistics and Correlations between Variables (N = 146)

	N Items	Mean	SD	1	2	3	4	5	6	7	8
1. Gender											
2. Age				-.22**							
3. Years in education				-.26**	.75**						
4. Affiliation				.07	.07	.04					
5. Years as teacher educator				-.20*	.53**	.54**	.05				
6. Working hours per week				-.15	.03	.08	.03	.06			
7. Broad professional identity	11	4.04	.46	.07	-.16	.02	.14	.05	.08		
8. Self-directed profess. Devel.	6	2.06	.37	-.10	.00	.12	.05	.16	.21*	.37**	
9. Broad coaching style	5	3.40	.59	.01	.11	.18*	-.03	.13	.04	.24**	.32**

Note: ** Correlation is significant at the 0.01 level (2-tailed); * Correlation is significant at the 0.05 level (2-tailed)

None of the control variables are significantly related to a broad professional identity. Self-directed professional development is significantly related to the hours per week the respondent works as a teacher educator ($r = .21$, $p < .05$). A broad coaching style is significantly related to number of years' work experience as a teacher educator ($r = .18$, $p < .05$).

The first hypothesis in this study assumed that a broad professional identity is positively related to self-directed professional development. This hypothesis was tested in a hierarchical regression analysis (see Table 13.3).

In step 1, we predicted professional development from the control variables gender, age, years of work experience in education, affiliation, years of work experience as teacher educator, hours per week working as teacher educator. In step 2 we added broad professional identity as a predictor of professionalization activities. To test for multi-collinearity between the

Table 13.3 Results of Regression Analyses Predicting Professionalization Activities from Broad Professional Identity

	Step 1	Step 2
	β	β
Gender	-.04	-.06
Age	-.25	-.10
Years work experience in education	.91	.10
Affiliation	.05	.00
Years work experience as teacher educator	.16	.12
Hours per week working as teacher educator	.19*	.16*
Broad professional identity		.33***
R^2	.09	.19
ΔR^2		.10***
F test	(4,79) (6,139) 2,40*	(7,138) 4,68***

Note: ***$p < .001$; **$p < .01$; *$p < .05$; $N = 146$

independent variables, the variance-inflation factors (VIF) were calculated (Belsley *et al.* 1980). All 'VIF' values were below 2.0, suggesting that multi-collinearity was not a problem in the analysis (Belsley *et al.* 1980). Clearly, step 2 shows a significant improvement in explained variance (R^2). Broad professional identity is positively related to self-directed professional development ($\beta = .33$, $p < .001$) (hypothesis 1 supported). Also, hours per week working as a teacher educator is positively related to self-directed professional development ($\beta = .16$, $p < .05$).

Hypotheses 2, 3, and 4 predict a positive relationship between a broad professional identity, professionalization activities, and a broad coaching style. In the second hypothesis it was held that professional development is positively related to a broad coaching style. In the third hypothesis a positive relationship between a broad professional identity and a broad coaching style was posited. According to the fourth hypothesis, professional development would have a (partially) mediating effect in the relationship between broad professional identity and broad coaching style. To investigate this mediation effect we applied the procedure as suggested by MacKinnon, Fairchild and Fritz (2007). These authors argue that a mediating effect exists if (1) the independent variable (broad professional identity) has a significant effect on the mediating variable (professionalization activities) and (2) the mediating variable has a significant effect on the dependent variable (broad coaching style) in a regression analysis of the independent and mediating variable on the dependent variable. If in this analysis the independent variable turns out to have no significant effect on the dependent variable, we have a case of pure mediation. If the independent variable (in addition to the mediating variable) does have a significant effect on the dependent variable, we have a case of partial mediation. Although older literature (Baron and Kenny 1986) argues that in case of a mediating effect, the independent and the dependent variables should correlate, according to more recent literature (Kenny *et al.* 1998; MacKinnon *et al.* 2007) this condition is not necessary as suppressor effects may occur.

To test the complete model, a hierarchical multiple regression analysis was conducted using broad coaching style as the dependent variable and broad professional identity and self-directed professional development as predictors, together with the control variables. The results are displayed in Table 13.4.

As we can see in Table 13.4, only self-directed professional development was a significant predictor of a broad coaching style ($\beta = .33$, $p < .001$), while the independent variable broad professional identity, as well as the control variables, failed to attain significance. The model explained 16 per cent of the variance in broad coaching style. It can be deduced from the analyses, therefore, first, that there is a positive relationship between self-directed professional development and a broad coaching style (hypothesis 2 accepted); second, that a broad professional identity has no direct effect on a broad coaching style (hypothesis 3 rejected); and, fourth, that

Table 13.4   Results of Regression Analyses Predicting Broad Coaching Style from Broad Professional Identity and Self-Directed Professional Development

	Step 1	Step 2
	β	β
Gender	.08	.08
Age	-.06	.08
Years work experience in education	.21	.11
Affiliation	-.04	-.08
Years work experience as teacher educator	.07	.00
Working hours per week	.06	-.00
Broad professional identity		.16
Professional development		.26**
R^2	.05	.16
ΔR^2		.11***
F test	(4,79) (6,139) 1.09	(8,137) 3,15**

Note: ***$p < .001$; **$p < .01$; *$p < .05$; $N = 146$

self-directed professional development has a purely mediating effect in the relationship between a broad professional identity on the one hand and broad coaching style on the other hand (hypothesis 4 supported). The main findings are summarized in Figure 13.2.

DISCUSSION

The present study has examined professional development as a mechanism between a broad professional identity and a broad coaching style in a sample of Dutch teacher educators.

Figure 13.2 Summary of empirical results.

As expected, a broad professional identity is a positive predictor of professional development, while actively engaging in professional development leads to a broader coaching style. Interestingly, a broad professional identity has no effect on a broad coaching style when professional development activities are also included as predictor (broad professional identity and broad coaching style are, however, significantly correlated). Probably, the way teacher educators actually behave with respect to their own development is a better predictor of the way they coach their students than what they deem important in their profession. The results show that professional development has a purely mediating effect in the relationship between professional identity, on the one hand, and a broad coaching style, on the other hand. This means that teacher educators who feel that they should play a role in innovation projects in schools have a better chance of being actively involved in self-directed professional development activities and will therefore want to prepare their students for learning behaviour in the context of their future school organization. As was shown in the correlation matrix, a broad professional identity was unrelated to teacher educator characteristics like age, gender, or years of work experience.

The results of this study are of interest for research and practice in the area of teacher education and might raise a discussion on the mission that teacher educators see for themselves (Korthagen 2004a). What do they want to educate for and how do they want to contribute to the quality of education? To what extent do teacher educators see themselves as 'change agents' who think analytically about the way the educational system functions and who critically assess how it can be redesigned in a positive way (Mulkeen and Copper 1992)? The knowledge that this study has generated may also be used for the purpose of human resources management within teacher training institutes or schools employing teacher educators, for example, for developing selection criteria in the recruitment process of (future) teacher educators, or for the development of learning interventions or assessment practices.

Many implementations of innovation in education have led to disappointments (Jongmans *et al.* 1998). In the end, the success of educational change relies on teachers. Research (Borko 2004; Garet *et al.* 2001) has shown that collective participation of groups of teachers from the same school in the innovation, coherence of their professional development activities, and encouragement of professional communication among teachers are crucial factors in the success of educational innovation. McLaughlin and Talbert (1993) show that secondary-school teachers who took risks and were continually inventing new ways of working with their students were, at the same time, developing a positive learning community with their peers and creating norms of openness and colleagueship. Teachers who were member of professional communities within the school were rethinking what they could do to change the way they were engaging students and were sharing what they were doing with their peers and supporting each other as they were learning together. When there was no such professional community within the school, teachers either tried new ideas in fragmented ways on their own or blamed students for their inabilities to learn. Also, it has been shown that teachers who work in a school that supports collaboration and teacher participation in decision making are more strongly committed to teaching and have stronger intentions to remain within the profession (Weiss 1999).

Making the shift from teacher education to actual professional practice is difficult for many novice teachers and often significantly influences the next career stages (Kelchtermans and Ballet 2002). Our study shows that if we want to prepare future teachers for their collective responsibility for processes of school innovation, they should be educated and coached by teacher educators who see school development and educational innovation as a part of their job and who are actively involved in professional development. To moderate the isolation of teaching (Cochran-Smith and Lytle 1999), student teachers should be trained to learn not only on an individual basis but also from the collaborative interactions that occur when groups of teachers work together to examine and improve their practice. In their educational program, core competencies relating to school leadership, educational politics, and change processes should be central.

Teachers are often considered as passive receivers of prescriptive programs for professional development and given little time or incentive to integrate these new programs into their classroom practice. Teacher networks, in contrast, involve their members in a variety of activities that reflect the purposes and changing needs of their participants (Lieberman 2000). Furthermore, the concept of teacher as researcher can disrupt traditional views about the relationships between knowledge and practice, blurring the boundaries between teachers and researchers, knowers and doers, and experts and novices (Cochran-Smith and Lytle 1999). Student educators should be coached to participate actively in research projects, to interrogating their own and others' practices and assumptions, and to learn how to improve one's teaching by collecting and analyzing the 'data' of daily life in schools (Cochran-Smith and Lytle 1999).

In line with the argument from Grossman *et al.* (2001) that we cannot expect teachers to create communities of learners among students if they do not have a parallel community to nourish their own growth, we might say the same about teacher educators. How can we expect young teachers to participate in teams of teachers with a shared goal of improving education if they were educated by teacher educators that do not participate in such communities themselves? If we want our future teachers to be capable of developing innovative ways of teaching, we should develop policies that stimulate teacher educators to have a broad perception of their role, and to be actively involved in professional communities. Special attention is needed for teacher educators who work part time as teacher educators, since our results show that these teacher educators are less active with respect to their professional development.

Our study is limited in that we only collected our data in the Netherlands. To be able to conclude to what extent our results can be generalized to teacher educators in other countries, this study would need to be replicated. Furthermore, we used only the perceptions of teacher educators of their own coaching style, instead of perceptions of student teachers. For future research it would be interesting to also include student evaluations of the coaching style of teacher educators.

KEY LEARNING POINTS

- Teacher educators with a broad professional identity are more involved in self-directed professional development.
- Teacher educators that are more actively involved in self-directed professional development tend to use a broader coaching style when coaching student teachers.
- Professional development has a purely mediating effect in the relationship between professional identity, on the one hand, and a broad coaching style, on the other hand.

ACKNOWLEDGEMENT

In remembrance of Prof. Dr. Johan van der Sanden, who took the initiative in the research project that is being reported in this chapter, but sadly passed away shortly after the data had been collected. I would like to thank our master students Debora Koelma and Nienke Brandsma, who helped us with the data collection.

APPENDIX

Items of the scales' broad professional identity, professionalization activities, and broad coaching style:

Broad Professional Identity

I find it important that a teacher educator . . .

1. participates in innovation projects in schools
2. advises schools in the area of school development
3. tries to establish relationships between personnel policies in schools and teacher education
4. tries to establish relationships between innovations in schools and teacher education
5. tries to establish relationships between educational or didactic research and teacher education
6. encourages schools to formulate research questions
7. supervises students in conducting research and development that are relevant to practice
8. is involved in projects that lead to an increased quality of teacher educators
9. keeps up with government policies on teacher education critically
10. keeps up with education policies of the government critically
11. participates in a team focused on improving the quality of teacher education

Self-Directed Professional Development

1. I conduct research
2. I keep up with recent research in the area of education
3. I develop new teaching materials with a network of colleagues
4. I point out new developments in the area of teacher education
5. I contribute to the development of teacher education courses
6. I keep up with new professional knowledge

Broad Coaching Style

How much attention do you give to the following activities?

1. Preparing students for the roles they will have to play as teachers in processes of school development
2. Supervising students in participating in innovations in schools
3. Encouraging students to form a well-founded opinion on the policies of their internship schools
5. Preparing students for the roles they can play as teachers in developing policies at the school level
6. Encouraging students to contribute to the performance of the team they are involved with at their internship schools

7. Preparing students for working in a self-managing team of teachers
8. Encouraging students to participate in activities of teams working on innovations at their internship schools
9. Supervising students in learning to bring about innovations in schools together with colleagues
10. Preparing students for the roles they will have to play as teachers in initiating and continuing processes of school improvement
11. Supervising students in learning to work in a team

14 Implications for Research and Practice

Marianne Van Woerkom and Rob Poell

The aim of this volume was to give an update on workplace learning research, a topic that has been highly popular in the last 20 years. After so many years of research spent on this topic it seems timely to draw up the balance sheet and look at what we as workplace learning researchers have accomplished. What is the state of affairs regarding theory development? What progression have we made in making workplace learning more tangible and measurable? What do we know about the work environments that are conducive to learning? And finally, what are promising new avenues for research? In this final chapter we intend to provide some answers to these questions, based upon the research that has been presented in the previous chapters.

WORKPLACE LEARNING AS AN INTERACTION BETWEEN THE INDIVIDUAL AND THE WORK CONTEXT

A central line of argument that emerges from several chapters in this volume is that learning should be understood as an interaction between personal and situational factors. The contribution by Stephen Billett (Chapter 2) makes it clear that learners can no longer be conceived of as passive individuals that learn by consuming and storing new concepts and skills. Instead, they need to be understood as active, agentic individuals that not only are shaped by the environment but also change the environment themselves as a result of individual agency, subjectivity, and intentionality. According to Chin and colleagues (Chapter 4), even novices take an active and pro-active role in the workplace, through a self-regulating process of submitting to the authority of experienced practitioners, mirroring the practitioner, and independently constructing patterns of actions and beliefs within the community. Fenwick (Chapter 3) also argues that individuals' learning is entangled in systems of continuous activity and emerges from people's relations and interactions with the social and material elements of particular contexts. In Bateson's theory as described by Tosey, Langley, and Mathison (Chapter 5), learning is also approached as something both individual and social in nature. Bateson even argues that 'mind' is located in connections and relations within systems, rather than in the brains of an individual. Berings, Van Veldhoven, and Poell (Chapter 6) conceptualize workplace learning as emerging from the interaction between psychological work conditions and intrinsic work motivation. They conclude that job demands and social support are not directly related to learning behaviour; rather, this relationship is mediated by the intrinsic work motivation of the learner.

Although most researchers tend to focus on the impact that the work environment has on the learner, several authors in this volume argue that it can also be the other way around. Andersson and Jansson (Chapter 11), for instance, show that learning processes can counter a problematic work situation by encouraging active participation and interaction. Hence, we should be aware that not only can workplace learning change the individual that engages in the learning process, but also individuals can change existing work activities and practices as a result of their learning behaviours.

Future research should place more emphasis on the way that individuals are nested within and interconnected with elements of the systems in which they participate, instead of focussing on the learning figure and dismissing all its complex interactions as context, as Fenwick suggests. Knowledge should not be understood as something contained in one actor or dimension of a system; rather, it is constantly emerging and spilling into other systems. HRD research should therefore focus more on the question of how to enable connections among elements of a system, in addition to the issue of how to train individuals that 'acquire' knowledge.

WORKPLACE LEARNING AS AN INDIVIDUAL AND COLLECTIVE PROCESS

When individual learning processes result in changes in the organization, organizational learning has occurred. Wang and Ellinger (Chapter 7) argue that organizational learning does not simply refer to a collection of individuals that have learned; rather, it points to an entity that is capable of learning on a collective basis. In the past, the focus of many publications on the topic of workplace learning, especially in the field of HRD, was on individual learning. The contributions in this volume reflect a tendency to broaden this perspective and include collective forms of learning. Van Engen and Van Woerkom (Chapter 9), for example, draw attention to learning as a collective team process. They refer to team learning as the processing of information and knowledge among team members, resulting in a change in the range of the team's potential behaviour. When team members share their knowledge and experiences with each other, this may result in new knowledge structures or routines. In her contribution on the self-directed professional development of teacher educators, Van Woerkom (Chapter 13) draws attention to the fact that didactic changes ask for more collaborative learning among teachers. Student teachers should therefore be prepared not only for their didactic and pedagogical roles, but also for the role they can play in the collective development of their school organization.

Upcoming research should pay attention to the issue of collective learning and to the many related questions that still have not been answered. Which factors determine whether collective entities are able to learn? To what extent is team learning influenced by, for example, task characteristics, such as task autonomy and task interdependency (Langfred 2005); psychological climate factors, such as psychological safety and trust (Edmondson 1999); the existence of relationship and/or task conflicts in the team (Van Woerkom and Van Engen 2009); teams having a problem-solving or blaming approach in relation to mistakes (Tjosvold 2004); or the presence of a coaching leader (Wageman *et al.* 2005)? Van Engen and Van Woerkom (Chapter 9) show that expertise diversity is one factor that contributes to collective learning. It is not yet clear, however, to what extent demographic diversity (age, gender, ethnicity) is related to expertise diversity and team learning.

Another relevant and current question is how diversity in teams and organizations should be dealt with and how collective learning is related to diversity management. Ely and Thomas (2001) identified three perspectives on workforce diversity. Within the discrimination-and-fairness perspective, diversity is a way to ensure justice and not a way to create extra value for the organization. The access-and-legitimacy perspective is characterized by the belief that diversity in organizations helps to gain access to diverse markets and has business value for the organization. Only in the integration-and-learning perspective, diversity is seen as a resource for learning, change, and renewal and is part of the organization's mission. Research should investigate which of these diversity perspectives yields most results in terms of learning processes and/or effectiveness.

Furthermore, one could argue that although collective learning has a positive connotation, its results are not always positive. Bapuji and Crossan (2004), for example, argue that organizations might fall into three different learning traps: the familiarity trap (tendency to employ known solutions), the maturity trap (tendency to employ proven solutions), and the propinquity trap (tendency to employ solutions closer to the known solutions). Future research should therefore focus on how these collective learning traps could be avoided.

WORKPLACE LEARNING AS COGNITION AND ACTION

Another related theme that is stressed in several chapters in this volume is that in studying workplace learning we cannot restrict ourselves to the cognitive aspects of learning, but we should also include the physical and affective aspects of learning. Clark (2001) argues that somatic knowing is at least as central to daily competence as the analytically discursive, distanced knowing that traditional schools cultivate. The kind of knowledge that is gained in workplace learning can be very different from the familiar declarative knowledge of the school classroom. It may include procedural and embodied knowledge; moreover, much of the knowledge required for success in the workplace is tacit.

This is clearly illustrated in the example given by Chin and colleagues (Chapter 4) of a co-op education student explaining how she learned to restrain an animal on the examining table at the veterinary clinic. Tosey and colleagues (Chapter 5) also conceptualize learning as an embodied experience in referring to Bateson's theory of learning as including cognition and behaviour; embodied, enacted change. Billett (Chapter 2) conceives of learning as a process through which individuals deploy and change their cognitive experiences, through participating in activities and interactions. Bauer and Mulder (Chapter 8) draw upon and integrate the cognitive perspective and the activity perspective. They operationalize the learning process as deliberate, overt, and cognitive activities that assumedly lead to the learning processes and outcomes described by the cognitive perspective. Wang and Ellinger (Chapter 7) differentiate between cognitive and social perspectives on organizational learning. The cognitive perspective focuses on the processes by which an organization collects, analyzes, and distributes information. Social perspectives focus on how learning emerges from social interactions and actions among organizational members.

Although human learning is traditionally conceived of as the acquisition of knowledge and skills, in the 1990s researchers started to refer to learning in terms of doing and/or knowing, indicating action, and leaving no room for a clear end point to the process of learning (Sfard 1998). On the one hand, this participational approach may be more helpful, as it challenges the traditional distinction between cognition and affect and brings social factors to the fore. On the other hand, it is extremely difficult, not to say impossible, to avoid the acquisition metaphor and related concepts such as knowledge, competence, and transfer of learning. When one refuses to view knowledge as a stand-alone entity and rejects the idea of context as a clearly delineated 'area', a concept like learning transfer does not have to exist, since there is simply nothing to be carried over and there are no definite boundaries to be crossed (Sfard 1998). Realizing that no one metaphor can cover the entire field, we see it as a strength of this book that both metaphors are represented, with, for example, Van Engen and Van Woerkom (Chapter 9) and Wang and Ellinger (Chapter 7) departing from a more acquisitive perspective and Billett (Chapter 2) and Fenwick (Chapter 3) representing a participative approach.

WORKPLACE LEARNING AS A POLITICAL PROCESS

Although a political approach was not apparent in every contribution, several authors in this volume draw attention to the fact that power relations influence what learning is valued, what counts as skill, and what knowledge remains marginal or unnamed. Smith and Preece (Chapter 12) show how political pressure on universities has led to a human capital vision of higher education and an emphasis on work-based learning. They also show, however, that resistance and a lack of awareness and interest from academic staff provide fundamental challenges to the government agenda for reform. Chin and colleagues (Chapter 4) demonstrate that also researchers themselves can make political choices, by making a plea for including at-risk youth and youth with disabilities in workplace learning research. The issues of power and politics are clearly conceptualized in the actor approaches described by Fenwick (Chapter 3) and Poell and colleagues (Chapter 10). Actor-network theory provides an insight in the issue of how knowledge is actually negotiated or 'translated' at each interaction; the politics influencing who or what can be seen and mobilized at any moment. Poell and colleagues draw attention to the fact that the question of the type of learning projects that emerge in organizations may depend on who is the dominant actor involved (the individual learner, the management, the team, or the professional association).

Politics is a natural feature of organizing and learning, and power relations directly mediate interpretative processes within organizations (Vince 2001). It is almost impossible to learn a practice and become a member in a community of practice if power relations impede or deny access to its more accomplished exponents (Contu and Willmott 2003). Future research should therefore take into account the political processes involved in learning, and especially in collective forms of learning. Under what conditions are learners prepared to withstand political pressure, to criticize the organization's espoused theories, and to reveal their theories in use? And how do processes of identity formation, in relation to class, gender, ethnicity, and age, operate to make large parts of the population of our society unable or unwilling to participate in certain occupational communities, thereby limiting the options for mastering their practices (Contu and Willmott 2003)?

MEASURING WORKPLACE LEARNING

The three chapters making up the second part of the book deal explicitly with the measurement of workplace-learning activities. Operationalizing learning in the workplace has been a major challenge for the field since the 1990s, when the topic gained renewed prominence. The often informal nature of workplace-learning settings made it difficult to capture exactly which activities mattered most. Unlike formal training, the field of workplace learning has lacked an agreed upon set of concepts and principles that have been clearly operationalized. Thus far, only two measurement instruments in the specific area of HRD have been used, researched, and published extensively; one is the Learning Transfer System Inventory (LTSI; see Holton, Bates and Ruona 2000) and the other is the Dimensions of the Learning Organization Questionnaire (DLOQ; see Marsick and Watkins 2003). Both do not, however, focus on measuring workplace learning activities as such; the LTSI looks at the factors involved in transferring knowledge and skills from training programmes to the workplace, and the DLOQ emphasizes the individual, team, and organizational factors associated with organizational learning. Instruments that describe actual workplace learning activities have been scarce and/or not well researched and published. This is where the three chapters in the second part of the current volume make their contribution.

Berings and colleagues (Chapter 6) present an instrument to measure nurses' on-the-job learning behaviour. Based on a range of previous studies that looked into what and how nurses learn on the job, a relatively simple diagnostic framework is put forward, which nurses and nurse educators can use to map their learning behaviour. Clearly set in the nursing context, the instrument nevertheless opens various opportunities for other professionals to operationalize their own on-the-job learning activities.

Wang and Ellinger (Chapter 7) propose an instrument to assess internal and external information acquisition activities conducted by employees. These activities are part of their informal workplace learning and can contribute to organizational learning. The measurement instrument was validated with a sample of product developers, designers, engineers, and marketing personnel. Like the workplace learning literature, the organizational learning literature has been criticized for failing to provide good empirical evidence to sustain its core concepts. This is exactly where the instrument put forward in this chapter (as well as the ones from Chapters 6 and 8) make their primary contribution to the body of knowledge.

Bauer and Mulder (Chapter 8) discuss an instrument that they developed to measure learning from errors at work, which can bring many opportunities for workplace learning. Only few studies address how and under which circumstances individuals learn from errors encountered in a naturalistic work context. The operationalization in the current study is based on theories of experiential learning at work and validated in a sample of nurses. Although further work in other settings is necessary to improve the generalizability of the instrument, here is another example of a promising measure for workplace-learning activities.

The practical implications of these three chapters seem obvious. Three validated measurement instruments are available for use by practitioners. Employees and HR professionals interested in encouraging workplace learning can find reliable operationalizations of the constructs of on-the-job learning behaviour, information acquisition activities, and learning from errors at work in the second part of this volume. These may be used by employees for self-diagnostic purposes or by HR professionals to support HR policies and practices.

WORK ENVIRONMENTS CONDUCIVE TO LEARNING

The five chapters in the third part of this volume deal with learning in various workplace settings, including multidisciplinary teams, work-related learning projects, call centres, work-based learning in university degree programmes, and coaching relationships. On the one hand, workplace learning is used within the context of organized programmes as a way of bridging theory and practice. On the other hand, workplace learning can also occur 'naturally' where the individual interacts with a workplace setting. A key question in both instances concerns the implications that various workplace settings have for employee learning. Roughly speaking, call centres and university degree programmes at first sight might not seem very conducive contexts for workplace learning, whereas multidisciplinary teams, work-related learning projects, and coaching are generally considered more favourable in terms of bringing about workplace learning. Under some conditions, however, so the chapters show, even settings that do not really seem geared to workplace learning can offer employees various opportunities in that area. Some chapters also provide us with an insight into the mechanisms and factors underlying workplace learning in various settings.

An example of the latter is provided by Marloes Van Engen and Marianne Van Woerkom (Chapter 9), who conclude from their study among 88 teams that team members who see differences in expertise in their teams perceive them as learning more, performing better, and being more innovative. These team members report more information acquisition, more information processing, and more storage and retrieval of information than do team members who experience low expertise diversity in their teams. Perceived team learning apparently mediates the relationship between expertise diversity experienced by team members and their perceptions of the performance and innovation of the team. This implies that perceived expertise diversity in work teams is associated not only with learning but also with performance outcomes.

In the same vein, Poell and colleagues (Chapter 10) conclude from eight learning-project case studies conducted in the Dutch and US contexts that, although the dominant actor and the intended level of reflection are important elements in designing learning projects, the role of individual agency may also be a crucial factor. The ways in which individual employees organize their own learning processes in various work and organizational contexts may even be more relevant than the project-design structures put forward by management and learning coaches. This would imply that individual needs, goals, and actions be given centre stage in shaping work-related learning projects.

Andersson and Jansson (Chapter 11) describe a project aimed at encouraging learning in call centres, a context not usually associated with much employee development. The project is based on a number of broad principles: a detached project, active participation, interaction, and usefulness. It seems that these principles make the project successful, at least in terms of individual learning. Participants thus gain a number of skills deemed important for developmental learning, including work planning, problem solving, dialoguing, and reflecting. Additionally, there are benefits for the organization in terms of a safe and efficient production, based on knowledge exchanges among individuals as well as among departments. The implication of this study is that, when using the right set of principles, even in Tayloristic work contexts it is possible to encourage learning both at the individual and the collective level.

Similarly, Smith and Preece (Chapter 12) address a problematic context for workplace learning. Their three case studies of UK universities offering work-based learning (WBL) programmes show a general lack of awareness among academic staff of, and even resistance to, WBL developments. Academics apparently see WBL as taking students from other disciplines and leading to lower intellectual standards; and they lack incentives to get involved in WBL programmes in the first place. The standard teaching delivery patterns, workload models, and government funding explain as well why innovative WBL programmes are still relatively few. Nevertheless, there are various benefits to be had from WBL programmes in universities that manage to overcome these problems, including financial returns to the university, flexibility, career development for students, and enhanced influence over the learning process and content for students. This implies that university contexts can be fruitful for workplace learning; however, only if a substantial number of problematic issues (mostly to do with their academic character) are resolved first.

Van Woerkom (Chapter 13) addresses the context of coaching, more specifically how teacher educators coach student teachers on the job. She concludes that a broad professional identity of teacher educators predicts their participation in professional development, which in turn leads to a broader coaching style vis-à-vis the student teachers. Also, how teacher educators engage in their own professional development is a better predictor of the way they coach student teachers than is their professional identity. Although student teachers themselves were not involved in this study, the conclusions seem to imply that the professional identity of teacher educators, and especially their self-directed professional development, are crucial factors in explaining how student teachers are coached into becoming qualified teachers.

Generally speaking, a lot of research still needs to be conducted to investigate which work contexts are beneficial, under which conditions, for workplace learning to occur. The answer to this question will undoubtedly be influenced by the power relations in the organizations under study. Who determines what is beneficial at all? Who shapes the work context and who decides about gaining access to it? Who establishes whether workplace learning has led to valuable outcomes? Organizations may differ considerably in how such questions would be answered. In any case, involving multiple actors in the investigation, working from the assumption that they will each have different perceptions and strategies of workplace learning, will add to the reliability and practical relevance of the study outcomes, Comparative studies, whether at the team, organization, sectoral, or even national level, should also help to shed more light on the conditions under which specific work contexts are most conducive to workplace learning.

Contributors

Eira Andersson is a PhD student, Department of Human Work Science, Luleå University of Technology, Sweden. She holds a master's degree in ergonomic production. Her thesis employs interactive research methods and focuses on safety and gender relations in the mining industry.

Johannes Bauer is a researcher, School of Education, Technische Universität München (TUM), Germany. In his research, he focuses on learning from errors, expertise, and teachers' professional development.

Marjolein Berings is interested in exploring how to create challenging and supportive working environments for staff in the health care sector in order to foster high staff motivation, significant on-the-job learning, high performance, and quality of care. She has conducted a PhD study on nurses' on-the-job learning and contributed to human resources for health issues in the development sector of Malawi. Currently she leads the training section for health care professionals of the Radboud University Medical Centre in the Netherlands.

Stephen Billett is Professor, Adult and Vocational Education, Faculty of Education, Griffith University, Australia. He investigates learning through and for work, the nature of work and working knowledge, and how this knowledge is best learnt through experiences in practice and educational settings.

Peter Chin is Associate Professor and Practicum Coordinator, Faculty of Education, Queen's University, Canada. His program of research is centred on workplace learning and how novices gain experience within new settings.

Andrea D. Ellinger is Professor, Human Resource Development, College of Business and Technology, University of Texas at Tyler, United States. Her research interests focus on managerial coaching, informal workplace learning, organizational learning, and the learning organization concept.

Tara Fenwick Professor of Professional Education, University of Stirling, Scotland. Her research focuses on learning in work, professionals' life-long learning, and teacher development in international contexts.

Nancy L. Hutchinson is Professor, Faculty of Education, Queen's University, Canada. She holds a PhD in educational psychology. Her research focuses on work-based education and workplace learning for youth with disabilities and at-risk youth.

Anna Berg Jansson is a PhD student, Department of Human Work Science, Luleå University of Technology, Sweden. She holds a master's degree in sociology. Her thesis concerns organizational changes within Swedish healthcare with a focus on nurses' working conditions and professional development.

Dawn Langley is a PhD student, School of Management, University of Surrey, United Kingdom; and organizational development practitioner. She works primarily in the arts and culture sector and has a particular interest in organizational learning in mission led organizations.

Victoria Marsick is Professor, Adult Learning and Leadership, Department of Organization and Leadership, Teachers College, Columbia University, United States; and co-director of the J. M. Huber Institute for Learning in Organizations. She researches and consults on action learning, informal learning, and organizational learning.

Jane Mathison is Visiting Research Fellow, School of Management, University of Surrey, United Kingdom; and trainer in NLP. Her main interests are developing new understandings of transformative learning and exploring innovations in the use of NLP in qualitative research.

Regina H. Mulder is Professor, Educational Science, Institute for Educational Science, University of Regensburg, Germany. Her research foci are on various aspects of vocational education and training and of learning in organizations.

Hugh Munby is Professor Emeritus, Queen's University, Canada. During his career he developed an extensive record of research and publication in science education, curriculum theory, teacher knowledge, and workplace learning.

Rob Poell is Professor, Human Resource Development, Department of Human Resource Studies, Tilburg University, Netherlands; and editor, *Human Resource Development International*. His main areas of expertise are workplace learning, learning networks, and HRD strategies, especially of employees.

David Preece is Professor, Technology Management and Organization Studies; Head, Centre for Leadership and Organizational Change; and DBA programme director, the Business School, University of Teesside, United Kingdom. His research has focussed on organizational and technological change and leadership development.

Paul Smith is Subject Group Leader, Strategy, Human Resources and Leadership, University of Teesside, United Kingdom, having previously worked in management development in the UK National Health Service. He has recently completed his PhD on work-based learning.

Paul Tosey is Senior Lecturer, School of Management, University of Surrey, United Kingdom; and Higher Education Academy national teaching fellow. He has published widely on organizational learning, transformative learning, the work of Gregory Bateson, and NLP.

Marloes Van Engen is Assistant Professor, Gender and Diversity in Organizations, Department of Human Resource Studies, Tilburg University, Netherlands. Her research interests are in the area of (the management of) diversity in teams and organizations, gender in organizations, gender and careers, and work-family issues in organizations.

Marc Van Veldhoven is Associate Professor, Work and Organizational Psychology, Department of Human Resource Studies, Tilburg University, Netherlands. He specializes in HRM, well-being, and performance.

Marianne Van Woerkom is Assistant Professor, Human Resource Development, Department of Human Resource Studies, Tilburg University, Netherlands. Her research interests are in the area of workplace learning, organizational learning, team learning and team performance, critical reflection, and coaching.

Joan Versnel is Assistant Professor, School of Occupational Therapy, Dalhousie University, Canada. She holds a PhD in education. Her research explores self-advocacy for adolescents and negotiating workplace accommodations for individuals with chronic illness and disability.

Yu-Lin Wang is Assistant Professor, Department of Business Administration, National Cheng Kung University, Taiwan. Her research interests focus on organizational learning and entrepreneurship in small and medium-sized enterprises.

Lyle Yorks is Associate Professor, Adult and Continuing Education, Department of Organization and Leadership, Teachers College, Columbia University, United States, where he teaches courses in human resource development, strategy development, and research. His research interests include action learning, collaborative inquiry, and learning transfer.

Bibliography

Abrahamsson, L. (2000) *Att Återställa Ordningen: könsmönster och förändring i arbetsorganisationer* [*To Restore the Order: gender patterns and change in work organizations*], Umeå, Sweden: Borea Bokförlag.

Adams, G.L. and Lamont, B.T. (2003) 'Knowledge management systems and developing sustainable competitive advantage', *Journal of Knowledge Management*, 7: 142–54.

Agrell, A. and Gustafson, R. (1994) 'The Team Climate Inventory (TCI) and group innovation: a psychometric test on a Swedish sample of work groups', *Journal of Occupational and Organizational Psychology*, 67: 143–51.

Akgün, A.E., Lynn, G.S. and Byrne, J.C. (2003) 'Organizational learning: a socio-cognitive framework', *Human Relations*, 56: 839–68.

Aldag, R.J. and Fuller, S.R. (1993) 'Beyond fiasco: a reappraisal of the groupthink phenomenon and a new model of group decision processes', *Psychological Bulletin*, 113: 533–52.

Allen, D. (2001) *The Changing Shape of Nursing Practice: the role of nurses in the hospital division of labour*, London: Routledge.

Ancona, D.G. and Caldwell, D.F. (1992) 'Demography and design: predictors of new product team performance', *Organization Science*, 3: 321–41.

Anderson, J.R. (1993) 'Problem solving and learning', *American Psychologist*, 48: 35–44.

Anderson, N. and West, M.A. (1996) 'The Team Climate Inventory: development of the TCI and its applications in teambuilding for innovativeness', *European Journal of Work and Organizational Psychology*, 5: 53–66.

Andersson, E. (2005) *Kompetensutveckling i call centres: genomförande och utvärdering av projekt helhetssyn vid Kalix Tele24* [*Competence Development in Call Centres: implementation and evaluation of an interactive project at Kalix Tele24*], Luleå, Sweden: Luleå University of Technology.

Antoncic, B. and Hisrich, R.D. (2004) 'Corporate entrepreneurship contingencies and organizational wealth creation', *Journal of Management Development*, 23: 518–50.

Aragón-Correa, J.A., García-Morales, V.J., & Cordón-Pozo, E. (2007). Leadership and organizational learning's role on innovation and performance: Lessons from Spain. *Industrial Marketing Management, 36*, 349–359.

Argote, L. and Todocara, G. (2007) 'Organizational learning', in G.P. Hodgkinson and J.K. Ford (eds) *International Review of Industrial and Organizational Psychology*, vol. 22, Chichester, NY: Wiley, pp. 193–234.

Argyris, C. (1991) 'Teaching smart people how to learn', *Harvard Business Review*, 69: 99–109.

———. (1993) *On Organizational Learning*, Cambridge, MA: Blackwell.

Argyris, C., Putnam, R. and Smith, D.M. (1985) *Action Science: concepts, methods, and skills for research and intervention,* San Francisco: Jossey-Bass.

Argyris, C. and Schön, D. (1978) *Organizational Learning,* Reading, MA: Addison-Wesley.

———. (1996). *Organizational learning II.* Reading, MA: Addinson-Wesley.

Arthur, M.B., DeFillippi, R.J. and Jones, C. (2001) 'Project-based learning as the interplay of career and company non-financial capital', *Management Learning,* 32: 99–117.

Ashby, W. (1965) *An Introduction to Cybernetics,* London: Methuen.

Ayas, K. and Zeniuk, N. (2001) 'Project-based learning: building communities of reflective practitioners', *Management Learning,* 32: 61–76.

Baldwin, J.M. (1894) 'Personality-suggestion', *Psychological Review,* 1: 274–79.

———. (1898) 'On selective thinking', *Psychological Review,* 5: 1–24.

Bandler, R. and Grinder, J. (1975) *The Structure of Magic: a book about language and therapy,* Palo Alto, CA: Science and Behavioural Books.

Bandura, A. (1997) *Self-efficacy: the exercise of control,* New York: Freeman.

Bantel, K. and Jackson, S. (1989) 'Top management and innovations in banking: does the composition of the team make a difference?', *Strategic Management Journal,* 10: 107–24.

Bapuji, H. and Crossan, M. (2004) 'From questions to answers: reviewing organizational learning research', *Management Learning,* 35: 397–417.

Barnett, R. (1994) *The Limits of Competence,* Buckingham, UK: SRHE and Open University Press.

———. (1997) 'Beyond competence', in F. Coffield and B. Williamson (eds) *Repositioning Higher Education,* Buckingham, UK: SRHE and Open University Press.

Baron, R.M. and Kenny, D.A. (1986) 'The moderator-mediator variable distinction in social psychological research: conceptual, strategic, and statistical considerations', *Journal of Personality and Social Psychology,* 51: 1173–82.

Barsade, S.G., Ward, A.J., Turner, J.D.F. and Sonnenfeld, J.A. (2000) 'To your heart's content: a model of affective diversity in top management teams', *Administrative Science Quarterly,* 45: 802–36.

Bartunek, J.M. and Moch, M.K. (1994) 'Third order organizational change and the Western mystical tradition', *Journal of Organisational Change Management,* 7: 24–41.

Bassi, L., Cheney, S. and Lewis, E. (1998) 'Trends in workplace learning: supply and demand in interesting times', *Training and Development,* 52(11): 51–77.

Bateman, T.S. and Crant, J.M. (1993) 'The proactive component of organizational behavior: a measure and correlates', *Journal of Organizational Behavior,* 14: 103–18.

Bates, R. and Holton III, E.F. (2004) 'Linking workplace literacy skills and transfer system perceptions', *Human Resource Development Quarterly,* 15: 153–70.

Bateson, G. (1973) *Steps to an Ecology of Mind: Collected Essays in Anthropology, Psychiatry, Evolution and Epistemology Paladin,* Granada, London.

———. (1979) *Mind and Nature,* Glasgow: Fontana/Collins.

———. (2000) *Steps to an Ecology of Mind: collected essays in anthropology, psychiatry, evolution and epistemology,* revised edn, Chicago: University of Chicago Press.

Bateson, G. and Bateson, M.C. (1988) *Angels Fear,* London: Rider Books.

Bateson, G., Jackson, D.D., Haley, J. and Weakland, J. (1956) 'Toward a theory of schizophrenia', *Behavioral Science,* 1: 251–64.

Bateson, M.C. (2005) 'The double bind: pathology and creativity', *Cybernetics and Human Knowing,* 12: 11–21.

Bauer, J. and Gruber, H. (2007) 'Workplace changes and workplace learning: advantages of an educational micro perspective', *International Journal of Lifelong Education*, 26: 675–88.

Bauer, J. and Mulder, R.H. (2007) 'Modelling learning from errors in daily work', *Learning in Health and Social Care*, 6: 121–33.

——. (2008) 'Conceptualization of learning through errors at work: a literature review', in S. Billett, C. Harteis and A. Eteläpelto (eds) *Emerging Perspectives on workplace learning* (pp. 115–128), Rotterdam, Netherlands: Sense Publishers.

Bauer, J., Rehrl, M. and Harteis, C. (2007) 'Measurement of learning culture: a motivational approach', in H. Gruber and T. Palonen (eds) *Learning at the Workplace: New Developments*, Turku, Finland: Finnish Educational Research Association, pp. 21–50.

Beckett, D. (2001) 'Hot action at work: understanding "understanding" differently', in T. Fenwick (ed.) *Socio-Cultural Understandings of Workplace Learning*, San Francisco: Jossey-Bass/Wiley, pp. 73–84.

Bedeian, A.G. (1986) 'Contemporary challenges in the study of organizations', *Journal of Management*, 12: 185–201.

Beijaard, D. and Verloop, N. (1999) 'Gebieden en ontwikkeling van de professionele identiteit van leraren: een cognitief perspectief' [Areas and development of the professional identity of teachers: a cognitive perspective], *Pedagogisch Tijdschrift*, 24: 433–50.

Belfiore, M.E., Defoe, T.A., Folinsbee, S., Hunter, J. and Jackson, N.S (2004) *Reading Work: literacies in the new workplace*, Mahwah, NJ: Lawrence Erlbaum Associates.

Belsley, D.A., Kuh, E. and Welsch, R.E. (1980) *Regression Diagnostics: identifying influential data and sources of collinearity*, New York: John Wiley and Sons.

Belt, W., Richardson, R. and Webster, J. (2002) 'Women, social skill and interactive service work in telephone call centers', *New Technology, Work and Employment*, 17: 20–34.

Berends, H., Boersma, K. and Weggeman M. (2003) 'The structuration of organizational learning', *Human Relations*, 56: 1035–56.

Berger, P.L. and Luckman, T. (1966) *The Social Construction of Reality*, Harmondsworth, UK: Penguin.

Bergers, G.P.J., Marcelissen, F.H.G. and de Wolff, C.J. (1986) *Vragenlijst Organisatiestress-d Handleiding* [*Work Stress Questionnaire Manual*], Nijmegen, Netherlands: University of Nijmegen.

Berings, M.G.M.C., Gelissen, J.P.T.M. and Poell, R.F. (2008) 'On-the-job learning in the nursing profession: developing and validating a classification of learning activities and learning themes', *Personnel Review*, 37: 442–59.

Berings, M.G.M.C., Poell, R.F., Simons, P.R.J. and van Veldhoven, M.J.P.M. (2007) 'The development and validation of the on-the-job learning styles questionnaire for the nursing profession', *Journal of Advanced Nursing*, 58: 480–92.

Berscheid, E. and Reis, H. (1998) 'Attraction and close relationships', in T. Gilbert, S.T. Fiske and G. Lindzey (eds) *The Handbook of Social Psychology*, 4th edn, vol. 2D, New York: McGraw-Hill.

Bhaskar, R. (1998) *The Possibility of Naturalism*, London: Routledge.

Biddle, M. (2004) 'Organizational learning in a fire and emergency training centre: examining knowledge creating activity', unpublished doctoral dissertation, University of Alberta, Canada.

Billett, S. (1994) 'Situated learning: a workplace experience', *Australian Journal of Adult and Community Education*, 34: 112–30.

———. (2001a) 'Knowing in practice: re-conceptualising vocational expertise', *Learning and Instruction*, 11: 431–52.

———. (2001b) *Learning in the Workplace: strategies for effective practice*, Sydney, Australia: Allen and Unwin.

———. (2002) Workplace pedagogic practices: Co-participation and learning. *British Journal of Educational Studies*, 50 (4) 457–481.

———. (2003a) 'Sociogeneses, activity and ontogeny', *Culture and Psychology*, 9: 133–69.

———. (2003b) 'Workplace mentors: demands and benefits', *Journal of Workplace Learning*, 15: 105–13.

———. (2004a) 'Co-participation at work: learning through work and throughout working lives', *Studies in the Education of Adults*, 36: 190–205.

———. (2004b) 'Workplace participatory practices. Conceptualizing workplaces as learning environments', *Journal of Workplace Learning*, 16: 312–24.

———. (2006a) 'Relational interdependence between social and individual agency in work and working life', *Mind, Culture and Activity*, 13: 53–69.

———. (2006b) 'Work, subjectivity and learning', in S. Billett, T. Fenwick and M. Somerville (eds) *Work, Subjectivity and Learning*, Dordrecht, Netherlands: Springer.

———. (2008). Learning throughout working life: A relational interdependence between social and individual agency. *British Journal of Education Studies*, 55 (1) 39–58.

Billett, S., Ehrich, L. and Hernon-Tinning, B. (2003) 'Small business pedagogic practices', *Journal of Vocational Education and Training*, 55 (2): 149–67.

Billett, S., Smith, R. and Barker, M. (2005) 'Understanding work, learning and the remaking of cultural practices', *Studies in Continuing Education*, 27: 219–37.

Birdhistle, N., & Fleming, P. (2005). Creating a learning organization within the family business: An irish perspective. *Journal of European Industrial Training*, 29(9), 730–750.

Bloom, J.W. (2004) 'Patterns that connect: rethinking our approach to learning, teaching and curriculum', *Curriculum and Teaching*, 19: 5–26.

Borko, H. (2004) 'Professional development and teacher learning: mapping the terrain', *Educational Researcher*, 33(8): 3–15.

Boshuizen, H.P.A., Bromme, R. and Gruber, H. (eds) (2004) *Professional Learning: gaps and transitions on the way from novice to expert*, Dordrecht, Netherlands: Kluwer.

Boud, D.J. and Garrick, J. (eds) (1999) *Understanding Learning at Work*, London: Routledge.

Boud, D. and Solomon, N. (2001), 'Future Directions for Work-based Learning: Reconfiguring Higher Education' in Boud, D. and Solomon, N. (ed.), (2001), WBL A New Higher Education?, SRHE and Open University, Buckingham.

Boud, D., Solomon, N. and Symes, C. (2001) 'New practices for new times', in D. Boud and N. Solomon (eds) *Work Based Learning: a new higher education?*, Buckingham, UK: SRHE and Open University Press.

Boud, D. and Symes, C. (2000) 'Learning for real', in C. Symes and J. McIntyre (eds) *Working Knowledge: the new vocationalism and higher education*, Buckingham, UK: SRHE and Open University Press.

Bowers, C.A., Pharmer, J.A. and Salas, E. (2000) 'When member homogeneity is needed in work teams: a meta-analysis', *Small Group Research*, 31: 305–27.

Bradley, J., White, B.J. and Mennecke, B.E. (2003) 'Teams and tasks. A temporal framework for the effects of interpersonal interventions on team performance', *Small Group Research*, 34: 353–87.

Braverman, H. (1974) Labor and monoploy capital: the degradation of work in the twentieth century. New York: Monthly Review Press.

Bredo, E. (1989) 'Bateson's hierarchical theory of learning and communication', *Educational Theory*, 39: 27–38.

Brennan, J. and Little, B. (1996) *A Review of Work-Based Learning in Higher Education*, London: Department for Education and Employment.

Brockbank, A. and McGill, I. (1998) *Facilitating Reflective Learning in Higher Education*, Buckingham, UK: Open University Press.

Brockman, J. (1977) *About Bateson*, New York: G.P. Dutton.

Brookfield, S. (1995) 'Adult learning: an overview', in A. Tuijnman (ed.) *International Encyclopedia of Education*, Oxford: Pergamon Press.

Brown, J.S., Collins, A. and Duguid, P. (1989) 'Situated cognition and the culture of learning', *Educational Researcher*, 18: 32–42.

Bryk, A.S. and Raudenbush, S.W. (1992) *Hierarchical Linear Models: applications and data analysis methods*, London: Sage.

Bryman, A. and Cramer, D. (1997) *Quantitative Data Analysis with SPSS for Windows*, London: Routledge.

Buchberger, F., Campos, B.P., Kallos, D. and Stephenson, J. (2000) *Green Paper on Teacher Education in Europe*, Umeå, Sweden: Thematic Network on Teacher Education in Europe.

Bunderson, J.S. (2003) 'Team member functional background and involvement in management teams: direct effects and the moderating role of power centralization', *Academy of Management Journal*, 46: 458–74.

Bunderson, J.S. and Sutcliffe, K.M. (2002) 'Comparing alternative conceptualizations of functional diversity in management teams: process and performance effects', *Academy of Management Journal*, 45: 875–93.

———. (2003) 'Management team learning orientation and business unit performance', *Journal of Applied Psychology*, 88: 552–60.

Bunning, C. (1992) 'Turning experience into learning', *Journal of European Industrial Training*, 16(6): 7–12.

Büssing, A. and Glaser, J. (2002) *Das Tätigkeits- und Arbeitsanalyseverfahren für das Krankenhaus: Selbstbeobachtungsversion (TAA-KH-S) [Activity and Work Analysis Methods for Hospitals: self-observation version]*, Göttingen, Germany: Hogrefe.

Byrne, D. (1971) *The Attraction Paradigm*, New York: Academic Press.

Campion, M.A., Medsker, G.J. and Higgs, A.C. (1993) 'Relations between work group characteristics and effectiveness: implications for designing effective work groups', *Personnel Psychology*, 46: 823–47.

Canadian Career Consortium (2007) Available HTTP: <http://www.careerccc. org/ccc/nav.cfm?l=e> (accessed 2 October 2007).

Canadian Human Rights Commission (2003) *A Place for All: a guide to creating an inclusive workplace*, Ottawa, Canada: Canadian Human Rights Commission.

Cannon, M.D. and Edmondson, A.C. (2001) 'Confronting failure: antecedents and consequences of shared beliefs about failure in organizational work groups', *Journal of Organizational Behavior*, 22: 161–77.

Capra, F. (1996) *The Web of Life: a new synthesis of mind and matter*, London: HarperCollins.

Carrillo, J.E. and Gaimon, C. (2004) 'Managing knowledge-based resource capabilities under uncertainty', *Management Science*, 50: 1504–18.

Casey, A. (2005) 'Enhancing individual and organizational learning', *Management Learning*, 36: 131–47.

Cell, E. (1984) *Learning to Learn from Experience*. Albany, NY: State University of New York Press.

Chaiklin, S. and Lave, J. (eds) (1993) *Understanding Practice: perspectives in activity and context,* Cambridge: Cambridge University Press.

Chappell, C., Tennant, M., Soloman, N. and Yates, L. (2003) *Reconstructing the Lifelong Learner: pedagogy and identity in individual, organisational and social change,* London: Routledge.

Charlton, N.G. (2008) *Understanding Gregory Bateson: mind, beauty, and the sacred earth,* Albany, NY: State University of New York Press.

Chin, P., Hutchinson, N.L., Versnel, J., Munby, H. and Stockley, D. (2007) 'Obligation and irony in workplace accommodations: a case study in a large corporate office', paper presented at the annual meeting of the American Educational Research Association, held in Chicago.

Chin, P., Munby, H. and Hutchinson, N.L. (2000) 'Workplace learning from a curriculum perspective', in C. Symes (ed.) *Working Knowledge: conference proceedings,* Sydney, Australia: University of Technology Sydney, pp. 317–23.

Chin, P., Munby, H., Hutchinson, N.L., Taylor, J. and Clark, F. (2004a) 'Where's the science?: understanding the form and function of workplace science', in E. Scanlon, P. Murphy, J. Thomas and E. Whitlegg (eds) *Reconsidering Science Learning,* London: Routledge, pp. 118–34.

Chin, P., Steiner Bell, K., Munby, H. and Hutchinson, N.L. (2004b) 'Epistemological appropriation in one high school student's learning in co-operative education', *American Educational Research Journal,* 41: 401–17.

Chiva, R. and Alegre, J. (2005) 'Organizational learning and organizational knowledge', *Management Learning,* 36: 49–68.

Cho, H., Hallfors, D.D. and Sanchez, V. (2005) 'Evaluation of a high school peer group intervention for at-risk youth', *Journal of Abnormal Child Psychology,* 33: 363–74.

Christenson, L.T. and Cheney, G. (2005) 'Integrated organizational identities: challenging the "bodily" pursuit', paper presented at the 4th Critical Management Studies conference, held in Cambridge.

Clardy, A. (2000) 'Learning on their own: vocationally oriented self-directed learning projects', *Human Resource Development Quarterly,* 11: 105–25.

Clark, J. (2001) 'De lerende verpleegkundige' [The learning nurse], Anna Reyvaan lecture, held May 8th at Academisch Medisch Centrum in Amsterdam, Netherlands.

Clark, M.C. (2001) 'Off the beaten path: some creative approaches to adult learning', *New Directions for Adult and Continuing Education,* 89: 83–92.

Clark, M.A., Amundsen, S.D. and Cardy, R.L. (2002) 'Cross-functional team decision-making and learning outcomes: a qualitative illustration', *Journal of Business and Management,* 8: 217–36.

Cochran-Smith, M. and Lytle, S.L. (1999) 'The teacher research movement: a decade later', *Educational Researcher,* 28: 15–25.

Coffield, F. (2000) 'Introduction: a critical analysis of a learning society', in Coffield, F. (ed.) *Differing Visions of a Learning Society,* Bristol: Policy Press.

Coffield, F., Moseley, D., Hall, E. and Ecclestone, K. (2004) *Should We Be Using Learning Styles? What the research has to say to practice,* London: Learning and Skills Research Centre.

Cole, M. (1998) 'Can cultural psychology help us think about diversity?', *Mind, Culture and Activity,* 5: 291–304.

Confessore, S. and Kops, W. (1998) 'Self-directed learning and the learning organization: examining the connection between the individual and the learning environment', *Human Resource Development Quarterly,* 9: 365–75.

Contu, A., Grey, C. and Örtenblad, A. (2003) 'Against learning', *Human Relations,* 56: 931–52.

Contu, A. and Willmott, H. (2003) 'Re-embedding situatedness: the importance of power relations in learning theory', *Organization Science,* 14: 283–96.

Cook, S.D.N., & Yanow, D. (1993). Culture and organization learning. *Journal of Management Inquiry,* 2(3), 373–399.

Cronbach, L.J. and Meehl, P.E. (1955) 'Construct validity in psychological tests', *Psychological Bulletin,* 52: 281–302.

Crossan, M.M., Lane, H.W., White, R.E. and Djurfeldt, L. (1995) 'Organizational learning: dimensions for a theory', *The International Journal of Organizational Analysis,* 3: 337–60.

Cummings, J.N. (2004) 'Work groups, structural diversity, and knowledge sharing in a global organization', *Management Science,* 50: 352–64.

Cunningham, I. and Dawes, G. (1997) 'Problematic premises, presumptions, pre-suppositions and practices in management education and training', in J. Burgoyne and M. Reynolds (eds) *Management Learning: integrating perspectives in theory and practice,* London: Sage, pp. 110–26.

Daft, R.L. and Huber, G.P. (1987) 'How organizations learn: a communication framework', in N. DiTomaso and S.B. Bacharach (eds) *Research in Sociology of Organizations,* vol. 5, Greenwich, CT: JAI Press, pp. 1–36.

Daft, R.L. and Weick, K.E. (1984) 'Toward a model of organizations as interpretation systems', *Academy of Management Review,* 9: 284–95.

Darrah, C.N. (1995) 'Workplace training, workplace learning: a case study', *Human Organization,* 54: 31–41.

Darwin, A. (2000) 'Critical reflection on meaning in work settings', *Adult Education Quarterly,* 50: 197–211.

Davidson, J.E. and Sternberg, R.J. (1998) 'Smart problem-solving: how metacognition helps', in D.J. Hacker, J. Dunlosky and A.C. Graesser (eds) *Metacognition in Educational Theory and Practice,* Mahwah, NJ: Lawrence Erlbaum Associates, pp. 47–68.

Davis, B. (2004). *Inventions of teaching: A geneology.* London: Routledge.

Davis, B. and Sumara, D.J. (2006) *Complexity and Education: inquiries into learning, teaching and research,* Mahwah, NJ: Lawrence Erlbaum Associates.

Davis, B., Sumara, D.J. and Luce-Kapler, R. (2000) *Engaging Minds: learning and teaching in a complex world,* Mahwah, NJ: Lawrence Erlbaum Associates.

de Dreu, C.K.W. and Weingart, L.R. (2003) 'Task versus relationship conflict, team performance, and team member satisfaction: a meta-analysis', *Journal of Applied Psychology,* 88: 741–49.

de Jonge, J. (1995) 'Job autonomy, well-being and health: a study among Dutch health care workers', unpublished PhD thesis, Maastricht University, Netherlands.

de Jonge, J., Landeweerd, J.A. and Nijhuis, F.J.N. (1995) *Constructie en Validering van de Vragenlijst ten Behoeve van het Project "Autonomie in het Werk"* [*Construction and Validation of the Questionnaire for the "Job Autonomy" Project*], Maastricht, Netherlands: Maastricht University.

de Lange, A., Taris, T., Jansen, P., Kompier, M., Houtman, I. and Bongers, P. (2005) 'Werk en motivatie om te leren: zijn er verschillen tussen jongere en oudere werknemers?' [Work and learning motivation: are there differences between younger and older employees?], *Gedrag and Organisatie,* 18: 309–25.

de Lange, A.H., Taris, T.W., Kompier, M.A.J., Houtman, I.L.D. and Bongers, P.M. (2003) 'The very best of the millennium: longitudinal research on the job demands-control model', *Journal of Occupational Health Psychology,* 8: 282–305.

de Leeuw, E.D. (2001) 'Reducing missing data in surveys: an overview of methods', *Quality and Quantity,* 35: 147–60.

Deery, S. & Kinnie, N. (eds) (2004) Call centres and human resource management: a cross-national perspective. Basingstoke: Palgrave Macmillan.

DeFillippi, R.J. (2001) 'Introduction: project-based learning, reflective practices and learning outcomes', *Management Learning,* 32: 5–10.

DeLuca, C., Hutchinson, N.L., deLugt, J.S., Thornton, A., Beyer, W., Chin, P., Versnel, J. and Munby, H. (2008) 'From disengagement to resilience: two cases of at-risk youth in work-based education', paper presented at the annual meeting of the Canadian Society for the Study of Education, Vancouver, Canada.

den Boer, P. and Hövels, B. (2001) *Benutting van Competenties in de Zorg- en Welzijnssector* [*Utilization of Competencies in Health and Social Care*], Tilburg, Netherlands: OSA.

Department for Education and Skills (2003) *The Future of Higher Education,* London: HMSO.

Dewey, J. (1925). *Experience and nature* (2nd ed.). Chicago: Open Court.

Diekmann, A. (2007) *Empirische Sozialforschung. Grundlagen, Methoden, Anwendungen* [*Empirical Social Research: fundamentals, methods, applications*], Reinbeck, Germany: Rowohlt.

Dilschmann, A., Falck, E. and Kraft, C. (2000) *Delaktighet, Lärande och Förändringsarbete: Lärandebok* [*Participation, Learning and Change Management*], Stockholm, Sweden: Liber.

———. (2000) Lärandebok: delaktighet, lärande och förändringsarbete. [Participation, Learning and Change Management]. Trygghetsfonden for kommuner och landsting. Stickhom: Liber.

Dilts, R.B. and Epstein, T.A. (1995) *Dynamic Learning,* Capitola, CA: Metapublications.

Dixon, N.M. (1992) 'Organizational learning: a review of the literature with implications for HRD professionals', *Human Resources Development Quarterly,* 3: 29–49.

Docherty, P. (1996) *Läroriket: vägar och vägval i en lärande organisation* [*Land of Learning: ways and strategies in a learning organization*], Stockholm, Sweden: Arbetslivsinstitutet.

Dodgson, M. (1993) 'Organizational learning: a review of some literatures', *Organization Studies,* 14: 375–94.

Dollard, M.F. and Winefield, A.H. (1998) 'A test of the demand-control/support model of work stress in correctional officers', *Journal of Occupational Health Psychology,* 3: 243–64.

Doornbos, A.J., Bolhuis, S. and Simons, P.R.J. (2004) 'Modeling work-related learning on the basis of intentionality and developmental relatedness: a non-educative perspective', *Human Resource Development Review,* 3: 250–74.

Druskat, V.U. and Kayes, D.C. (2000) 'Learning versus performance in short-term project teams', *Small Group Research,* 31: 328–53.

Ducharme, E.R. (1993) *The Lives of Teacher Educators,* New York: Teachers College Press.

Dunphy, D. and Bryant, B. (1996) 'Teams: panaceas or prescriptions for improved performance?', *Human Relations,* 49: 677–99.

Dyck. B., Starke, F.A., Mischke, G.A. and Mauws, M. (2005) 'Learning to build a car: an empirical investigation of organizational learning', *Journal of Management Studies,* 42: 387–416.

Earley, P.C. and Mosakowski, E. (2000) 'Creating hybrid team cultures: an empirical test of transnational team functioning', *Academy of Management Journal,* 43: 26–49.

Easterby-Smith, M. (1997) 'Disciplines of organizational learning: contributions and critiques', *Human Relations,* 50: 1085–1113.

Easterby-Smith, M. and Araujo, L. (1999) 'Organizational learning: current debates and opportunities', in M. Easterby-Smith, J. Burgoyne and L. Araujo (eds) *Organizational Learning and the Learning Organization: developments in theory and practice*, Thousand Oaks, CA: Sage, pp. 1–21.

Edmondson, A.C. (1996) 'Learning from mistakes is easier said than done: group and organizational influences on the detection and correction of human error', *Journal of Applied Behavioral Science*, 32: 5–28.

———. (1999) 'Psychological safety and working behaviour in work teams', *Administrative Science Quarterly*, 44: 350–83.

———. (2004) 'Learning from errors in health care: frequent opportunities, pervasive barriers', *Quality and Safety in Health Care*, 13: 3–9.

Edmondson, A., Bohmer, R.M. and Pisano, G.P. (2001a) 'Speeding up team learning', *Harvard Business Review*, 79: 125–32.

———. (2001b) 'Disrupted routines: team learning and new technology implementation in hospitals', *Administrative Science Quarterly*, 46: 685–716.

Edwards, R. (2006) 'Beyond the moorland? Contextualising lifelong learning', *Studies in the Education of Adults*, 38: 25–36.

Edwards, E. and Nicoll, K. (2004) 'Mobilizing workplaces: actors, discipline and governmentality', *Studies in Continuing Education*, 26: 159–73.

Egan, K. (1978) 'Some presuppositions about curriculum', *Curriculum Studies*, 10: 123–33.

Eisenhardt, K.M. and Tabrizi, B.N. (1995) 'Accelerating adaptive processes: product innovation in the global computer industry', *Administrative Science Quarterly*, 40: 84–110.

Ekberg, K. and Barajas, J. (2000) 'Hälsobefrämjande omorganisation: vilka är förutsättningarna?' [Health promotion reorganization: what are the conditions?], in K. Barklöf (eds) *Vägval? En Antologi om Förändringsprocesser i Magra Organisationer* [*An Anthology about Change Management in Lean Organisations*], Stockholm, Sweden: Rådet för Arbetslivsforskning.

Elkjaer, B. and Wahlgren, B. (2006) 'Organizational learning and workplace learning-similarities and differences', in E. Antonacopoulou, P. Jarvis, V. Andersen, B. Elkjaer and S. Høyrup (eds) *Learning, Working, and Living: mapping the terrain of working life learning*, New York: Palgrave Macmillan, pp. 15–32.

Ellinger, A.D. (2005) 'Contextual factors influencing informal learning in a workplace setting: the case of "Reinventing itself Company" ', *Human Resource Development Quarterly*, 16: 389–415.

Ellinger, A.D. and Cseh, M. (2007) 'Contextual factors influencing the facilitation of others' learning through everyday work experiences', *Journal of Workplace Learning*, 19: 435–52.

Ellinger, A.D., Watkins, K.E. and Bostrom, R.P. (1999) 'Managers as facilitators of learning in learning organizations', *Human Resource Development Quarterly*, 10: 105–25.

Ellström, P.E. (1992) *Kompetens, Utbildning och Lärande i Arbetslivet: problem, begrepp och teoretiska perspektiv* [*Competence, Education and Learning in Working Life: problems, concepts and theoretical perspectives*], Stockholm, Sweden: Norstedts.

———. (2001) 'Integrating learning and work: problems and prospects', *Human Resource Development Quarterly*, 12: 421–35.

———. (2002) 'Lärande: i spänningsfältet mellan produktionens och utvecklingens logik' [Learning: the interplay of production and development logic], in K. Abrahamsson, L. Abrahamsson, T. Björkman, P.E. Ellström and J. Johansson (eds) *Utbildning, Kompetens och Arbete* [*Education, Competence and Work*], Lund, Sweden: Studentlitteratur.

Ely, R.J. and Thomas, D.A. (2001) 'Cultural diversity at work: the effects of diversity perspectives on work group processes and outcomes', *Administrative Science Quarterly*, 46: 229–73.

Engeström, Y. (1987). Learning by expanding. An activity Theoretical Approach to Developmental Research. Orienta Konsultit Oy: Helsinki.

———. (1999) 'Innovative learning in work teams', in Y. Engeström, R. Miettinen and R.-L. Punamaki (eds) *Perspectives on Activity Theory*, Cambridge: Cambridge University Press, pp. 377–406.

———. (2001) 'Expansive learning at work: toward an activity theoretical reconceptualization', *Journal of Education and Work*, 14: 133–46.

Enos, M.D., Kehrhahn, M.T. and Bell, A. (2003) 'Informal learning and the transfer of learning: how managers develop proficiency', *Human Resource Development Quarterly*, 14: 369–87.

Eraut, M., Alderton, J., Cole, G. and Senker, P. (1998) *Development of Knowledge and Skills in Employment*, Brighton, UK: University of Sussex, Institute of Education.

———. (2002) 'The impact of the manager on learning in the workplace', in R. Harrison, F. Reeve, A. Hanson and J. Clarke (eds) *Supporting Life Long Learning: organizing learning*, Milton Keynes, UK: Open University, pp. 91–108.

Evans, K. (2002) 'Taking control of their lives? Agency in young adult transitions in England and the New Germany', *Journal of Youth Studies*, 5: 245–69.

Faul, F., Erdfelder, E., Lang, A.-G. and Buchner, A. (2007) 'G*power 3: a flexible statistical power analysis program for the social, behavioral, and biomedical sciences', *Behavior Research Methods*, 39: 175–91.

Fenwick, T. (2008). Understanding relations of individual-collective learning in work: A review of research. *Management Learning* 39 (3), 227–243.

Fernie, S. and Metcalf, D. (1998) *(Not) Hanging on the Telephone: payment systems in the new sweatshops,* London: Centre of Economic Performance, London School of Economics.

Field, J. (2000) 'Governing the ungovernable: why lifelong learning promises so much yet delivers so little', *Educational Management and Administration*, 28: 249–61.

Fiol, C.M. (1994) 'Consensus, diversity and learning in organizations', *Organization Science*, 5: 403–20.

Flanagan, J.C. (1954) 'The critical incident technique', *Psychological Bulletin*, 51: 327–58.

Forrester, K., Payne, J. and Ward, K. (1995) *Workplace Learning: perspectives on education, training and work*, Aldershot, UK: Avebury.

French, R. and Bazalgette, J. (1996) 'From "learning organization" to "teaching-learning organization"?', *Management Learning*, 27: 113–28.

Frese, M. and Zapf, D. (1994) 'Action as the core of work psychology: a German approach', in H.C. Triandis, M.D. Dunette and L.M. Hough (eds) *Handbook of Industrial and Organizational Psychology*, 2nd edn, vol. 4, Palo Alto, CA: Consulting Psychologists Press, pp. 271–340.

Furze, G. and Pearcey, P. (1999) 'Continuing education in nursing: a review of the literature', *Journal of Advanced Nursing*, 29: 355–63.

Garcia-Prieto, P., Bellard, E. and Schneider, S.C. (2003) 'Experiencing diversity, conflict, and emotions in teams', *Journal of Applied Psychology*, 52: 413–40.

Garet, M.S., Porter, A.C., Desimone, L., Birman, B.F. and Yoon, K.S. (2001) 'What makes professional development effective? Results from a national sample of teachers', *American Educational Research Journal*, 38: 915–45.

Garrick, J. (1998) 'Informal learning in the workplace: unmasking human resource development', London: Routledge.

———. (1999) 'The dominant discourses of learning at work', in D. Boud and J. Garrick (eds) *Understanding Learning at Work*, London: Routledge.

Gates, L.B. (2000) 'Workplace accommodation as a social process', *Journal of Occupational Rehabilitation*, 10: 85–98.

Gee, J.P. (2000) 'New people in new worlds: networks, capitalism and school', in B. Cope and M. Kalantzis (eds) *Multiliteracies: literacy learning and the design of social futures*, London: Routledge, pp. 43–69.

Geijsel, F. and Meijers, F. (2005) 'Identity learning: the core process of educational change', *Educational Studies*, 31: 419–30.

George, G., Zahra, S.A., Wheatley, K.K., & Khan, R. (2001). The effects of alliance portfolio characteristics and absorptive capacity on performance: A study of biotechnology firms. *Journal of High Technology Management Research*, 12, 205–226.

Gherardi, S. and Nicolini, D. (2000) 'To transfer is to transform: the circulation of safety knowledge', *Organization*, 7: 329–48.

Gibb, S. (2004) 'Imagination, creativity, and HRD: an aesthetic perspective', *Human Resource Development Review*, 3: 53–74.

Giddens, A. (1991) *Modernity and Self-Identity: self and society in the late modern age*, Stanford, CA: Stanford University Press.

Gilhooly, A., Irving, H. and Molloy, S. (2004) 'Learning partnerships for holistic work-based learning', *Widening Participation and Lifelong Learning*, 6: 25–34.

Glendon, I., Clarke, S.G. and McKenna, E.F. (2006) *Human Safety and Risk Management*, Boca Raton, FL: Taylor & Francis.

Gnyawali, D.R. and Stewart, A.C. (2003) 'A contingency perspective on organizational learning: integrating environmental context, organizational learning processes, and types of learning', *Management Learning*, 34: 63–89.

Grossman, P., Wineburg, S. and Woolworth, S. (2001) 'Toward a theory of teacher community', *Teachers College Record*, 103: 942–1012.

Gruber, H. (2001) 'Acquisition of expertise', in J.J. Smelser and P.B. Baltes (eds) *International Encyclopedia of the Social and Behavioral Sciences*, Oxford: Elsevier, pp. 5145–50.

Guest, D.E., Michie, J., Conway, N. and Sheehan, M. (2003) 'Human resource management and corporate performance in the UK', *British Journal of Industrial Relations*, 41: 291–314.

Guskey, T.R. (2002) 'Professional development and teacher change', *Teachers and Teaching: Theory and Practice*, 8: 381–91.

Gustavsen, B. (1990) *Vägar till ett Bättre Arbetsliv [Ways to a Better Working Life]*, Stockholm, Sweden: Arbetslivscentrum.

Habermas, J. (1984). *The theory of communicative action* (Vol. 1, T. McCarthy, Trans.). Boston: Beacon Press.

Hager, P. (2004) 'Lifelong learning in the workplace? Challenges and issues', *Journal of Workplace Learning*, 16: 22–33.

Hambrick, D.C., Cho, T.S. and Chen, M.J. (1996) 'The influence of top management team heterogeneity on firms' competitive moves', *Administrative Science Quarterly.*, 41: 659–84.

Hargreaves, P. and Jarvis, P. (1998) *Human Resource Development Handbook*, London: Kogan Page.

Harries-Jones, P. (1995) *A Recursive Vision: ecological understanding and Gregory Bateson*, Toronto, Canada: University of Toronto.

Harrison, D.A. and Klein, K.J. (2007) 'What's the difference? Diversity constructs as separation, variety, or disparity in organizations', *Academy of Management Review*, 32: 1199–1228.

Harrison, R., & Kessels, J. (2003). Human resource development: key organizational process in a knowledge economy. *Proceedings of the Fourth International Conference on HRD Research and Practice across Europe*. Toulouse, France.

Harteis, C., Bauer, J. and Haltia, P. (2007) 'Learning from errors at the workplace: insights from two studies in Germany and Finland', in H. Gruber and T. Palonen (eds) *Learning at the Workplace: New Developments*, Turku, Finland: Finnish Educational Research Association, pp. 119–38.

Higher Education Academy Report (2006) *Work-Based Learning: illuminating the higher education landscape*, York, UK: Higher Education Academy.

Higher Education Council for England (2006a) *Workplace Learning in the North East*, report to HEFCE by the KSA Partnership, London: Higher Education Council for England.

Higher Education Council for England. (2006b) *HEFCE Strategic Plan*, London: Higher Education Council for England.

Higher Education Funding Council for England. (2003) *HEFCE Strategic Plan*, London: Higher Education Council for England.

Higher Education Funding Council for England. (2006) *Towards a Strategy for Workplace Learning*, Report to HEFCE by Centre for Higher Education Research and KPMG, London: Higher Education Council for England.

Hodges, D.C. (1998) 'Participation as dis-identification with/in a community of practice', *Mind, Culture and Activity*, 5: 272–90.

Hoegl, M. and Gemuenden, H.G. (2001) 'Teamwork quality and the success of innovative projects: a theoretical concept and empirical evidence', *Organization Science*, 12: 435–49.

Holman, D.J. and Wall, T.D. (2002) 'Work characteristics, learning related outcomes, and strain: a test of competing direct effects, mediated, and moderated models', *Journal of Occupational Health Psychology*, 7: 283–301.

Holton, E.F., Bates, R.A. and Ruona, W.A. (2000) 'Development of a generalized learning transfer system inventory', *Human Resource Development Quarterly*, 11: 333–58.

Honey, P. and Mumford, A. (1992) *A Manual of Learning Styles*, Maidenhead, UK: Peter Honey Publications.

Horwitz, S.K. and Horwitz, I.B. (2007) 'The effects of team diversity on team outcomes: a meta-analytic review of team demography', *Journal of Management*, 33: 959–86.

Houlihan, M. (2000) 'Eyes wide shut? Querying the depth of call centre learning', *Journal of European Industrial Training*, 24: 228–40.

Hoyle, E. (1980) *Professionalization and Deprofessionalization in Education*, London: Kogan Page.

Hoyle, E. and John, P. (1995) *Professional Knowledge and Professional Practice*, London: Cassell.

Huber, G.P. (1991) 'Organizational learning: the contributing processes and the literatures', *Organization Science*, 2: 88–115.

Human Resources Development Canada (1998) *Ensuring Opportunities: access to post-secondary education (Response to the first report of the Standing Committee on Human Resources Development and the Status of Persons with Disabilities)*, Ottawa, Canada: Human Resources Development Canada.

Hung, D.W.L. (1999) 'Activity, apprenticeship, and epistemological appropriation: implications from the writings of Michael Polyani', *Educational Psychologist*, 34: 193–205.

Huselid, M.A. (1995) 'The impact of human resource management practices on turnover, productivity, and corporate financial performance', *Academy of Management Journal*, 38: 635–72.

Hutchinson, N.L. (2007) *Inclusion of Exceptional Learners in Canadian Schools: a practical handbook for teachers*, Toronto, Canada: Prentice Hall.

Hutchinson, N.L., Berg, D., Versnel, J., Wintermute, J., Munby, H., Chin, P. and Stockley, D. (2005) 'Creating enabling workplaces for workers with disabilities: a review of the literature and an emerging model', paper presented at the annual conference of the Canadian Society for Studies in Education, held in London, Canada.

Hutchinson, N.L., Poth, C., Munby, H., Chin, P., deLugt, J.S., Berg, D., Versnel, J. and Stockley, D. (2006) ' "They want to come to school": Work-based education programs for students with disabilities and for at-risk students', paper presented at the annual meeting of the American Educational Research Association, held in San Francisco.

Hutchinson, N.L., Steiner-Bell, K., Munby, H., Chin, P., Versnel, J. and Chapman, C. (2001) 'Multiple perspectives on the purposes of high school cooperative education: a qualitative study', *Journal of Cooperative Education*, 36: 73–85.

Hutchinson, N.L., Versnel, J., Chin, P. and Munby, H. (2008) 'Negotiating accommodations so that work-based education facilitates career development for youth with disabilities', *Work: A Journal of Prevention, Assessment and Rehabilitation*, 30: 123–36.

Hutchinson, N.L., Versnel, J., deLugt, J.S., Chin, P., Munby, H., Stockley, D. and Berg, D. (2007) 'Creating enabling workplaces for workers with disabilities: education for negotiating accommodations', paper presented at the annual meeting of the American Educational Research Association, held in Chicago.

International Labour Office (2006) *Global Employment Trends for Youth*, Geneva, Switzerland: International Labour Office.

Ivanovas, G. (2007) 'Still not paradigmatic', *Kybernetes*, 36: 847–51.

Jackson, N. (1991) *Skills Formation and Gender Relations: the politics of who knows what*, Geelong, Australia: Deakin University Press.

——. (2004) 'Developing the concept of metalearning', *Innovations in Education and Teaching International*, 41: 391–403.

Jackson, S.E. (1996) 'The consequences of diversity in multidisciplinary work teams', in M.A. West (ed.) *Handbook of Work Group Psychology*, Chichester, UK: Wiley.

Jackson, S.E., Brett, J.F., Sessa, V.I., Cooper, D.M., Julin, J.A. and Peyronnin, K. (1991) 'Some differences make a difference: individual dissimilarity and group heterogeneity as correlates of recruitment, promotions, and turnover', *Journal of Applied Psychology*, 76: 675–89.

Jacobs, R.L. and Washington, C. (2003) 'Employee development and organizational performance: a review of literature and directions for future research', *Human Resource Development International*, 6: 343–54.

Jacobsen, D.I. and Thorsvik, J. (2002) *Hur Moderna Organisationer Fungerar* [*The Function of Modern Organizations*], Lund, Sweden: Studentlitteratur.

Janis, I.L. (1985) 'International crisis management in the nuclear age', *Applied Social Psychology Annual*, 6: 63–86.

Jansson, A. (2006) *Lärandemiljö vid Callcenters: kartläggning av arbets- och lärandemiljön vid callcenters i Norrbotten, våren 2004* [*Learning Environment in Call Centres. A mapping study of call centres in the Northern part of Sweden, spring 2004*], Luleå, Sweden: Luleå University of Technology.

Janz, B.D. (1999) 'Self-directed teams in IS: correlates for improved systems development work outcomes', *Information and Management*, 35: 171–92.

Jarvis, P. (2007) *Globalisation, Lifelong Learning and the Learning Society: sociological perspectives*, Abingdon, UK: Routledge.

Jehn, K.A. and Bezrukova, K. (2004) 'A field study of group diversity, work-group context, and performance', *Journal of Organizational Behaviour,* 25: 703–29.

Johnson, S. (1998) *Who Moved My Cheese,* London: Vermilion, Random House.

———. (2001) *Emergence: The Connected Lives of Ants, Brains, Cities and Software.* New York: Scribner.

Jones, O. and Macpherson, A. (2005) 'Organizational learning and strategic renewal in owner-managed SMEs: institutionalizing network knowledge', paper presented at the sixth international conference on HRD research and practice across Europe, held in Leeds.

Jongmans, C.T. and Beijaard, D. (1997) 'De professionele oriëntatie van leraren en hun betrokkenheid bij het schoolbeleid' [The professional orientation of teachers and their involvement in school policy], *Pedagogische Studiën,* 74: 97–107.

Jongmans, C.T., Biemans, H.J.A., Sleegers, P.J.C. and Jong, F.P.C.M. (1998) 'De professionele oriëntatie van docenten en hun betrokkenheid bij onderwijsvernieuwingen' [The professional orientation of teachers and their involvement in educational reforms], *Pedagogisch Tijdschrift,* 23: 25–38.

Jung, D.I., Sosik, J.J. and Baik, K.B. (2002) 'Investigating work group characteristics and performance over time: a replication and cross-cultural extension', *Group Dynamics: Theory, Research, and Practice,* 6: 153–71.

Kang, S., Morris, S.S. and Snell, S.A. (2007) 'Relational archetypes, organizational learning, and value creation: extending the human resource architecture', *Academy of Management Review,* 32: 236–56.

Karasek, R.A. (1985) *Job Content Instrument: questionnaire and user's guide,* revision 1.1 edn, Los Angeles: University of Southern California.

———. (1989) 'Control in the workplace and its health-related aspects', in S.L. Sauter, J.J. Hurrell and C.L. Cooper (eds) *Job Control and Work Health,* New York: Wiley, pp. 129–59.

Karasek, R. and Theorell, T. (1990) *Healthy Work: stress, productivity, and the reconstruction of working life,* New York: Basic Books.

Karmel, T. and Maclean, R. (eds) (2006) *Technical and Vocational Education and Training in an Ageing Society: experts meeting proceedings.* Adelaide, Australia: National Centre for Vocational Education Research.

Karpiak, I. (2000) 'Evolutionary theory and the new sciences', *Studies in Continuing Education,* 22: 29–44.

Katzenbach, J. and Smith, D. (1993) *The Wisdom of Teams,* Boston, MA: Harvard Business School Press.

Kauffman, S. (1995) *At Home in the Universe: the search for laws of complexity,* London: Penguin.

Keegan, A. and Turner, J.R. (2001) 'Quantity versus quality in project-based learning practices', *Management Learning,* 32: 77–98.

Keeney, B. (1983) *Aesthetics of Change,* New York: Guilford Press.

Keith, N. and Frese, M. (2005) 'Self-regulation in error management training: emotion control and metacognition as mediators of performance effects', *Journal of Applied Psychology,* 90: 677–91.

Kelchtermans, G. and Ballet, K. (2002) 'The micropolitics of teacher induction. A narrative-biographical study on teacher socialisation', *Teaching and Teacher Education,* 18: 105–20.

Kenny, D.A., Kashy, D.A. and Bolger, N. (1998) 'Data analysis in social psychology', in D. Gilbert, S. Fiske and G. Lindzey (eds) *The Handbook of Social Psychology,* 4th edn, vol. 1, Boston, MA: McGraw-Hill, pp. 233–265.

Kieft, M. and Nijhof W.J. (2000) *HRD-Profielen 2000: een onderzoek naar rollen, outputs en competenties van bedrijfsopleiders* [*HRD Profiles 2000: an investigation into the roles, outputs and competencies of corporate trainers*], Enschede, Netherlands: Twente University Press.

King, R. (2004) 'Globalization and the university', in R. King (ed.) *The University in the Global Age*, Basingstoke, UK: Palgrave Macmillan.

Kinnie, N., Hutschinson, S. and Purcell, J. (2000) ' "Fun and surveillance": the paradox of high commitment management in call centres', *International Journal of Human Resource Management*, 11: 967–85.

Klaassen, C., Beijaard, D. and Kelchtermans, G. (1999) 'Perspectieven op de professionele identiteit van leraren' [Perspectives on the professional identity of teachers], *Pedagogisch Tijdschrift*, 24: 375–99.

Kolb, D.A. (1984) *Experiential Learning*, Englewood Cliffs, NJ: Prentice Hall.

Kolodner, J. (1983) 'Towards an understanding of the role of experience in the evolution from novice to expert', *International Journal of Man-Machine Studies* 19: 497–518.

Kornfield, J. (2000) *After the Ecstasy, the Laundry: how the heart grows wise on the spiritual path*, London: Rider Books.

Korthagen, F.A.J. (2004a) 'In search of the essence of a good teacher: towards a more holistic approach in teacher education', *Teaching and Teacher Education*, 20: 77–97.

———. (2004b) 'Zin en onzin van competentiegericht opleiden' [Sense and nonsense of competence-based training], *VELON Tijdschrift voor Lerarenopleiders*, 25(3): 13–23.

Krull, J.L. and MacKinnon, D.P. (2001) 'Multilevel modeling of individual and group level mediated effects', *Multivariate Behavioral Research*, 36: 249–77.

Kwakman, C.H.E. (1999) 'Leren van docenten tijdens de beroepsloopbaan: studies naar professionaliteit op de werkplek in het voortgezet onderwijs' [Continuing teacher learning: studies into professionalism at the workplace in secondary education], unpublished PhD thesis, University of Nijmegen, Netherlands.

———. (2003) 'Factors affecting teachers' participation in professional learning activities', *Teaching and Teacher Education* 19: 149–70.

Kwakman, K. and Van den Berg, E. (2004) 'Professionele ontwikkeling als kennisontwikkeling door leraren: naar een betere interactie tussen praktijk en theorie', *VELON Tijdschrift voor Lerarenopleiders*, 25(3): 6–12.

Lai, K., Cheng, T.C.E. and Yeung, A.C.L. (2004) 'Relationship stability and supplier commitment to quality', *International Journal of Product Economics*, 96: 397–410.

Lakeoff, G. & Johnson, M. 1999, Philosophy in the Flesh: the embodied mind and its challenge to Western thought Basic Books, New York.

Lambert, R. and Peppard, J. (1993) 'Information technology and new organisational forms: destination but no road map?', *Journal of Strategic Information Systems*, 2: 180–205.

Langfred, C.W. (2005) 'Autonomy and performance in teams: the multilevel moderating effect of task interdependence', *Journal of Management*, 31: 513–29.

Latour, B. (2005) *Re-Assembling the Social: an introduction to actor network theory*, London: Oxford University Press.

Laursen, E. (2006) 'Knowledge, progression and the understanding of workplace learning', in E. Antonacopoulou, P. Jarvis, V. Andersen, B. Elkjaer and S. Høyrup (eds) *Learning, Working, and Living: mapping the terrain of working life learning*, New York: Palgrave Macmillan, pp. 69–84.

Lave, J. (1993) 'The practice of learning', in S. Chaiklin and J. Lave (eds) *Understanding Practice: perspectives on activity and context*, Cambridge: Cambridge University Press, pp. 3–32.

Lave, J. and Wenger, E. (1991) *Situated Learning: legitimate peripheral participation*, Cambridge: Cambridge University Press.

Law, J. and Hassard, J. (1999) *Actor Network Theory and After*, Oxford: Blackwell.

Lawrence, B.S. (1997) 'The black box of organizational demography', *Organization Science*, 8: 1–22.

Lawton, S. and Wimpenny, P. (2003) 'Continuing professional development: a review', *Nursing Standard*, 17(24): 41–4.

Lee, M., Letiche, H., Crawshaw, R. and Thomas, M. (1996) *Management Education in the New Europe: boundaries and complexity*, London: Routledge.

LeGrand, C., Szulkin, R. and Tåhlin, M. (2002) 'Har jobben blivit mer kvalificerade? Kvalifikationskravens förändringar i Sverige under tre decennier' [Has work become more qualified? Three decades of changing demands for qualification in Sweden], in K. Abrahamsson, L. Abrahamsson, T. Björkman, P.E. Ellström and J. Johansson (eds) *Utbildning, Kompetens och Arbete* [*Education, Competence and Work*], Lund, Sweden: Studentlitteratur.

Leonard-Barton, D. (1995) *Wellspring of Knowledge: building and sustaining the sources of innovation*, Boston, MA: Harvard Business School Press.

Levine, P. and Wagner, M. (2005) 'Transition for young adults who received special education services as adolescents: a time of challenge and change', in D.W. Osgood, E.M. Foster, C. Flanagan and G.R. Ruth (eds) *On Your Own Without a Net: the transition to adulthood for vulnerable populations*, Chicago: University of Chicago Press, pp. 202–71.

Lieberman, A. (2000) 'Networks as learning communities: shaping the future of teacher development', *Journal of Teacher Education*, 51: 221–7.

Lindgren, A. and Sederblad, P. (2001) *Work organisation, control and qualifications in travel agencies and call centres*, 19th annual International Labour Process conference, held March 26–28 at the School of Management, Royal Holloway, University of London.

Lipset, D. (1980) *Gregory Bateson: the legacy of a scientist*, London: Prentice Hall.

Lipshitz, R., Popper, M. and Friedman, V.J. (2002) 'A multifacet model of organizational learning', *Journal of Applied Behavioral Science*, 38: 78–98.

Little, R.J.A. and Rubin, D.B. (1990) 'The analysis of social science data with missing values', *Sociological Methods and Research*, 18: 292–326.

Livingstone, D. (1999) *The Education-Jobs Gap: underemployment or economic democracy*, Toronto, Canada: Garamond Press.

Liyanage, S. and Barnard, R. (2002) 'What is the value of firms' prior knowledge? Building organizational knowledge capabilities', *Singapore Management Review*, 24(3): 35–116.

Locke, E.A., & Latham, G.P. (1990). *A theory of goal setting and task performance*. Englewood Cliffs, NJ: Prentice Hall.

Lopez, S.P., Peon, J.M.M. and Ordas, C.J.V. (2005) 'Organizational learning as a determining factor in business performance', *The Learning Organization*, 12: 227–45.

Lowe, G. (2000) *The Quality of Work. A people-centred agenda*, Toronto, Canada: Oxford University Press.

Lundvall, B.A. (1995) *National Systems of Innovations: towards a theory of innovation and interactive learning*, London: Printer.

Lunenberg, M. and Korthagen, F.A.J. (2003) 'Teacher educators and student-directed learning', *Teaching and Teacher Education* 19: 29–44.

Lunenberg, M., Snoek, M. and Swennen, A. (2000) 'Between pragmatism and legitimacy: developments and dilemmas in teacher education in the Netherlands', *European Journal of Teacher Education*, 23: 251–60.

McDermott, R. (1998) 'Learning across teams: the role of communities of practice in team organization', *Knowledge Management Review*, 8: 32–6.

McPhail, B. (2002). What is 'on the line' in call centre studies: A review of key issues in the acdemic literature. Faculty of Information Studies: University of Toronto.

MacKinnon, D.P., Fairchild, A.J. and Fritz, M. (2007) 'Mediation analysis', *Annual Review of Psychology*, 58: 593–614.

McLaughlin, M.W. and Talbert, J.W. (1993) *Contexts that Matter for Teaching and Learning*, Palo Alto, CA: Context Center on Secondary School Teaching.

McPhail, B. (2002) *What Is 'on the Line' in Call Centres Studies? A review of key issues in the academic literature*, Toronto, Canada: Faculty of Information Studies, University of Toronto.

McWhinney, W. (2005) 'The white horse: a reformulation of Bateson's typology of learning', *Cybernetics and Human Knowing*, 12: 22–35.

McWhinney, W. and Markos, L. (2003) 'Transformative education: across the threshold', *Journal of Transformative Education*, 1: 16–37.

Madaus, J.W., Ruban, L.M., Foley, T.E. and McGuire, J.M. (2003) 'Attributes contributing to the employment satisfaction of university graduates with learning disabilities', *Learning Disability Quarterly*, 26: 159–70.

Major, D. (2002) 'A more holistic form of higher education: the real potential of work-based learning', *Widening Participation and Lifelong Learning*, 4(3): 26–34.

Marcelis, B.A.C.R. (2006). The relation between action-learning programs types and the level of reflection that occurs. Master's thesis, Radboud University, Nijmegen, Netherlands.

Marsick, V.J. (1987) *Learning in the workplace*, New York: Croon Helm.

Marsick, J. and O'Neil, J. (1999) 'The many faces of action learning', *Management Learning*, 30: 159–76.

Marsick, V.J. and Volpe, M. (eds) (1999) *Informal Learning on the Job*, San Francisco: Berrett-Koehler.

Marsick, V.J. and Watkins, K.E. (1990). *Informal and incidental learning in the workplace*. London, UK: Routledge.

———. 2003) 'Demonstrating the value of an organization's learning culture: the dimensions of the learning organization questionnaire', *Advances in Developing Human Resources*, 5: 132–51.

Marsick, V., Cederholm, L., Turner, E. and Pearson, E. (1992) 'Action-reflection learning', *Training and Development*, 46(8): 63–6.

Maturana, H.R. and Varela, F.J. (1998) *The Tree of Knowledge, the Biological Roots of Human Understanding*, revised edn, Boston, MA: Shambhala Publications.

Maurer, T.J. (2002) 'Employee learning and development orientation: toward an integrative model of involvement in continuous learning', *Human Resource Development Review*, 1: 9–44.

Maurer, T.J., Weiss, E.M. and Barbeite, F.G. (2003) 'A model of involvement in work-related learning and development activity: the effects of individual, situational, motivational, and age variables', *Journal of Applied Psychology*, 88: 707–24.

Meurier, C.E., Vincent, C.A. and Parmar, D.G. (1997) 'Learning from errors in nursing practice', *Journal of Advanced Nursing*, 26: 111–19.

Meyer, A.D. (1982) 'Adopting the environmental jolts', *Administrative Science Quarterly*, 27: 515–37.

Mezirow, J. (1991) *Transformative Dimensions of Adult Learning*, San Francisco: Jossey-Bass.

Mezirow, J. and Associates (2000) *Learning as Transformation: critical perspectives on a theory in progress*, San Francisco: Jossey-Bass.

Mikkelsen, A., Øgaard, T. and Landsbergis, P. (2005) 'The effects of new dimensions of psychological job demands and job control on active learning and occupational health', *Work and Stress*, 19: 153–75.

Milliken, F. and Martins, L. (1996) 'Searching for common threads: understanding the multiple effects of diversity in organizational groups', *Academy of Management Review*, 21: 402–33.

Mojab, S. & Gorman, R. (2003). Women and Consciousness in the "Learning Organization": Emancipation or Exploitation? *Adult Education Quarterly*, 53 (4) 228–24.

Montagnini, L. (2007) 'Looking for "scientific" social science', *Kybernetes*, 36: 1012–21.

Moon, J. (2005) *We Seek It Here: a new perspective on the elusive activity of critical thinking: a theoretical and practical approach*, Bristol, UK: ESCalate.

Morrison, D.L., Cordery, J. and Girardi, A. (1998) *How Work Design Influences Psychological Well Being: a longitudinal study supporting the mediating role of skill utilization*, Sheffield, UK: Institute of Work Psychology, University of Sheffield.

Mulkeen, T.A. and Copper, B.S. (1992) 'Implications of preparing school administrators for knowledge work organizations', *Journal of Educational Administration*, 30(10): 17–29.

Munby, H., Chin, P. and Hutchinson, N.L. (2003a) 'Co-operative education, the curriculum, and working knowledge', in D. Trueit, W. Doll, H. Wang and W. Pinar (eds) *The Internationalization of Curriculum*, New York: Peter Lang, pp. 205–18.

Munby, H., Hutchinson, N.L. and Chin, P. (2007a) 'Workplace learning, work-based education, and the challenges to educational psychology', in J. Kincheloe and R. Horn (eds) *Praeger Handbook of Education and Psychology*, Westport, CT: Praeger, pp. 540–7.

———. (2009) 'Workplace learning: metacognitive strategies for learning in the knowledge economy', in R. Maclean and D. Wilson (eds) *International handbook of education for the changing world of work: Bridging academic and vocational learning* (pp. 1763–1775). New York: Springer.

Munby, H., Versnel, J., Hutchinson, N.L., Chin, P. and Berg, D. (2003b) 'Workplace learning and the metacognitive function of routines', *Journal of Workplace Learning*, 15: 94–104.

Munby, H., Zanibbi, M., Poth, C., Hutchinson, N.L., Chin, P. and Thornton, A. (2007b) 'Enhancing workplace learning for adolescents: the use of metacognitive instruction', *Education and Training*, 49: 8–24.

Munro, A., Holly, L. and Rainbird, H. (2000) ' "My ladies aren't interested in learning": managers, supervisors and the social context of learning', *International Review of Education*, 46: 515–28.

Mutch, A. (2003) 'Communities of practice and habitus: a critique', *Organization Studies*, 24: 383–95.

Nafukho, F.M., Hairston, N.R. and Brooks, K. (2004) 'Human capital theory: implications for human resource development', *Human Resource Development International*, 7: 545–51.

Nevis, E.C., A.J. DiBella & J.M. Gould (1995). Understanding organizations as learning systems. *Sloan Management Review*, 36(2), 73–85.

Nezlek, J.B. and Zyzniewski, L.E. (1998) 'Using hierarchical linear modeling to analyze grouped data', *Group Dynamics: Theory, Research, and Practice*, 2: 313–20.

Nielsen, K.A. and Svensson, L. (2006) *Action Research and Interactive Research: beyond practice and theory*, Maastricht, Netherlands: Shaker Publishing.

Niemi, H. (2002) 'Active learning: a cultural change needed in teacher education and schools', *Teaching and Teacher Education*, 18: 763–80.

Nonaka, I. and Takeuchi, H. (1995) *The Knowledge-Creating Company: how Japanese companies create the dynamics of innovation*, New York: Oxford University Press.

Norman, K. (2005) *Call Centre Work: characteristics, physical and psychosocial exposure, and health related outcomes,* Stockholm, Sweden: Arbetslivsinstitutet.

O'Connor, B.P. (2000) 'Using parallel analysis and Velicner's MAP test', *Behavior Research Methods, Instruments, and Computers*, 32: 396–402.

Ohlsson, S. (1996) 'Learning from performance errors', *Psychological Review*, 103: 241–62.

O'Neil, J. (1999) 'The role of the learning advisor in action learning', unpublished doctoral dissertation, Teachers College, Columbia University, New York.

O'Neil, J. and Marsick, V.J. (1994) 'Becoming critically reflective through action learning', *New directions for Adult and Continuing Education*, 63: 17–30.

——. (2007). *Understanding action learning*. New York: American Management Association.

Ontario Ministry of Training, Colleges and Universities (2008) *Second Career*. Available HTTP: <http://www.edu.gov.on.ca/eng/tcu/secondcareer/newcareer.html> (accessed 25 July 2008).

O'Reilly, C.A., Snyder, R.C. and Boothe, J.N. (1993) 'Executive team demography and organizational change', in G.P. Huber and W.H. Glick (eds) *Organizational Change and Redesign*, New York: Oxford University Press, pp. 147–75.

Organisation for Economic Co-operation and Development (1996) *Lifelong Learning for All*, Paris, France: Organisation for Economic Co-operation and Development.

Osberg, D. and Biesta, G.J.J. (2007) 'Beyond presence: epistemological and pedagogical implications of "strong" emergence', *Interchange*, 38: 31–51.

Osterman, P. (1994) 'How common is workplace transformation and who adopts it?', *Industrial and Labor Relations Review*, 47: 173–88.

Ostroff, C. and Schmitt, N. (1993) 'Configurations of organizational effectiveness and efficiency', *Academy of Management Journal*, 36: 1345–61.

Park, M.G. and Dhameja, S. (2006) 'Technical entrepreneurship development for the aged', in T. Karmel and R. Maclean (eds) *Technical and Vocational Education and Training in an Ageing Society: experts meeting proceedings*, Adelaide, Australia: National Centre for Vocational Education Research, pp. 102–17.

Parker, S.K. and Sprigg, C.A. (1999) 'Minimizing strain and maximizing learning: the role of job demands, job control, and pro-active personality', *Journal of Applied Psychology*, 84: 925–39.

Patton, M. (1990) *Qualitative Evaluation and Research Methods*, Thousand Oaks, CA: Sage.

Pearce, J.A. and Ravlin, E.C. (1987) 'The design and activation of self-regulating work groups', *Human Relations*, 40: 473–88.

Pedler, M., Burgoyne, J. and Boydell, T. (2001) *A Manager's Guide to Self-Development*, London: McGraw-Hill.

Pegels, C.C., Song, Y.I. and Yang, B. (2000) 'Management heterogeneity, competitive interaction groups, and firm performance', *Strategic Management Journal*, 21: 911–23.

Pelled, L.H., Eisenhardt, K.M. and Xin, K.R. (1999) 'Exploring the black box: an analysis of work group diversity, conflict and performance', *Administrative Science Quarterly*, 44: 1–28.

Peterson, T.E. (1999) 'Whitehead, Bateson and readings and the predicates of education', *Educational Philosophy and Theory*, 31: 27–41.

Pfeffer, J. (1994) 'Competitive advantage through people', *California Management Review*, 36(2): 9–28.

Pham, N.T. and Swierczek, F.W. (2006) 'Facilitators of organizational learning in design', *The Learning Organization*, 13: 186–201.

Pilbeam, S. and Corbridge, M. (eds) (2006) *People Resourcing: contemporary HRM in practice*, 3rd edn, Harlow, UK: Pearson Education.

Pillay, H., Brownlee, J. and McCrindle, A. (1998) 'The individuals' beliefs about learning and nature of knowledge on educating an intelligent workforce', *Journal of Education and Work*, 11: 239–54.

Poell, R.F. (1998) 'Organizing work-related learning projects: a network approach', unpublished PhD thesis, University of Nijmegen, Netherlands.

———. (1999) 'The learning organisation: a critical evaluation', in J.P. Wilson (ed.) *Human Resource Development: learning and training for individuals and organisations*, London: Kogan Page.

Poell, R.F. and van der Krogt, F.J. (2003) 'Learning strategies of workers in the knowledge-creating company', *Human Resources Development International*, 6: 387–403.

———. (2008) 'The role of social networks in managing organizational talent, knowledge and employee learning', in V. Vaiman and C. Vance (eds) *Smart Talent Management*, London: Edward Elgar, pp. 93–118.

———. (2009) 'An empirical typology of hospital nurses' individual learning paths', in J. Calvin and S. Carter (eds) *Top Ten Best Papers from the 2008 Academy of HRD International Research Conference*, Bowling Green, OH: AHRD.

Poell, R.F., Yorks, L. and Marsick, V.J. (2005) 'Conducting action-learning research from a cross-cultural multi-theory perspective: theory and data from the US and the Netherlands compared', in M.L. Morris, F.M. Nafukho and C.M. Graham, *Proceedings of the 2005 International Research Conference of the Academy of HRD*, Bowling Green, OH: Academy of HRD.

———. (2009) 'Organizing project-based learning in work contexts: a cross-cultural cross analysis of data from two projects', *Adult Education Quarterly*, 60 (1), 77-93.

Porst, R. (2001) *Wie Man die Rücklaufquote bei Postalischen Befragungen Erhöht [How To Increase the Return Rate of Postal Surveys]*, Mannheim, Germany: Zentrum für Umfragen, Methoden und Analyzen.

Powell, J. H. (1989) 'The reflective practitioner in nursing', *Journal of Advanced Nursing*, 14: 824–32.

Probert, B. (1999) 'Gendered workers and gendered work: implications for women's learning', in D. Boud and J. Garrick (eds) *Learning in Work*, London: Routledge, pp. 98–116.

Quintini, G., Martin, J.P. and Martin, S. (2007) *The Changing Nature of the School-to-Work Transition Process in OECD Countries*, Bonn, Germany: Institute for the Study of Labor (IZA).

Räftegård, K. (1998) *Pratet som Demokratiskt Verktyg: om möjligheten till en kommunikativ demokrati [Talk as a Democratic Tool: on the possibility of a communicative democracy]*, Stockholm, Sweden: Gidlunds.

Rainbird, H., Fuller, A. and Munro, A. (2004) *Workplace Learning in Context*, London: Routledge.

Raizen, S.A. (1991) 'Learning and Work: the research base', in Organisation for Economic Co-operation and Development (ed.) *Vocational Education and Training for Youth: towards coherent policy and practice*, Paris, France: Organisation for Economic Co-operation and Development, pp. 69–114.

Ranhagen, U. (1995) *Att Arbeta i Projekt: om planering och projektering inför stora förändringar [Project Work: planning and design for major changes]*, Göteborg, Sweden: Novum Grafiska AB.

Rasmussen, J. (1987) 'The definition of human error and a taxonomy for technical system design', in J. Rasmussen, K. Duncan and J. Leplat (eds) *New Technology and Human Error*, Chichester, UK: Wiley, pp. 23–30.

Ray, W.A. and Govener, M.R. (2007) 'Legacy: lessons from the Bateson team meetings', *Kybernetes*, 36: 1026–36.

Reason, J.T. (1990) *Human Error*, Cambridge: Cambridge University Press.

———. (1995) 'Understanding adverse events: human factors', *Quality in Health Care*, 4: 80–9.

Reeve, F. and Gallacher, J. (2003) 'Exploring understandings of university and employer "partnerships" within work-based learning programmes', paper presented at the third international conference on Researching Work and Learning, held at the University of Tampere, Finland.

Resnick, L. (1987) 'Learning in school and out', *Educational Researcher,* 16(9): 13–20.

Revans, R.W. (1982) *The Origin and Growth of Action Learning,* London: Chartwell Bratt.

Richardson, R. and Belt, V. (2001) 'Saved by the bell? Call centers and economic development in less favoured regions', *Economic and Industrial Democracy,* 22: 67–98.

Rimanoczy, I. & Turner, E. (2008). Action reflection learning: Solving real business problems by connecting learning with earning. Mountain View, CA: Davies-Black.

Roach, D.W. and Bednar, D.A. (1997) 'The theory of logical types: a tool for understanding levels and types of change in organizations', *Human Relations,* 50: 671–99.

Rogoff, B. (1990) *Apprenticeship in Thinking: cognitive development in social context,* New York: Oxford University Press.

Rogoff, B. and Lave, J. (eds) (1984) *Everyday Cognition: its development in social context,* Cambridge, MA: Harvard University Press.

Rybowiak, V., Garst, H., Frese, M. and Batinic, B. (1999) 'Error orientation questionnaire (EOQ): reliability, validity, and different language equivalence', *Journal of Organizational Behavior,* 20: 527–47.

Sadler-Smith, E. (2006) *Learning and Development for Managers: perspectives from research and practice,* Malden, MA: Blackwell.

Sadler-Smith, E., Gardiner, P., Badger, B., Chaston, I. and Stubberfield, J. (2000) 'Using collaborative learning to develop small firms', *Human Resource Development International,* 3: 285–306.

Säljö, R. (2000) Lärande i praktiken. Ett sociokulturellt perspektiv [Learning in practice. A sociocultural perspective]. Prisma: Stockholm.

Salomon, G. (1997) *Distributed Cognitions: psychological and educational considerations,* Cambridge: Cambridge University Press.

Sambrook, S. and Stewart, J. (eds) (2007) *Human Resource Development in the Public Sector: the case of health and social care,* London: Routledge.

Sandgren, S. (2000) 'Competence demands in the new economy: a call centre case study', paper presented at the eighth international Joseph A. Schumpeter Society (Millennium) conference, held in Manchester, June 28–July 1.

Santos-Vijande, M.L., Sanzo-Pérez, M.J., Álvarez-González, L.I. and Vázquez-Casielles, R. (2005) 'Organizational learning and marketing orientation: interface and effects on performance', *Industrial Marketing Management,* 34: 187–202.

Saru, E. (2005) 'Organizational learning and strategic HRD: how are they valuable for small firms', paper presented at the Sixth International Conference on HRD Research and Practice across Europe, held in Leeds.

Sawchuk, P. (2003) *Adult Learning, Technology, and Working Class Life,* Cambridge: Cambridge University Press.

Sawchuk, P., Duarte, N. and Elhammoumi, M. (eds) (2005) *Critical Perspectives on Activity: explorations across education, work and everyday life,* Cambridge: Cambridge University Press.

Scarbrough, H., Bresnen, M., Edelman, L.F., Laurent, S., Newell, S. and Swan, J. (2004a) 'The processes of project-based learning: an exploratory study', *Management Learning,* 35: 491–506.

Scarbrough, H., Swan, J., Laurent, S., Bresnen, M., Edelman, L.F. and Newell, S. (2004b) 'Project-based learning and the role of learning boundaries', *Organization Studies*, 25: 1579–1600.

Schank, R.C. (1999) *Dynamic Memory Revisited*, Cambridge: Cambridge University Press.

Schön, D. (1983) *The Reflective Practitioner. how professionals think in action*, London: Temple Smith.

Schreurs, P.J.G. and Taris, T.W. (1998) 'Construct validity of the demand-control model: a double cross-validation approach', *Work and Stress*, 12: 66–84.

Schumacker, R.E. and Lomax, R.G. (2004) *A Beginner's Guide to Structural Equation Modeling*, Mahwah, NJ: Lawrence Erlbaum Associates.

Schwab, J.J. (1972) 'The practical: translation into curriculum, *School Review*, 81: 501–22.

Scott, P. (1998) 'Massification, internationalization and globalization', in P. Scott (ed.) *The Globalization of Higher Education*, Buckingham, UK: SRHE and Open University.

Scott-Morgan, P. (1994) The Unwritten Rules of the Game, McGraw-Hill, London.

Scribner, S. (1985a) 'Knowledge at work', *Anthropology and Education Quarterly*, 16: 199–206.

———. (1985b) 'Vygostky's use of history', in J.V. Wertsch (ed.) *Culture, Communication and Cognition: Vygotskian perspectives*, Cambridge: Cambridge University Press, pp. 119–45.

Seezink, A. and van der Sanden, J.M.M. (2005) 'Lerend werken in de docentenwerkplaats: praktijktheorieën van docenten over competentiegericht voorbereidend middelbaar beroepsonderwijs' [Learning and working within a "teachers' workplace": teachers' practical theories about competence-oriented prevocational secondary education], *Pedagogische Studiën*, 82: 275–92.

Senders, J.W. and Moray, N.P. (1991) *Human Error: cause, prediction, and reduction*, Hillsdale, NJ: Lawrence Erlbaum Associates.

Senge, P. (1990) The fifth discipline: the art and practice of the learning organization. New York: Doubleday/Currency.

Sfard, A. (1998) 'On two metaphors for learning and the dangers of choosing just one, *Educational Researcher*, 27(2): 4–13.

Shaw, W.S. and Feuerstein, M. (2004) 'Generating workplace accommodations: lessons learned from the integrated case management study', *Journal of Occupational Rehabilitation*, 14: 207–16.

Simons, P.R.J. and Ruijters, M.C.P. (2004) 'Learning professionals: towards an integrated model', in H.P.A. Boshuizen, R. Bromme and H. Gruber (eds) *Professional Learning: gaps and transitions on the way from novice to expert*, Dordrecht, Netherlands: Kluwer, pp. 207–29.

Simons, T., Pelled, L.H. and Smith, K.A. (1999) 'Making use of difference: diversity, debate, and decision comprehensiveness in top management teams, *Academy of Management Journal*, 42: 662–73.

Sitkin, S.B. (1992) 'Learning through failure: the strategy of small losses', *Research in Organizational Behavior*, 14: 231–66.

Skule, S. (2004) 'Learning conditions at work: a framework to understand and assess informal learning in the workplace', *International Journal of Training and Development*, 8: 8–20.

Slater, S.F. and Narver, J.C. (1995) 'Market orientation and the learning organization', *Journal of Marketing*, 59: 63–74.

Smith, A., Oczkowski, E., Macklin, R. and Noble, C. (2003) 'Organisational change and the management of training in Australian enterprises', *International Journal of Training and Development*, 7: 2–15.

Snijders, T.A.B. and Bosker, R.J. (1999) *Multilevel Analysis: an introduction to basic and advanced multilevel modeling*, London: Sage.

Snyder, B.R. (1971) *The Hidden Curriculum*, New York: Knopf.

Sosik, J.J. and Jung, D.I. (2002) 'Work-group characteristics and performance in collectivistic and individualistic cultures', *Journal of Social Psychology*, 142: 5–23.

Spencer, B.A. (1994) 'Models of organization and total quality management: a comparison and critical evaluation', *Academy of Management Review*, 19: 446–71.

Stacey, R.D. (2005) *Experiencing Emergence in Organizations: local interaction and the emergence of global pattern*, London: Routledge.

Stake, R.E. (2000) 'Case studies', in N.K. Denzin and Y.S. Lincoln (eds) *Handbook of Qualitative Research*, 2nd edn, Thousand Oaks, CA: Sage, pp. 435–54.

Stasz, C. and Stern, D. (1998) *Work-Based Learning for Students in High Schools and Community Colleges*, Berkeley, CA: University of California, National Center for Research in Vocational Education.

Stewart, J. and McGoldrick J. (1996) *Human Resource Development: perspectives, strategies and practice*, London: Pitman.

Stewart J., McGoldrick, J. and Watson, S. (eds) (2001) *Understanding Human Resource Development: a research based approach*, London: Routledge.

Straka, G.A. (1999) 'Perceived work conditions and self-directed learning in the process of work', *International Journal of Training and Development*, 3: 240–9.

——. (2000) 'Conditions promoting self-directed learning at the workplace', *Human Resources Development International*, 3: 241–51.

Streumer, J.N. (ed.) (2006) *Work-Related Learning*, Dordrecht, Netherlands: Springer.

Swanborn, P.G. (1996) *Case-Study's: wat, wanneer en hoe? [Case Studies: what, when, and how?]*, Meppel, Netherlands: Boom.

Swanborn, P.G. and Rademaker, L. (1982) *Sociologische Grondbeginselen [Fundamentals of Sociology]*, Utrecht, Netherlands: Spectrum.

Swanson, R.A. and Holton, III, E.F. (2001) *Foundations of Human Resource Development*, San Francisco: Berrett-Koehler.

Symes, C. (2001) 'Capital degrees: another episode in the history of work and learning', in D. Boud and N. Solomon (eds) *Work Based Learning: a new higher education?*, Buckingham, UK: SRHE and Open University Press.

Tajfel, H. and Turner, J.C. (1986) 'The social identity theory of intergroup behavior', in S. Worchel and W.G. Austin (eds) *Psychology of Intergroup Relations*, Chicago: Nelson-Hall, pp. 7–24.

Taris, T.W. and Feij, J.A. (2005) 'Learning and strain among newcomers: a three-wave study on the effects of job demands and job control', *Journal of Psychology*, 138: 543–63.

Taris, T.W. and Kompier, M.A.J. (2004) 'Job characteristics and learning behavior', in P.L. Perrewé and D.C. Ganster (eds) *Research in Occupational Stress and Well-Being: exploring interpersonal dynamics*, Vol. 4, Amsterdam, Netherlands: JAI Press, pp. 127–66.

Taris, T.W., Kompier, M.A.J., de Lange, A.H., Schaufeli, W.B. and Schreurs, P.J.G. (2003) 'Learning new behaviour patterns: a longitudinal test of Karasek's active-learning hypothesis among Dutch teachers', *Work and Stress*, 17: 1–20.

Taylor, R., Barr, J. and Steele, T. (2002) *For a Radical Higher Education: after postmodernism*, Buckingham, UK: SRHE and Open University Press.

Templeton, G.F., Lewis, B.R. and Snyder, C.A. (2002) 'Development of a measure for the organizational learning construct', *Journal of Management Information System*, 19: 175–218.

Tengblad, P., Wiberg, A., Herrman, L. and Backström, M. (2002) *Hållbart Arbete i Informationssamhället. Slutrapport från projektet "Call center i utveckling: långsiktigt hållbart arbete med kunder på distans" [Sustainable Employment in the Information Society: final report of the project "Call centers in develop-ment: sustainable work with clients at a distance"*], Stockholm, Sweden: VIN-NOVA.

Test, D., Fowler, C., Wood, W., Brewer, D. and Eddy, S. (2005) 'A conceptual framework of self-advocacy for students with disabilities', *Remedial and Special Education*, 26: 43–54.

Thomas, F.N., Waits, R.A. and Hartsfield, G.L. (2007) 'The influence of Gregory Bateson: legacy or vestige?', *Kybernetes*, 36: 871–83.

Thompson, P. and Warhurst, C. (1998) *Workplace of the Future*, Wiltshire, UK: Macmillan Business.

Tillema, H.H. (1997) 'Promoting conceptual change in learning to teach', *Asian-Pacific Journal of Teacher Education*, 25: 7–16.

Tjepkema, S., Stewart, J., Sambrook, S., Mulder, M., ter Horst, H. and Scheerens, J. (2002) *HRD and Learning Organisations in Europe*, London: Routledge.

Tjosvold, D., Yu, Z.Y. and Hui, C. (2004) 'Team learning from mistakes: the con-tribution of cooperative goals and problem solving', *Journal of Management Studies*, 41: 1223–45.

Torraco, R.J. (1999) 'Integrating learning with working: a reconception of the role of workplace learning', *Human Resource Development Quarterly*, 10: 249–70.

Torrington, D., Hall, L. and Taylor, S. (2004) *Human Resource Management*, 6th edn, Harlow: Pearson Education.

Tosey, P. and Mathison, J. (2008) 'Do organisations learn? Some implications for HRD of Bateson's levels of learning', *Human Resource Development Review*, 7: 13–31.

Tosey, P., Mathison, J. and Langley, D. (2008) ' "Flesh and blood and action": organ-isations, learning and aesthetics', paper presented at the ninth international con-ference on HRD research and practice across Europe, held in Lille, France.

Tosey, P., Mathison, J. and Michelli, D. (2005) 'Mapping transformative learn-ing: the potential of neuro-linguistic programming', *Journal of Transformative Education*, 3: 335–52.

Toulmin, S. and Gustavsen, B. (1996) *Beyond Theory: changing organization through participation*, Amsterdam, Netherlands: John Benjamins.

Tsang, E.W.K. (1997) 'Organizational learning and the learning organization: a dichotomy between descriptive and prescriptive research', *Human Relations*, 50: 73–89.

Tucker, A.L. and Edmondson, A.C. (2003) 'Why hospitals don't learn from fail-ures: organizational and psychological dynamics that inhibit system change', *California Management Review*, 45: 55–72.

Tummers, G.E.R., Landeweerd, J.A. and van Merode, G.G. (2002) 'Work organ-isation, work characteristics and their psychological effects on nurses in the Netherlands', *International Journal of Stress Management*, 9: 183–206.

Turnbull, H.R., Turnbull, A.P. and Wehmeyer, M.L. (2003) 'A quality of life framework for special education outcomes', *Remedial and Special Education*, 24: 67–74.

Turner, J.C., Hogg, M.A., Oakes, P.J., Reicher, S.D. and Wetherell, M. (1987) *Rediscovering the Social Group: a self-categorization theory*, Oxford: Black-well.

Urry, J. (2000) *Sociology beyond Societies*, London: Routledge.

Valsiner, J. (1994) 'Bi-directional cultural transmission and constructive sociogen-esis', in W. de Graaf and R. Maier (eds) *Sociogenesis Re-examined*, New York: Springer, pp. 101–34.

——. (2000) *Culture and Human Development*, London: Sage.

Valsiner, J. and van der Veer, R. (2000) *The Social Mind: the construction of an idea*, Cambridge: Cambridge University Press.

van Buren, M.E. (2002) 'From cost to investment: workplace learning has new significance', *Employment Relations Today,* 29: 63–71.

van de Wiel, M.W.J., Szegedi, K.H.P. and Weggeman, M.C.D.P. (2004) 'Professional learning: deliberate attempts at developing expertise', in H.P.A. Boshuizen, R. Bromme and H. Gruber (eds) *Professional Learning: gaps and transitions on the way from novice to expert,* Dordrecht, Netherlands: Kluwer, pp. 181–206.

van der Klink, M.R. and Streumer, J.N. (2002) 'Effectiveness of on-the-job training', *Journal of European Industrial Training,* 26: 196–99.

van der Krogt, F.J. (1995) *Leren in Netwerken: veelzijdig organiseren van leernetwerken met het oog op humaniteit en arbeidsrelevantie* [*Learning in Networks: versatile organisation of learning networks with a view to humanity and work relevance*], Utrecht, Netherlands: Lemma.

———. (1998) 'Learning network theory: the tension between learning systems and work systems in organizations', *Human Resource Development Quarterly,* 9: 157–77.

———. (2007). *Organiseren van leerwegen: Strategieën van werknemers, managers en leeradviseurs in dienstverlenende organisaties* [Organizing learning paths: Strategies of workers, managers, and consultants in service organizations]. Rotterdam, Netherlands: Performa.

van der Vegt, G.S. and Bunderson, J.S. (2005) 'Learning and performance in multidisciplinary teams: the importance of collective team identification', *Academy of Management Journal,* 48: 532–47.

van der Vegt, G.S., Bunderson, J.S. and Oosterhof, A. (2006) 'Expertness diversity and interpersonal helping in teams: why those who need the most help end up getting the least', *Academy of Management Journal,* 49: 877–93.

van Dijk, H., van Engen, M.L. and van Knippenberg, D. (2009) 'Work group diversity and group performance: a meta-analysis'. Paper presented at the Academy of Management Annual Meeting, August 7–11, Chicago, Ill, USA.

van Dyck, C., Frese, M., Baer, M. and Sonnentag, S. (2005) 'Organizational error management culture and its impact on performance: a two-study replication', *Journal of Applied Psychology,* 90: 1228–40.

van Ginkel, J.R. (2007) 'Multiple imputation for incomplete test, questionnaire, and survey data', unpublished PhD thesis, Tilburg University, Netherlands.

van Ginkel, J.R., Sitsma, K., van der Ark, L.A., & Vermunt, J.K. (in press). Incidence of missing item scores in personality measurement, and simple item-score imputation. *Methodology.*

van Knippenberg, D., de Dreu, C.K.W. and Homan, A.C. (2004) 'Work group diversity and group performance: an integrative model and research agenda', *Journal of Applied Psychology,* 89: 1008–22.

van Knippenberg, D.L., Haslam, S.A. and Platow, M.J. (2007) *Unity through Diversity: value-in-diversity beliefs, work group diversity, and group identification,* Rotterdam, Netherlands: Erasmus University, ERIM.

van Knippenberg, D. and Schippers, M.C. (2007) 'Work group diversity', *Annual Review of Psychology,* 58: 515–41.

van Offenbeek, M. (2001) 'Processes and outcomes of team learning', *European Journal of Work and Organizational Psychology,* 10: 303–17.

van Veen, K., Sleegers, P., Bergen, T. and Klaassen, C. (1999) 'Opvattingen van docenten in het voortgezet onderwijs over hun professionaliteit' [Beliefs of teachers in secondary education about their professionalism], *Pedagogisch Tijdschrift,* 24: 401–31.

Van Woerkom, M. (2003) *Critical Reflection at Work: bridging individual and organizational learning,* unpublished PhD thesis, Twente University, Netherlands.

Van Woerkom, M. and Croon, M. (2008) 'Operationalising critically reflective work behaviour', *Personnel Review,* 37: 317–33.

Van Woerkom, M. and van Engen, M. (2009) 'Learning from conflicts: the effect of task and relationship conflicts on team learning and team performance', *European Journal of Work and Organizational Psychology*, 18, 381–404.

Van Woerkom, M., Nijhof, W.J. and Nieuwenhuis, L. (2003) 'The relationship between critical reflection and learning: experiences within Dutch companies', in B. Nyhan, P. Cressey, M. Kelleher and R.F. Poell (eds) *Facing Up to the Learning Organisation Challenge: selected European writings*, Luxembourg: Office for Official Publications of the European Communities, pp. 184–98.

Vera, D. & Crossan, M. (2004). Strategic leadership and organization learning, *Academy of Management Review*, 29, 222–240.

Varela, F.J., Thompson, E. and Rosch, E. (1993) *The Embodied Mind: cognitive science and human experience*, Cambridge, MA: MIT Press.

Velde, C. and Cooper, T. (2000) 'Students' perspectives of workplace learning and training in vocational education', *Education and Training*, 42: 83–92.

Verdonschot, S. (2005). Method for identifying learning processes in innovation processes. *Proceedings of the Sixth international conference on HRD research and practice across Europe.* Leeds, England.

Versnel, J. (2002) 'An analysis of routines observed in a range of workplaces', unpublished paper, Queen's University, Kingston, Canada.

Versnel, J. and Hutchinson, N.L. (2001) 'Preparing for the world: self-determination at work', paper presented at the annual provincial conference of the Council for Exceptional Children, Stratford, Canada.

Versnel, J., Hutchinson, N.L., Munby, H. and Chin, P. (2008) 'Work-based learning for adolescents with learning disabilities: creating a context for success, *Exceptionality Education Canada*, 18: 113–34.

Vince, R. (2001) 'Power and emotion in organizational learning', *Human Relations*, 54: 1325–51.

Visser, M. (2003) 'Gregory Bateson on deutero-learning and double bind: a brief conceptual history', *Journal of History of the Behavioural Sciences*, 39: 269–78.

———. (2007) 'Deutero-learning in organizations: a review and reformulation', *Academy of Management Review*, 32: 659–67.

Voronov, M. (2008) 'Toward a practice perspective on strategic organizational learning', *The Learning Organization*, 15: 195–221.

Waddell, D.L. (1993) 'Why do nurses participate in continuing education? A meta-analysis', *Journal of Continuing Education in Nursing*, 24: 52–6.

Wageman, R., Hackman, J.R. and Lehman, E. (2005) 'Team diagnostic survey: development of an instrument', *Journal of Applied Behavioral Science*, 41: 373–98.

Wagner, W.G., Pfeffer, J. and O'Reilly, C.A. (1984) 'Organizational demography and turnover in top-management groups', *Administrative Science Quarterly*, 29: 74–92.

Walton, J. (1999) *Strategic Human Resource Development*, Harlow: Prentice Hall.

Warr, P.B., Cook, J. and Wall, T.D. (1979) 'Scales for the measurement of some work attitudes and aspects of psychological well-being', *Journal of Occupational Psychology*, 52: 129–48.

Watkins, K.E. (1991) *Facilitating Learning in the Workplace.* Geelong, Australia: Deakin University.

Watkins, K.E and Marsick, V.J. (1993) *Sculpting the Learning Organization*, San Francisco: Jossey-Bass.

Watzlawick, P., Weakland, J. and Fisch, R. (1974) *Change: principles of problem formation and problem resolution,* New York: W.W. Norton & Co.

Weiss, E.M. (1999) 'Perceived workplace conditions and first-year teachers' morale, career choice commitment, and planned retention: a secondary analysis—When teaching is more than a job', *Teaching and Teacher Education*, 15: 861–79.

Wenger, E. (1998) *Communities of Practice: learning, meaning and identity*, Cambridge: Cambridge University Press.

Wertsch, J.V. (1998) *Mind as Action*. Oxford University Press: Oxford.

Whitmore, J. (2002) *Coaching for Performance*, 3rd edn, London: Nicolas Brealey.

Wielenga-Meijer, E.G.A., Taris, T.W., Kompier, M.A.J. and Wigboldus, D.H.J. (2006) 'Understanding task related learning: when, why, how and who?', in S. McIntyre and J. Houdmont (eds) *Occupational Health Psychology: European perspectives on research, education and practice*, vol. 1, Maia: ISMAI, pp. 59–81.

Wiener, N. (1965) *Cybernetics, or Control and Communication in the Animal and the Machine*, 2nd edn, Cambridge, MA: MIT Press.

Wiethoff, C. (2004) 'Motivation to learn and diversity training: application of the theory of planned behavior', *Human Resource Development Quarterly*, 15: 263–78.

Wijnhoven, F. (2001) 'Acquiring organizational learning norms: a contingency approach for understanding deutero learning', *Management Learning*, 32: 181–200.

Williams, K.Y. and O'Reilly, C.A. (1998) 'Demography and diversity in organizations: a review of 40 years of research', *Research in Organizational Behavior*, 20: 77–140.

Williams, P., Barclay, L. and Schmeid, V. (2004) 'Defining social support in context: a necessary step in improving research, intervention, and practice', *Qualitative Health Research*, 14: 942–60.

Williamson, B. and Coffield, F. (1997) 'Repositioning higher education', in F. Coffield and B. Williamson (eds) *Repositioning Higher Education*, Buckingham, UK: SRHE and Open University Press.

Wilson, J.P. (ed.) (1999) *Human resource development: Learning and training for individuals and organisations*. London: Kogan Press.

———. (ed.) (2005) *Human Resource Development: learning and training for individuals and organisations*, 2nd edn, London: Kogan Page.

Wright, K. (2003) *Exploring learning through work processes of expert workers*, unpublished doctoral dissertation, University of Alberta, Canada.

Yorks, L. (2005) *Strategic Human Resource Development*, Mason, OH: Thomson South-Western.

Yorks, L., O' Neil, J. and Marsick, V.J. (1999) 'Action learning: theoretical bases and varieties of strategies for individual, team and organizational development', *Advances in Developing Human Resources*, 1: 1–18.

Yorks, L., O'Neil, J., Marsick, V.J., Nilson, G.E. and Kolodny, R. (1996) 'Boundary management in action reflection learning research: taking the role of a sophisticated barbarian', *Human Resource Development Quarterly*, 7: 313–29.

Zanibbi, M., Munby, H., Hutchinson, N.L., Versnel, J. and Chin, P. (2006) 'Exemplary practice in work-based education: a validation study', *Journal of Vocational Education and Training*, 58: 65–81.

Zapf, D., Frese, M. and Brodbeck, F.C. (1999) 'Fehler und Fehlermanagement' [Error and error management], in C. Hoyos and D. Frey (eds) *Organisationspsychologie* [*Organizational Psychology*], Weinheim, Germany: Beltz PVU, pp. 398–411.

Zellmer-Bruhn, M. and Gibson, C. (2006) 'Multinational organization context: implications for team learning and performance', *Academy of Management Journal*, 49: 501–18.

Zhao, B. and Olivera, F. (2006) 'Error reporting in organizations', *Academy of Management Review*, 31: 1012–30.

Zuber-Skerritt, O. (2002) 'The concept of action learning', *The Learning Organization*, 9: 114–24.

Index